OBJECT-ORIENTED PROGRAMMING FOR WINDOWS™

Ernest R. Tello

John Wiley & Sons, Inc.

New York · Chichester · Brisbane · Toronto · Singapore

In recognition of the importance of preserving what has been written, it is a policy of John Wiley & Sons, Inc. to have books of enduring value published in the United States printed on acid-free paper, and we exert our best efforts to that end.

Windows is a Trademark of Microsoft Corporation.

This publication is designed to provide accurate and authoritative information in regard to the subject matter covered. It is sold with the understanding that the publisher is not engaged in rendering legal, accounting, or other professional service. If legal advice or other expert assistance is required, the services of a competent professional person should be sought. FROM A DECLARATION OF PRINCIPLES JOINTLY ADOPTED BY A COMMITEE OF THE AMERICAN BAR ASSOCIATION AND A COMMITTEE OF PUBLISHERS.

Library of Congress Cataloging-in-Publication Data

Tello, Ernest R.
    Object-oriented programming for Windows / Ernest Tello.
        p.   cm.
    Includes index.
    ISBN 0-471-52957-5. — ISBN 0-471-52754-8 (pbk.)
    1. Object-oriented programming (Computer science)   2. Microsoft
    windows (Computer program)   I. Title.
QA76.64.T44   1991
004.4'3—dc20   90-23729

Printed in the United States of America

91 92 10 9 8 7 6 5 4 3 2 1

*This book is dedicated
to my nephew Devin
and others of his generation
who will probably be reading it
and benefiting from it
long before I realize.*

CONTENTS

PREFACE   xiii

1

INTRODUCTION TO WINDOWS   1

Introduction to Windows 3.0 / 1
What's New With 3.0? / 2
Multitasking / 2
The Program Manager / 2
The Main Group / 3
The File Manager / 4
Clipboard / 5
Screen Capture / 6
Calculator / 6
Numbers / 8
The Macro Recorder / 9
Printer Manager / 10
Control Panel / 11
386 Enhanced Mode Controls / 11
Multitasking Controls / 11
Initialization Files / 12
The PIF Editor / 14
Application Shortcut Keys / 14
Memory Management / 15
Microsoft Word for Windows / 15
Outlining / 15
NewWave / 16

Office Tools / 17
Toolbook / 17
Wingz: A Next-Generation Spreadsheet / 21
A Session With Windows 3.0 / 25

2

OBJECT-ORIENTED PROGRAMMING: WHAT IS IT?   29

Introduction / 29
Programming Paradigms / 29
The Object-Oriented Paradigm / 30
Object-Oriented Programming Metaphors / 32
Active Data / 32
Message Passing / 33
Classes, Instantiation, and Inheritance / 34
Types of Object-Oriented Systems / 35
How Object-Oriented Systems Work / 36
Using an Object-Oriented System / 37
Why Object-Oriented Programming? / 37
Some Conclusions / 38
Additional Programming Responsibilities / 40

3

OBJECT-ORIENTED LANGUAGES AND DEVELOPMENT TOOLS   43

C++ 2.0: An Overview / 43
Structs and Classes / 44
Multiple Inheritance / 44
Member Functions / 45
Privacy and Protection / 45
Friends / 45
Operator and Function Overloading / 46
Prototyping / 47
Virtual Functions and Virtual Classes / 47
Constructors and Destructors / 48
The Zortech Compiler / 50
Memory Models / 51
The Memory Map of Programs / 51
The C++ Debugger / 52
Zortech Tools Classes / 53
Conclusions About C++ / 54
Objective-C / 55

Class Hierarchy / 57
Collection Data Structures / 59
Graphics / 61
Symbolic Debugging / 63
Discussion / 63
Ctalk / 65
Ctalk Syntax / 67
Ctalk Foundation Classes / 68
Run-Time Applications / 70
Conclusions About Ctalk / 71
VIEWS: An Object-Oriented C Development Tool for
Windows / 71
The C++ VIEWS Browser / 72
The MVC User Interface Model / 74
The AppView Class / 74
What VIEWS Windows Do / 76
The View Classes / 76
Creating Dialogs with The Interface Generator / 77
Setting Up Menus / 77
Text Editing Classes / 78
Timer / 78
Communications Class / 79
Graphics / 79
The Application Streamliner / 79
Conclusions About VIEWS / 80

4

WINDOWS 3.0 SOFTWARE DEVELOPMENT 81

What's New With the Windows 3.0 SDK? / 81
How the Windows System Works / 82
Functions that Create Things / 83
Window Classes / 83
Messages / 83
Windows Function / 85
Display Contexts / 86
Elements of Windows User Interfaces / 86
Owner-Draw Controls / 87
Icons / 87
Menus / 87
Controls / 88
Buttons / 88
Scroll Bars / 88
Dialogs / 89

LIST BOXES / 89
Combo Boxes / 90
Floating Popup Menus / 90
GDI / 90
Multi-Document Interface / 91
Dynamic Link Libraries / 92
Dynamic Data Exchange / 93
Device-Independent Color Graphics / 93
The Help-Building System / 94
The Resource Compiler / 94
Resource Editors and Tools / 95
The Dialog Editor / 95
SDKPaint / 96
The Font Editor / 96
Zoomin / 97
Profiler / 97
Spy / 98
HeapWalker / 99
Swap / 100
Shaker / 100
Codeview for Windows / 101
The Symdeb Real Mode Debugger / 102
Maintaining Compatibility with Versions 2.0 and 3.0 / 102
The Structure of Windows Programs / 102
Windows User Interface Style / 103
Writing Resource Scripts / 103
Conclusions / 103
Windows Editing Control Messages / 105
New Windows 3.0 Functions / 105
New Windows 3.0 Messages / 111
New Windows 3.0 Structures / 114

5

INTRODUCTION TO THE ACTOR PROGRAMMING SYSTEM

The Actor Language Version 3.0 / 117
The Actor Programming Environment / 117
Actor's Browser / 118
Inspectors / 120
Actor Classes / 120
MS-Windows Classes / 121
Controls / 123
Dynamic Menus and Dialogs / 124

Callbacks / 124
List Structures / 125
Programming in Actor / 125
Actor Syntax Basic / 126
A Little Music? / 128
Code Blocks / 128
File Formats / 128
Actor Workouts / 129
Number Class Session / 129
Strings / 130
Control Structures / 131
Loops / 131
Collections / 133
Arrays / 133
Other Collections / 134
Ordered Collections / 135
Dictionaries / 136
Text Collections / 136
Queues / 137
Class Variables / 138
Calling Dynamic Link Libraries / 138
Representing Knowledge / 139
Debugging / 140
The Profiler / 140
Executing External Programs / 140
Sealing Off Applications / 141
The Application Class / 141
Adding Primitives to Actor / 143
Managing Time / 144
Working with Dates and Times / 145
What Time Is It? / 152
Digital Clocks / 152
Time Management Class Descriptions / 154
Additional Sample Code / 157

6
OBJECT-ORIENTED USER INTERFACES FOR WINDOWS   161

Creating Windows / 161
Text Windows / 164
EditWindows / 166
FileEditor / 168
Class Descriptions / 168
The ActorApp Class / 170

Buttons, Dialogs, and Other Controls / 171
Creating Buttons / 172
Creating File Dialogs / 175
WorkSpaces / 176
The TextFile Class / 176
Creating Dynamic Menus / 177
Creating Dynamic Dialogs / 178
Modeless Dialogs / 179
Custom Dynamic Dialogs / 180
Creating List Boxes / 181
Creating Combo Boxes / 181
Creating Main Window Menu Bars / 183
Simple Executive Controller / 186
Sample Resource File Selections / 190
DOS Directories / 194

7

OBJECT-ORIENTED GRAPHICS PROGRAMMING FOR WINDOWS

217

Built-in Graphics Classes / 217
The Point Class / 218
Scribble / 218
The Scribble Class Description / 220
Rectangles / 220
Round Rectangles / 222
Ellipses / 223
Polygons / 224
Color Bitmaps / 227
Point3-D / 228
Charts / 230
Animation / 232
Observations / 234
Graphics Class Descriptions / 234

8

PROGRAMMING WITH OBJECT GRAPHICS

243

An Overview of Object Graphics / 244
SampleDraw / 244
Adding a Menu and More Shapes to SampleDraw / 245
ObjectDraw / 247
Extending Actor / 250

Platform Filters / 251
Color / 252
Bitmaps / 252
Rectangles / 253
Shapes / 253
Graph Spaces / 254
Icons / 255
PolyShapes and PolyLines / 255
Curves / 256
Drawing Triangles / 256
Pictures / 262
Regions / 262
Palettes / 263
Groupings / 264
Applying Rendering Tools / 266
PolyMarks / 271
Object Graphics Class Hierarchy / 272
Object Graphics Window Class Extensions / 274

9

A SAMPLE WINDOWS 3.0 APPLICATION   277

Executive Control: A Brief Overview / 277
Multiple-Document Interface (MDI) / 279
Actor MDI Support / 279
MDIFrameWindow / 280
MDIFileWindow / 281
MDI Class Hierarchy / 282
Handling Large Complex Menu Systems / 283
Hierarchical Menus / 284
Combining Static and Dynamic Menus / 285
Dynamic File Dialogs / 286
Factoring Command Methods / 286

10

TOPICS IN OBJECT-ORIENTED WINDOWS DESIGN   311

Designing for Users / 311
What's the Computer Really Doing? / 312
Partitioning Procedures and Protocols / 313
Designing Classes / 314
Multiple Application Instances / 314
Object-Oriented Design for GUIs / 314

Example: Designing An Object-Oriented Spreadsheet / 315
Open Activity Chains / 316
Factoring Command Methods / 317
Object-Oriented Design for MS-Windows / 317
Hierarchical Menus / 319
Handling Large Complex Menu Systems / 319
CommonView / 319
C++ Views Classes / 320
CommonView Classes / 321
Windows Memory Management Design / 323
Types of Data Storage / 324
Discardable Memory / 324
Advanced Memory Management / 325
Standard Mode / 325
386 Enhanced Mode / 325
Some Rules of Thumb / 325
The WINMEM32.DLL Library / 326
Memory Management with Actor / 326
Swapping Static Memory / 328
Actor Memory Classes / 328
Memory Class Descriptions / 329
Designing Indexed Sequential File Databases 1947 / 333
Wintrieve: An Overview / 333
Object-Oriented Relational Database Systems / 335
Designing Relational Databases with Wintrieve / 335
Wintrieve Classes / 336
Underlying Classes Used by Wintrieve / 337
Wintrieve Class Descriptions / 338
Sample Class Descriptions / 339

INDEX   343

PREFACE

This book is designed to serve the needs of both beginning and intermediate programmers. For less experienced readers, clear, detailed explanations are offered to get them up and running with a minimum of frustration. Also, general methods are illustrated that can allow the programming novice to have a working scheme from which new programs can be constructed. Object-oriented programming (OOP) is well suited for this sort of thing because of its extreme modularity. For the more advanced programmer, all the methods for using the OOP paradigm to take the capabilities of the Windows environment to the limits are covered.

■ WHY OBJECT-ORIENTED PROGRAMMING FOR WINDOWS?

Microsoft Windows has emerged as the *de facto* standard user environment for the millions of MS-DOS machines worldwide. Currently most of the important applications such as Excel, Pagemaker, Designer, Ami, Corel Draw, and hundreds of other applications are ported to the Windows environment. Object-oriented programming is also rapidly emerging as the state-of-the-art programming model, and companies such as Lotus, AT&T, Microsoft, Borland, Apple, and Next are adopting it as the most progressive current programming methodology.

Chapter 1 is intended to give programmers an overview of the key aspects of how the Windows environment functions. It will provide examples of various applications already written under Windows and discusses some of the technical issues, such as the differences in memory management, in the different running modes, the regular, the real mode, and 386 Enhanced Modes.

In Chapter 2, a basic discussion of the advantages of OOP will be given (there are a number of them) as well as the disadvantages (there are a few). The advantages stem largely from the increased modularity of the OOP approach and most of them benefit programmers, though there are some advantages that can also be directly enjoyed by end users. I will discuss both. Then, I will generally enumerate and explain the essential defining features of true object-oriented systems and show why they are important for reaping the benefits of OOP.

The OOP tools that will be covered include VIEWS from CNS, a Windows development tool for Object-Oriented C; Actor from the Whitewater Group; and Zortech C++ from Zortech. Since C is currently the most popular commercial programming language, it is appropriate to devote a chapter to programming in Object-Oriented C and to discuss the different dialects, such as C++, Objective-C, and Ctalk. Also, since a number of the example programs will be written in Object-Oriented C, I will try to help readers along here. However, it will not be assumed that you are using any one of these tools in particular. Since the dialects are relatively similar, I will provide some special sections on converting programs from one dialect to another. In cases where this is far from trivial, I will include versions in different dialects.

As a graphic user interface environment, Windows lends itself to incorporating various graphics into applications. From business charts to Computer Aided Display (CAD) and animation, graphics are becoming an increasingly important part of today's state-of-the-art tools. Object-oriented programming has already had an impressive history in the graphics field. This chapter will cover the essentials of how to take advantage of OOP's strength for dealing with various issues that arise in the Windows environment.

User Interface programming in environments like Windows has become one of the most time-consuming parts of a programmer's task. Object-oriented programming is particularly valuable for minimizing this tendency because it has the ability to avoid redundant code by reusing program parts and customizing existing code. Windows lends itself extremely well to the OOP approach. It is very natural to define user interface elements like windows, dialogs, buttons, menus, and so on as object classes, and then to define specialized subclasses of these elements, ready to use for a variety of purposes. Approaches for extending the user interface facilities provided by Windows will also be discussed.

As a natural follow-up to the techniques already supplied a systematic method will be provided for designing application programs along OOP lines. Although the reader will be cautioned against trying to force applications into a given model, and encouraged to find creative solutions to unique problems, there is a core of general principles that have been developed over the last ten years or so that have considerable general validity. The emphasis here will be on those aspects of OOP design that specifically make optimum use of the advanced modularity that true OOP tools provided in the MS Windows environment.

Important advanced Windows programming techniques include being able to write programs that read relevant information from a user's WIN.INI file, writing your own custom versions of standard Windows objects, and allowing your program to execute when a user clicks the mouse on any one of its data files. Also important is knowing how to design memory management parameters that are appropriate for given applications.

One of the most difficult problems in developing the user interface is properly sealing off the application. Object-oriented programming lends itself to an automated solution to this problem. The answer is to write a set of classes that allow you to define all the seal-off methods necessary for a large class of applications, which can be customized as needed. The result is a program that can seal off your program automatically.

The advantages of OOP become especially evident in larger programming projects, for instance as in the major project of this book found in Chapter 9. It will be a program that complements the Windows environment and extends its use considerably. By providing a program that readers can actually use, I believe that greater benefits from the programming point of view will be provided. First, the application domain will not be limited to just a few users. Second, because the readers typically will use the application themselves on an ongoing basis, they will have a greater understanding of it. Finally, they will be more likely to extend and customize the program. It is then, of course, when the advantages of OOP will become most apparent to the user.

A key issue in environments like Windows is that of memory management. Here again, the OOP approach is of special importance. The key to efficient memory management in Windows is the modular design of programs. The OOP approach provides the maximum opportunity to a programmer for modular design and coding.

1

INTRODUCTION
TO WINDOWS

■ INTRODUCTION TO WINDOWS 3.0

With this major new release of the Windows Graphics User Interface (GUI), there is now precious little real difference between the software styles of the leading computers, and therefore, precious little reason to pay extra for it. This environment is bound to delight all sorts of Windows users, from neophytes to power users, to programmers.

Windows has now emerged as the standard GUI for low-cost computers. Now that there is just one version of the program instead of three, the time is right for new classic applications to appear, and to take a place alongside Word for Windows, Excel, and Pagemaker. Unlike Presentation Manager for OS/2, Windows does not require users to buy additional hardware and learn a new operating system. Currently, nearly all important new application programs are being ported to Windows. With the enormous size of the installed base of the machines on which it runs, and the nearly indiscernible functional difference between this and the popular Macintosh GUI, the popularity of this environment is ensured well into the nineties.

This chapter will cover many of the things users need to understand about the Windows environment and what it can do for them. It explains the three Windows operating modes, and when and how to use them. Also, basic concepts and metaphors are explained, such as the concept of a Graphic User Interface (GUI). Finally, an overview is given of the key features of the Windows product, and what they mean in practical terms. The chapter also tries to explain why windows and Windows are useful things to have and describes how to work with them. Icons are also explained, pointing out the difference between them and windows. The different types of windows are explained, as are interactions with windows, and the mouse and the keyboard. Scroll bars and collapsing and expanding windows are also explained. Another basic part of working with windows is interacting with the menu bars and menus that are attached to them. The Windows Help system is also described.

■ WHAT'S NEW WITH 3.0?

There is an entirely new look to the Windows 3.0 desktop. All buttons are shaded for a 3-D appearance and give the actual visual feedback of having been pushed. The old MS-DOS Executive program has been dropped and replaced with two others, the Program Manager and the File Manager. One of the watchwords for the new Windows environment is icons. Another is color. Still another of the new watchwords is device-independence. And certainly one of the more important ingredients in the new look of Windows is the adoption of proportional fonts.

To the end user, Windows 3.0 appears as just one program. There is no longer special Windows products for 286 and 386 machines. You buy one Windows product now and get them all. But you can run Windows in one of three different modes: Standard Mode, Real Mode, and 386 Enhanced Mode. An important difference from earlier versions is that there is much more that you can do with non-Windows applications now, particularly in the 386 Enhanced Mode. Help is also a ubiquitous presence in Windows 3.0. The standardized Help facilities have allowed even the smallest Windows accessories to have their own readily available help systems. The result is that detailed information about any application is readily available whenever you need it. And Multitasking has arrived in a big way, especially for those who are able to run Windows in 386 Enhanced Mode.

Before becoming an expert Windows programmer you should first attempt to become an expert Windows user. By becoming familiar with what the environment can do well and those things that it does not do so well, you can improve your ability to write effective applications for the new Windows environment.

■ MULTITASKING

Just double clicking on the desktop background is sufficient to get the Task List window to pop up. This is the window that gives the list of all processes currently running under Windows. Various options are available, but usually what you want to do with this window is select the application you want to bring into the foreground. For most users, this Task List becomes a very familiar sight in their Windows sessions. In the close box in the upper left of every window, there is now a **"Switch to . . ."** option that allows one to transfer control to any of the other Windows applications currently loaded. The result of this ease in transferring from one application to another is that, in effect, separate applications become as though they are part of one big program, instead of several different ones.

■ THE PROGRAM MANAGER

The Program Manager (Figure 1.1) displays groups of programs with icons that can be opened into windows that contain other icons, which represent application programs. Group windows can be resized just like any other window. There is also a facility for

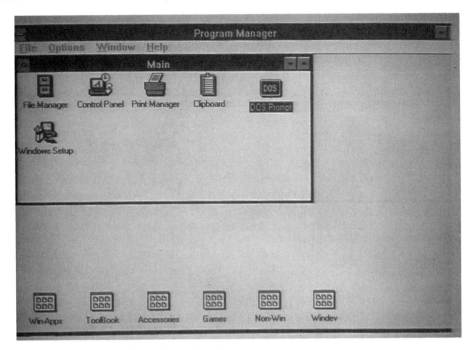

Figure 1.1 The Windows Program Manager.

rearranging group windows in either a cascaded or tiled configuration. The standard groups that come with the Windows package as it is shipped are the Main, Accessories, Games, Windows Applications, and Non-Windows Applications groups. However, you can change these arrangements and add to them as you see fit. When more than one window group of the Program Manager is open at a time, the group windows can be rearranged in either the tiled or cascading window styles.

■ THE MAIN GROUP

The programs that come assigned to the Main Group are: the File Manager, the Print Manager, the Clipboard, the DOS Prompt, Windows Setup, and the Control Panel. To create a new group, all that is necessary is to choose New from the File menu and give a descriptive name for the group. If you do not provide a file name, Windows does so automatically. Adding programs to a group is similar, but here a directory and executable file must be provided. In the case of Windows applications, their associated icons will be immediately displayed in the group folder. In cases where you would like to open a document or other data file when you launch an application, the Run command from the File menu can be used, in which case you simply enter the full command line with the name of the file to be loaded, as you would from the DOS prompt if the program were a regular DOS application.

■ THE FILE MANAGER

The File Manager (Figure 1.2) can be used for all the usual kinds of file maintenance and manipulation, but also for creating new groups or modifying existing ones. While applications can be launched from either the Program Manager or the File Manager, the former makes it much more convenient to do. Clicking on the folder icons to the left of any executable file in the tree will launch that application.

Like the Program Manager, the File Manager lets you arrange windows in either the tiled or cascading window styles. One very worthwhile use of the tiled window style is for displaying both the source and target directories simultaneously when you are copying or moving several files. Its use for this purpose is diminished by the fact that Windows insists that all the upper branches of a directory tree have to be open for the bottom branches to remain open too. This can tend to clutter up the screen. In such cases you can still grab, drag, and resize the child windows to make them more accessible for the purpose of viewing source and target directories.

One technique for minimizing screen clutter is to take advantage of the facility for expanding subdirectories as much as needed in the directory tree display. Those directories that have a subdirectory structure are identified by a plus sign (+) on their folder icon. A single mouse click on the plus sign expands the directory so that all of its immediate subdirectories are displayed. Double clicking on the icon as you do when

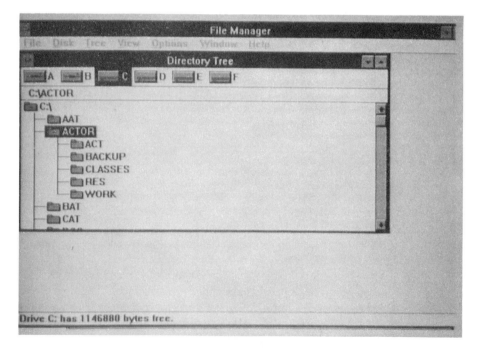

Figure 1.2 The Windows File Manager.

there are no subdirectories indicated will cause a separate window to open for the subdirectory display. Another way of expanding directory levels is to use the options on the Tree menu, which include: Expand One Level, Expand Branch, Expand All, and Collapse Branch.

A very welcome feature of the File Manager is the fact that the amount of free disk space is displayed at the bottom of the root directory windows. Another is the inclusion of a Move operation, which ends the necessity of first copying and then deleting files. In general, the default behavior for operations on more than one file at a time is for confirmation dialogs to open for each individual file. These confirmations can be suppressed by a selection on the Options menu. The File Manager also supports copying entire directories at a time simply by selecting the directory, choosing the copy function from the File menu, and supplying the name of a destination directory.

The File Manager also allows you to associate data files of a given extension with a specified application so that when those files are selected, the application is automatically loaded with the file. This is a function that formerly required the user to edit the WIN.INI file.

Printers are now installed from the Control Panel. With the Control Panel open, a user selects the Printers icon, which opens the Printers dialog box. From there a printer is installed by selecting from a list of supported printers, or the Generic or Unlisted Printer options chosen. Font sets are also installed in a similar way by selecting the Fonts icon.

There are a variety of different ways that the Windows environment can be customized to suit one's personal preferences and work habits. I will cover many of them here. The main exception is memory management, which is handled in Chapter 10. First I will explain the four Windows initialization files. I will also explain how to use the Control Panel and Macro Recorder for personalizing the environment. With the Control Panel users can create custom backgrounds for their Windows setup, with custom color schemes. It's almost like decorating an office or apartment. Special fonts can be added and selected, the time and date can be set, and the behavior of printers can be configured.

Windows comes with a set of powerful desk accessory programs that immediately make the advantages of the Windows environment obvious. I will cover all of the desk accessory groups except the Cardfile and the Write programs. Those that will be covered here are the: Clock, Paintbrush, Notepad, Calendar, Clipboard, Terminal, PIF Editor, and Recorder.

■ CLIPBOARD

The Windows Clipboard is one of the primary things that gives the environment its ability to share data and images between applications. It is now a visible presence on the Windows desktop with its own icon that opens into a window allowing you to see, but not modify, the Clipboard's contents. The reason direct editing of the Clipboard is not allowed may have been to safeguard the integrity of its contents while keeping the mechanism as simple as possible, as ample tools are available for editing data and images both before and after their passage through the Clipboard. Also, it is now possible to save the contents of the Clipboard to disk. Being able to save the Clipboard as a disk file allows programs that run in a different Windows mode to share data. When in the mode of the data source, you copy the data to the Clipboard and save it as a file. Then you exit Windows, launch it again in the mode of the target application, load the file into the Clipboard, and paste it in. The Clipboard also now has a provision for viewing its contents in different formats. For example, in the text mode, if you have something loaded in the Clipboard and pull down the Display menu you will see the Owner Display, Text, and OEM Text options. Your text will indeed have a different appearance depending on which option you select.

It is now also possible to copy selected information in non-Windows applications to the Clipboard if the application is running in a window in 386 Enhanced Mode. Non-Windows application information also transfers in the opposite direction. A couple of different facilities make this possible. First, whenever you are in a non-Windows application that occupies the entire screen, you can collapse this program down to a DOS icon on the Windows desktop without disturbing its screen's contents. If you pop up the control menu of this icon, you will see some new options, namely the Edit and Settings options. If you select the Settings option, a dialog opens that gives you the option of displaying the current screen of the non-Windows application in a window. If you do this, you can use the mouse to highlight an area to be copied to the Clipboard. Choosing the Edit option from the Control menu spawns a submenu with the Copy option. Paste works in a similar way.

■ SCREEN CAPTURE

In Windows 3.0, if you want to capture the entire screen at any time, all you have to do is press Shift-Printscreen. For Windows applications, you can also specify how to capture just the contents of a particular window. To do this, the Alt-Printscreen key combination is used. Even for non-Windows applications running under Windows, you can capture entire data screens in the Clipboard. In the 386 Enhanced Mode if a program is running in a window then you have the option of capturing just that window. This applies to graphics programs too, but not in all display modes. In general, only the most advanced video graphics array (VGA) modes don't allow the screen capture of graphic images.

■ CALCULATOR

The most dramatic thing about the new calculator is undoubtedly the scientific mode. Without losing any stored values, you can shift back and forth between this and the regular mode. In the scientific mode you have numerous math functions available and three different number lengths to choose from: Dword, Word, and Byte. The Calculator also makes full use of the keyboard's function keys. Math function keys include trig and log functions, as well as square roots, cubes, and exponents. Typing 'h' toggles between regular and hyperbolic trig functions. One of the nicest features on this whole calculator is the Inverse function that reverses whatever the function is that you used last, which can be used as an 'Undo' key for calculations.

Numbers can be computed in the Calculator, copied to the Clipboard, and then pasted into a spreadsheet in Excel, or any other application. Clipboard copying and pasting also works in the other direction. Numbers developed in a spreadsheet can be pasted into the calculator for further processing.

In the scientific mode the Calculator can also do statistical operations. If the Sta key is selected, another window called the Statistics Box pops open, which can record stored lists of numbers and statistics computed about them. You can compute sums, averages, standard deviations, and some "advanced" functions. The Calculator is especially useful for programmers because of its support for four different number systems: decimal, binary, hexadecimal, and octal. Selecting a number system automatically converts the number currently displayed into a value in that system.

The Calendar accessory is now displayed to look like a regular calendar with days in squares arranged in columns according to the days of the week. Various marker styles are available for marking different days in ways that make the appointments on those days identifiable by a visual code. The calendars available for your perusal go as far into the future as you could possibly want, even if you were an author of exotic science fiction. However, they cannot go back before 1980, so unfortunately the Calendar cannot be used for looking up days and dates of the past.

One of the most useful features of the Cardfile accessory is the ability to transfer graphic images to it from the Clipboard. This gives it innumerable uses besides that of a simple address and phone directory. With the right hardware installed on your computer, you can use digitized photographs of people, objects, places, and so on. Unfortunately, though, the graphics are only displayed in monochrome, no matter what you are using for the text area color.

Depending on what type of machine is being used and how it's configured, different options can be specified to make the most memory available for applications. Since there are a number of different things that interact to produce different results, this can be a little confusing. In planning the memory management for an application, programmers should be familiar with all the ways that a user can configure the memory that Windows uses, and when and how to use them in combination to obtain the best results. Programmers need to be especially aware of the different Microsoft drivers for memory management, such as HIMEM.SYS, SMARTDRV.SYS, and EMM386.SYS, and what effect they have on one another—and your application—when used in combination.

Windows programmers also need to be particularly familiar with the graphics and video issues involved with the Windows environment. For programmers without any background in graphics at all, a place to start might be learning to use the new color Paintbrush program. It is the only Windows accessory that uses two mouse buttons rather than just one. I will teach its use by actually creating a finished drawing, step by step, that uses most of the features of the program, explaining them as I go along. Some of the advanced features illustrated will include shrinking and enlarging cutouts, creating custom colors, converting files from Microsoft Paint, and printing drawings in parts.

This section is a good place to discuss some of the general issues of graphics under Windows. There are already several excellent graphics programs currently available for the environment, such as Designer, Corel Draw, Zing, Drafix CAD, and Picture Publisher. Another matter to mention here is the new category of image database software, of which there are already several examples, that run under Windows. We will look at some of the best tools and methods currently available for the purpose of editing bitmap images and icons, such as the Icon Editor. Windows has now become the definitive environment for preparing state-of-the-art multimedia presentations, so Windows programmers will often need to be aware of those issues.

■ NUMBERS

Number processing in all its glory has many handy assistants in the Windows environment. As we have seen, there is the desk accessory Calculator, featuring both a regular mode, and a scientific mode. I mentioned that the Microsoft Excel spreadsheet program, can be used in conjunction with the Calculator accessory. One of the things users can profit from is the way multiple windows and linking can give another dimension to using spreadsheets. Also of interest is the option of using the macro recorder to automate repeated operations that move across different number processing applications. A powerful product for handling numbers is Macrocalc, from Anderson Consulting, and scientific users will appreciate some of the powerful things it can do.

Word for Windows, the state-of-the-art document processor, is a superb example of an application program that takes full advantage of Windows capabilities. Knowing how to use a tool like this effectively can save enormous amounts of time. Just the Glossary facility alone can eliminate much repetitive typing. Other impressive text processing applications that run under Windows are Ami and Legend. Today, text processing is one link in the "production chain" that makes up "desktop publishing." Pagemaker is one desktop publishing program that has continued to evolve to keep up with the latest trends in this rapidly changing field. I'll talk about its pluses and minuses and discuss the practical matter of the types of projects for which it is best suited. Finally, the subject of scanners and optical character recognition hardware and software will complete the picture of text processing under Windows.

Windows offers support for many different aspects of interfacing, from information and image transfer using the Dynamic Data Exchange (DDE) to printing. This will also be the chapter where the new network support is covered. Knowing how to use the Print Manager is central to knowing how to get the best results from printing under Windows. Another important program for communicating with the outside world is the Terminal. A special copy of the Setup program is provided for those using networks. The process of using this for installing Windows on nodes in the network will be described here.

Finally, third party communication packages like Crosstalk will be discussed to give the reader guidance in which ones to select.

It should start to be apparent how the synergy of the Windows environment pays off. It would be impossible to enumerate all the ways that you can create integral methods of accomplishing useful things, which combine various application programs into a single process with many repeated elements automated. As an example, imagine a desktop publishing application that uses the Macro Recorder to bring into Pagemaker contributions from Word for Windows, Paintbrush, and Excel. Or consider the field of graphic design. With the Clipboard, screen capture, and format conversion utilities; images and artwork can migrate from one program to another, picking up various detailed effects, by taking advantage of what each program does best. This is possibly one of the most important advantages of all that Windows provides. Programmers of a given application can just do so much. In even the best programs, we can always find something to wish for. With an integrated environment like Windows it's possible to combine the best features of all the best programs for various tasks within a single project.

The real advantage of Windows is enjoyed when used with the best programs available for it in a unified working environment, which derives the best from each application. The best way of illustrating the power of Windows is by demonstrating what can be done when using the best of the applications that run under it.

∎ THE MACRO RECORDER

This accessory is a global recorder for the Windows environment that allows the recording of both keystrokes and mouse operations. The recorder sequence can be assigned to a hot key and stored in a file with other related macros. Although the Recorder can record mouse movements, this is a potential source of problems and should be avoided whenever it is possible to do the same thing another way. It is recommended that shortcut keys be used whenever possible in recording macros.

One excellent feature of the Recorder is the ability to interrupt a macro recording at any point and store the macro you have recorded so far. This seems essential, because otherwise you are in the awkward position of having to record whatever movements are needed to get into a position of stopping the recording. In some cases, you want a macro that takes you to a screen or window display that you have to leave before the Recorder could be accessed. With this feature, as soon as you get to where you want the macro to end, you press CTRL-BREAK and a dialog pops up, which lets you end the macro right there.

Recording a macro for playback in a multiple application environment like Windows can be a complex task. For this reason a number of different record and playback options are provided. You can decide whether mouse movements should be recorded relative to a particular window or to the whole screen, whether to play the macro back as quickly as possible or at the speed it was recorded, and so on. The Recorder is designed to be able to make long recordings suitable for use in preparing demonstrations that can be used as sales floor or exhibit demos. There are undoubtedly numerous purposes for which this program can be effectively used, which were not foreseen by its designers.

When a macro is called from within an application there may be a wait while the hourglass icon appears before the macro actually executes. Obviously this can defeat the purpose of the macro in the first place. Where waiting occurs, obviously only more elaborate macros can be justified.

■ PRINTER MANAGER

Once a printer has been installed from the Control Panel, it is possible to print under Windows via the Printer Manager (Figure 1.3). This program handles printing in the background so that, once an application has been told to print a document, you can go on doing other work. When non-Windows applications run under Windows, printing is done the way these programs normally would, that is, without the Printer Manager.

Selecting the Printer Manager icon opens a window in which all relevant information about current printing operations is displayed. This includes the printer currently installed, where it is connected to the computer, and its current status. After each printer

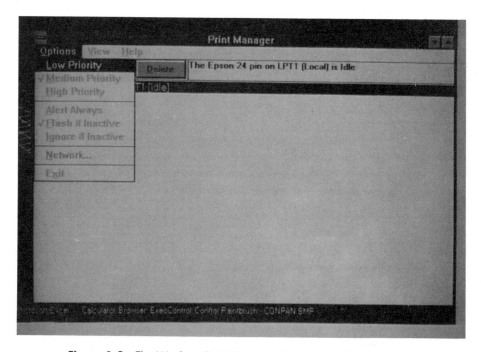

Figure 1.3 The Windows Print Manager showing the Options menu.

name is a current print queue list of files to be printed on that printer. If a file is currently being printed, the amount that has printed so far is displayed as a percentage. If desired, you can change the position of any file in the print queue by dragging that file to a new position with the mouse.

■ CONTROL PANEL

The Control Panel has been completely redone with Version 3.0. The Font editor now supports proportional font sets. Font sets are a collection of sizes for a given typeface, customized for particular displays and printers. There are both screen *(raster)* and printer *(vector)* fonts supplied with Windows. The Fonts dialog box allows you to see a sample of the font you select in the window pane below.

Clicking on the Colors icon opens the dialog that lets you customize the color scheme used on standard window controls as well as the foreground and background of text areas. The method for selecting colors is completely interactive. A mockup of a Windows screen is provided for selecting the area whose color you want to change, and an array of color boxes to choose from is displayed. If the color you are interested in does not appear, there is also a screen where you can mix your own colors. Once done, you can save the color settings to a file. Windows comes with several alternate color schemes in files already provided.

Opening the Desktop icon allows you to change the appearance of the desktop background on which Windows objects appear, either by selecting a wallpaper pattern or a graphics bitmap image.

■ 386 ENHANCED MODE CONTROLS

If you are running in 386 Enhanced Mode, the Control Panel (Figure 1.4) automatically displays that icon. One of the things you can configure in this mode is the rule by which applications contend for output devices such as printers. The options on the Control Panel are only concerned with arbitrating this when one of the applications is a non-Windows application. The Always Warn option means that when an application tries to take over use of one of the I/O (input/output) ports, you will be interrupted from what you are doing to select which application should get use of the facility. The Never Warn option is a risky one, because there is a chance that two applications could use your printer or modem at the same time, giving you some garbled hieroglyphics as a result. The Idle option allows you to specify the amount of time that an application should wait from when a port becomes available until it actually tries to use it. Some printers might need more reset time than others. The other main options for 386 Enhanced Mode are involved with multitasking issues, which will be discussed next.

■ MULTITASKING CONTROLS

The Minimum Time-Slice option allows you to specify the number of milliseconds that an application under Windows will run before control is given to another application. Not having a precise way of measuring milliseconds, I decided not to try testing the

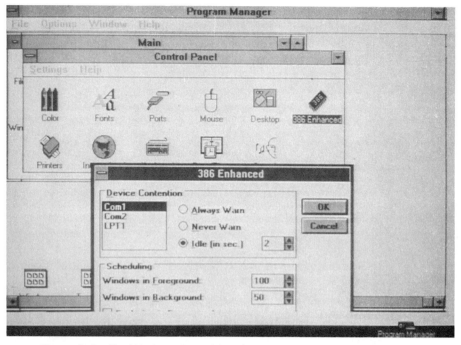

Figure 1.4 The Windows Control Panel accessory showing the options for 386 Enhanced Mode.

accuracy of this setting. The Windows in Foreground and Windows in Background options have to do with the relative amount of the time-sharing pie allocated between Windows and non-Windows applications, depending on whether Windows is in the foreground or background. The settings are measured in the proportion of total time-slices. Generally, each application is assigned one time-slice, whether it is a Windows or a non-Windows application. The Exclusive in Foreground option allows you to specify that when Windows is in the foreground it always gets 100 percent of the processing time.

The Windows multitasking does not extend to things like disk operations. Writing files to disk or formatting them cannot be done in the background while you do other work. It is probably a safe thing that this is so, because otherwise there might be situations when disk operations would not complete themselves (Figure 1.5).

∎ INITIALIZATION FILES

The following are the initialization files for Windows 3.0:

CONTROL.INI

PROGRAM.INI

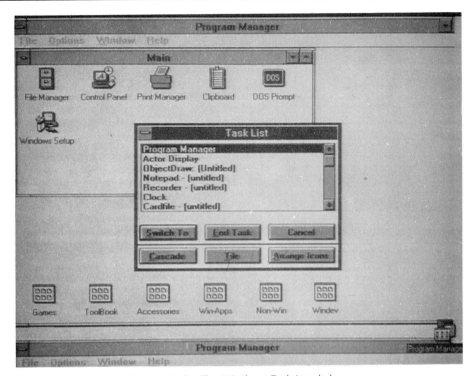

Figure 1.5 The Windows Task List dialog.

SYSTEM.INI

WIN.INI

WINFILE.INI

The two standard Windows initialization files are SYSTEM.INI, which has the settings for customizing Windows for your specific hardware configuration, and WIN.INI, which has the settings for altering your Windows environment according to your software needs and preferences. Sections are used to break settings into logical groups. The enclosing brackets ([ ]) are required. A keyname=value statement is used to specify the value that each of the settings will take. A keyname is simply the name of a setting. It may be formed of any combination of characters, both letters and digits, and must be followed by an equal sign (=). Value is the setting's value. It may be an integer, a string, or a quoted string, depending on the parameter in question.

There are four different types of applications for Windows:

1. Windows 3.0 applications

2. Earlier Windows applications

3. Non-Windows applications

4. Memory-resident programs

Although this is basically correct, there are some important differences even among applications written specifically for Windows 3.0 and later. There are some applications that might require either protected 286 or 386 modes. To make the user's life easier in configuring their system for such variations in application requirements, there are special provisions in the PIF Editor for handling different Windows operating modes.

■ THE PIF EDITOR

Every PIF has two sets of options, one set for running an application in real or standard modes, and another set for running in 386 enhanced mode. The PIF Editor automatically displays the right options for the mode you are currently running in. However, you can change modes from within the editor if you need to.

One interesting PIF application is for use with DOS batch files that you want to launch from Windows. The PIF memory requirement minimum tells Windows how much memory it must have to be able to even start an application. It does not limit how much Windows will make available to it once it is launched. PIF files have some interesting uses, because you can launch an application by clicking on its icon with a mouse. You can define alternate PIF files for the same application and have all of them available from a group window for launching the program with different configurations.

Multitasking settings include the ability to set the background and foreground priorities as well as to toggle the Detect Idle Time option. Background and foreground priorities are numbered between 0 and 1,000 and are used only for relative comparisons in determining how to break up the central processing unit (CPU) time-sharing pie. So, for example, if you have four tasks running with priorities of 150, 100, 50, and 50, then to calculate how much processing time each application is assigned, you first add all the priorities (which in this case is 350) and then use the priority number of any task to estimate the percentage of the total that it will be getting. If the Detect Idle Time is toggled on, then Windows will give processing time to other applications whenever the current application is sitting idle waiting for user input.

■ APPLICATION SHORTCUT KEYS

This convenience feature is available only in the 386 Enhanced Mode. Windows allows you to assign shortcut keys to applications in this mode so that once they are loaded, you can instantly make them the foreground application by hitting the key. The application shortcut key works globally no matter what application or what part of the Windows environment you currently are in.

■ MEMORY MANAGEMENT

What are the issues that affect the amount of memory you have available to use under Windows? There are actually quite a few now. Here is a convenient checklist:

- The amount of RAM installed in your computer
- The type of memory
- The mode in which you are running Windows
- Which drivers you have installed

In real mode, Windows can use expanded memory of the LMI (Lotus-Intel-Microsoft) standard. When you start up in real mode, Windows automatically determines what it thinks will be the best way to use the expanded memory. If you want to have more control over the memory management of expanded memory, command line options are one way of doing that.

■ MICROSOFT WORD FOR WINDOWS

The best way for the aspiring Windows programmer to get an appreciation for the important issues of programming for this environment is to gain some practical familiarity with one or more state-of-the-art applications. Microsoft Word for Windows is one of the programs that uses the features of the Windows 3.0 environment to the fullest. For this reason, I will describe some of the more interesting features the program offers.

Word for Windows is a state-of-the-art word processing program that writers in all professions can well benefit from. There are quite a few things about this program that make it suitable for many varied purposes. For one thing, it has a built-in outline processor. In case you're not quite sure what that is, an outline processor is a special type of text processing program that allows you to create a structure of headings and subheadings and store any amount of text under each, making this text visible or invisible as the need requires. Word for Windows also has most of the capabilities of desktop publishing programs as well.

■ OUTLINING

I'll begin with the outline processor, because this is a rather unique feature of the program, and one that many professionals can particularly benefit from. Regardless of what type of document you are writing, it will most likely be divided into various parts or segments. Even though the final readers may not be aware of these divisions, it is often important for the writer to be aware of them during the development process. The outline processor lets you look at only those parts of the document you are interested in. Imagine for a moment that you are writing some kind of multimedia presentation. So, for example, if you are using the Act and Scene type of organization used in large productions, then you can make visible only those scenes that are important for a particular task. You may decide to make a change in a certain speaker. If so, you can make visible only those scenes or sequences in which that speaker appears.

At any time, you can collapse the whole document into just its skeleton. As you can see there are some very powerful uses to which an outline processor can be put. For programmers the built-in outline processor is very useful for keeping the structure of programs clear. The Arrange All option in the Windows menu allows all the open document windows to become visible on the screen at the same time, arranged as tiled windows. From this display it is possible to interact with any of them with the click of the mouse.

■ NEWWAVE

One company that is not content to copy the essentials of the graphic user interface popularized by Apple, and leave it at that, is Hewlet-Packard. The NewWave environment takes a number of key steps beyond the Xerox-Macintosh model. The overall design of NewWave is decidedly object-oriented, but with this system the meaning of that term takes on yet a new twist. Objects have a meaning for the end user that is analogous to the meaning they have for the programmer in object-oriented programming (OOP). In NewWave, an object means represents both a data file and the executable program that utilizes that file. This relationship goes beyond the convenience of being able to select the data file and have the program load itself already opened to that file. Creating such an active object allows the Object Management Facility to handle various operations automatically, such as handling various links between applications. When a composite document has been prepared that includes, say, text, statistics, and graphics, even though separate programs are used to print each type of element, they are all handled automatically. It also paves the way for the Agent, a facility that allows operations across different applications to be recorded and subsequently automated.

When a document is composed of elements from different applications, such as text from a word processor, numbers from a spreadsheet, and charts from a graphics program, it is called a Compound object. NewWave also has another type, called a Container object. A Container object is one that holds other objects and displays their names or icons. When object A contains object B there is a containment link between those objects. Objects can also have information links between them. When data is shared between different applications, this is not accomplished as a one time only copying operation. It is done instead through information links so that only the original need be updated, and all the objects that share this data are automatically given the updated version. Notice that a consequence of this is that the Object Manager is needed for making backup copies of compound objects to ensure that all the components are included.

To enjoy the full range of facilities provided in NewWave, applications have to be written to specifically run in this environment. However, there are different degrees to which applications can benefit from them even if they are not specifically written as

NewWave applications. It's also possible to upgrade the degree to which an existing application can utilize the NewWave environment by a process called encapsulation. The NewWave Office is the main window, analogous to the MS Windows Executive. It has icons such as a file drawer and wastebasket meant to remind the user of an office environment.

∎ OFFICE TOOLS

A unique type of object in NewWave is the Office Tool. It could be considered a superobject in the sense that once created, there is no other object like it. Office tools look different from other objects in the NewWave Office because their icons are styled to look like 3-D objects seen in perspective. Tools are also different in that they can only be created by developers. Users cannot create or destroy tools.

The standard NewWave tools include the File Drawer, the WasteBasket, the Printers, and the Dictionaries. The File Drawer is a container object that can hold up to 200 objects, regardless of their contents. These objects usually contain folders, since each folder can hold 200 additional objects, including other folders. However, apparently the same object can only appear in one folder. The Printers tool allows you to print as many objects as you choose on any printer set up for NewWave, including those on a network. The Dictionaries tool is used to create lists of vocabulary words that can be used in conjunction with the main spelling checker dictionary.

The WasteBasket object is an interesting one in that it is a container object, but one that is used to "get rid" of objects rather than to hold onto them. Although you can use it to dispose of files, they do not immediately vanish and can be retrieved.

There are also some impressive applications that have already been specifically ported to the NewWave environment by the programmers. Naturally, the most important are initially those programs that are already popular to users, such as the Microsoft Excel spreadsheet program. Also, Samna is not only providing a version of their Ami program, but a new version called Ami Professional, which is for advanced word processing chores. Other applications that look very promising include the Graph Plus program from Micrografix, an intelligent database from Channel Computing called Forest & Trees, and a desktop video program from New Media Graphics called Video New Wave that boasts full motion video for the PC.

∎ TOOLBOOK

Toolbook is a software construction set for creating electronic books and other software applications. By using software construction, custom applications can be written with little or very light programming. More sophisticated programming can obviously provide substantially greater results. The basic program screens are created interactively, and various utility scripts are written to provide added functionality. Toolbook also has hypertext capability, which utilizes the book metaphor, making it a welcome im-

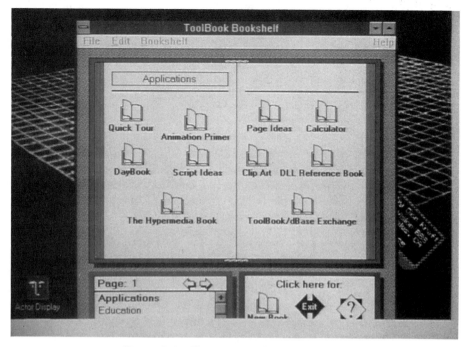

Figure 1.6 The iconic Toolbook Bookshelf.

provement in providing hypertext-oriented software construction for people with little or no programming background. Developing applications is much more accessible to nonprogrammers when they can think of the program screens in terms of books, something already familiar to most people. The metaphor of a book is an advance over stacks of cards offered by other programmers because a book is a sophisticated, unified tool with various recognized parts, such as an index, a table of contents, a bibliography, and appendixes. Books are more sophisticated, more complex, and more unified tools than stacks of cards. Now it is possible to easily build electronic books that combine many of the strengths of both paper and electronic information media.

Toolbook and Windows 3.0

Software construction with a program like Toolbook is particularly appropriate for producing applications for Windows 3.0. Although not all applications can or should be written this way, a surprising number of them can be. Prototypes can be put together in a matter of days where otherwise they may have taken weeks or even months. Although this may sound like familiar hype, I know for a fact that it is true.

Objects and Messages in Toolbook

The design of Toolbook applications is also made easier by the fact that they are built with objects and messages. Every Toolbook application has a hierarchy of objects that is consistently maintained, and that has a built-in scheme for routing messages throughout it. Books and other applications developed with Toolbook are constructed as a hierarchy of objects, which can send and receive messages that mirror and extend the messages at the Windows level. You can use the OpenScript language to define handlers that specify how objects will respond to messages, and you can also use it to send messages, both from within OpenScript programs and interactively from the Command Window. Although the object system in Toolbook does not have the Class concept, and therefore lacks inheritance, there are tricks that can compensate for this somewhat. The system of programming utilized in this book makes the most of the tricks at one's disposal to compensate as much as possible for the absence of classes.

Graphics and Animation

One of the strongest and most appealing aspects of Toolbook is its superior capability for utilizing object-oriented graphics and animation. With animation, electronic books can be created that literally come to life. Their parts move before the reader, making this kind of book something quite different than just a passive book. No longer just a dry, inert accumulation of text, electronic books appear to dance on the screen before the reader. Toolbook provides a number of functions for animating graphics and text, including optical effects like wipes and dissolves, so that considerable variety can be introduced in the way that one page of a book gives way to another (Figure 1.6).

Getting the most out of Toolbook graphics will inevitably lead to preparing and using a library of images that can be easily found and accessed. Toolbook provides a collection of clip art with an accompanying manager. Unfortunately, this application is "locked up" in some ways. You can add and subtract images and pages, but you cannot add new categories for images or new scripts.

The animation feature is best used by keeping things moving whenever possible. Text and images can be hidden and then shown according to a prearranged plan, or at the decision of the user. They can change size and position, appear to rotate, or even be made to distort.

OpenScript

The Toolbook script language is a versatile tool and has been designed to resemble English as much as it is feasible to do with a simple language. One of the frequent uses of OpenScript is writing handlers for messages. Ordinarily there is a flurry of messages circulating in the system that register user interaction. The default behavior is for these messages to be ignored unless there is a script that specifies how to respond to them. An OpenScript handler is a piece of code that defines what actions an object will take in response to a message. A typical example of this is writing a script for a button that specifies what the button will do when it receives a buttonUp message.

There are three main ways that software construction scripts like OpenScript can make use of the resources of other MS Windows applications: 1) using the Dynamic Data Exchange (DDE) protocol, 2) executing functions in application command languages externally, and 3) calling functions in Dynamic Link Libraries (DLLs). The following paragraphs spell out the basics of how these three techniques work.

Dynamic Data Exchange

Exchanging data between Toolbook applications and other Windows programs is a two-way street, as it should be. You can use it to have outside programs request data from the Toolbook environment and you can have your application built with Toolbook receiving data from other programs. This can be designed as a give and take process that is quite useful. So, for example, you might want to take advantage of some number crunching feature of a spreadsheet that Toolbook doesn't have. In this type of situation, you could combine the external execution feature with the data exchange feature to get the optimum results.

Accessing DLLs

One of the things that make Windows based script languages like OpenScript powerful is the availability of what are called Windows Dynamic Link Libraries (DLLs). A DLL provides a modular way of reusing code by several applications that can be loaded in Windows at once. Each program does not have to have its own compiled copies of the code. The one copy of code in the DLL can serve all of them at once. A script language can call upon the functions provided in DLLs quite readily and use functionality provided there. An example of a DLL that comes with Windows 3.0 is PBRUSH.DLL, which provides code used by the Paintbrush accessory program. There are a total of eight dynamic link libraries supplied with Toolbook. There are three with Windows 3.0 itself, and many Windows applications provide at least one additional DLL that in principle can be used.

External Execution

OpenScript provides the ability to issue commands in other Windows applications such as the Excel spreadsheet. This offers another important way that applications crossing over boundaries of many different products can be assembled to integrate the process of problem solving. Ideally, a user should be able to focus on a problem and not be distracted by the tools that are used to solve it. Up until now, computer software has been very obtrusive in the sense that users must always keep in mind which program they are using as well as what problem they are trying to solve. The increasing integration and standardization of graphic user interfaces makes it possible to take important steps toward an environment where it is not necessary that the user know at each step what program is being run. A higher level user interface at work can insulate the user from the need to know which program is active at any given time. The external execution feature of languages like OpenScript makes it possible for software systems like this to be constructed.

Practical procedures for modular development can be provided, many of which can be recorded or coded as scripts so that as much as possible of the development effort can be automated. An example of such a procedure is the creation of new page backgrounds based on an existing background, which can be edited within the same book without changing the original background too. Although this technique and others like it are not terribly difficult procedures, they are not self-evident.

Probably the most tedious and time-consuming tasks in the Toolbook development cycle are the creation of hotwords and the scripts that go with them. It would be great if a way to automate the process of inserting all the instances where a given hotword appears in the text could be found. The difficulty is that it is hard to know at the time of coding all the details that are important to a user. One possible approach would be for a program to stop at each page within a range provided by the user and to prompt for whether the hotword should be added to a specified field. This type of program can be rather readily programmed in OpenScript.

Electronic Libraries

With the capabilities provided by the Windows environment and OpenScript, it is possible to go beyond electronic books to electronic libraries by providing a user interface designed to manage not just books but systems of books, such as an encyclopedia. One basic limitation of Toolbook is that the number of open files is limited to ten, so large applications have to be designed with this in mind. In an application that accesses and loads other books, a provision can be made to keep count of the number of books loaded at a given time and, when the number reaches ten, to query the user which book they want to unload before loading the new one.

■ WINGZ: A NEXT-GENERATION SPREADSHEET

Another state-of-the-art Windows program programmers should be aware of is Wingz (Figure 1.7), from Informix, a spreadsheet that makes several innovations in an application area that has been surprisingly stable compared to other types of product in the software industry. What follows should help aspiring programmers see what a graphics environment like Windows means from the user's point of view.

With all the powerful and attractive spreadsheet programs now on the market, you might think the last thing we need is still another one. However, the truth of the matter is that in the past ten years there have been precious few important changes in the basic way spreadsheets are made. Most of the advances have been largely embellishments on the original idea rather than substantial improvements. So my feeling is that there is plenty of room for innovation here, and it's not surprising that we're finally beginning to really see something new in the field.

Wingz is a next-generation spreadsheet originally developed on the Macintosh and now available in an MS-DOS version for Windows 3.0 as well as for the Sun workstation platform. In three areas, it marks an important breakthrough in spreadsheet technology: 1. fast, versatile 3-D charts, 2. multicolor custom worksheets, and 3. a powerful built-in programming language called Hyperscript. And any overview of the innovative new spreadsheet features provided in Wingz should not fail to mention the Tool Box Icons and Operator Icons that allow spreadsheets to be made almost entirely with the mouse.

Taking Wingz

Once you understand what Wingz is all about, the question you're most likely to ask is why no one did this sooner. Questions like this are bound to be rhetorical, but the point is that we have something new and important here that's going to be the way all

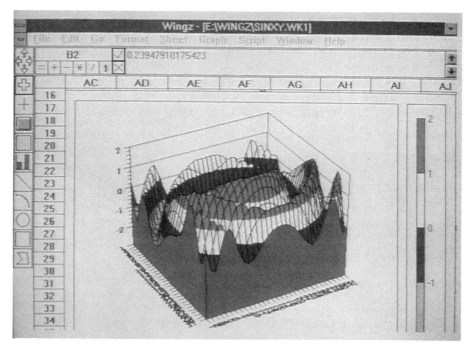

Figure 1.7 A 3-D graph created with Wingz.

spreadsheets will be expected to perform in the near future. What has Wingz added to the usual complement of spreadsheet capabilities? Quite a few things, actually. The most noticeable thing right away is the addition of powerful and esthetically beautiful 3-D charts and graphics, twenty different types. But there's quite a bit more. For one thing, there's color like there has never been color before on a worksheet. Any cell can be whatever combination of foreground and background colors you like, including custom colors you mix by hand. For those with color monitors, this opens up a whole new way to make worksheets clear, understandable, and quite attractive too. But the best is still to come. Wingz includes a built-in Hyperscript programming language that leaves other spreadsheet macro languages very far behind. These things alone would make Wingz revolutionary, but there's even more that will be touched upon later.

The average Excel user will fall in love with Wingz immediately and not find it very difficult to catch on to it. What makes this an attractive product is the right combination of presentation capability and power. As I mentioned above, after ten years, spreadsheets haven't seen many significant breakthroughs. There is still tremendous drudgery and time involved in doing anything really useful with them. But in the case of a spreadsheet with a language like Hyperscript, there is an opportunity to change this in a substantial way. With the right use of this simple but powerful language, quite a bit can be automated. Even more importantly, it is possible to make generic applications that can serve a wide variety of purposes and evolve over time, improved continually.

This is why the technology really makes sense. Now that spreadsheets are designed to handle really huge amounts of data, ways of taking advantage of that without endless hours of work are needed. With this in mind, it is clear that Wingz and its imitators will have a long future.

Novel Editing of Worksheets

Wingz provides some new editing features for spreadsheets, particularly its array of icon-based tools. For example, with its Operator Icons, all the basic arithmetical operators, as well as the dollar sign used to signify absolute cell references, can be inserted into formulas by a single mouse click on the appropriate icon. Pasting functions has also been improved from the method used in Excel. The Wingz function paste dialog has a number of buttons for selecting the formula type, so that usually most of those of a given type are available on the screen at once and ready for grabbing. Resizing rows and columns is also possible by first clicking on the row or column boundary and then simply dragging the element until it reaches its new size. Links can be made between cells to those in any other worksheet. The worksheet must be currently active though, and recalculation after changes in the external sheet is not automatic.

Power Graphics

In the field of 3-D graphics, as a stand-alone spreadsheet, Wingz does just that: it stands alone. As mentioned, it gives you twenty different types of spectacular 3-D charts, including even topographic charts. Charts using polar coordinates are also supported. With any 3-D chart, it is possible to interactively change the angle of view using a slider dialog. This option also allows for adding perspective. But it doesn't stop there. There is a free graphics drawing capability too. Wingz allows external drawings and "clip art" to be imported and pasted onto worksheets as picture objects. A powerful facility is also provided for mixing custom palette colors and assigning them to "color picker" controls. Words, of course, can't be expected to rival the visuals themselves in conveying the dramatic results attainable even by rather modest means and skill.

Custom Controls and Dialogs

Wingz allows you to create controls such as buttons interactively, and mount them right on your worksheets. Things like adding a scroll bar to a text field of a worksheet are routine. You can record operations into an automatic script and attach this to a custom button. Controls and other objects can also be joined together into groups and acted upon as a unit. Objects are literally attached to the cell ranges to which they are assigned. This means that if those cells are resized, the objects get resized with them. For this reason, they are usually left until after the layout of a worksheet has been completed. Various visual styles are available for the objects and controls, such as the 3-D Drop, which uses a shadow effect to give the appearance of added dimensionality. The full use of these enhancements is made possible with Hyperscript.

Tricks of the Trade

With Wingz, just about anything that enhances a worksheet is called an object. Objects are created by the different tools in the Wingz Tool Box. Completely custom screens can be created that bring out the full potential of graphics oriented worksheets. Some things that might be overlooked at first in a product like Wingz are: using multiple formula search criteria with databases, using multiple windows, forming double variable tables, creating custom number formats, and making custom grid displays. With Wingz, for example, all cells in a worksheet do not have to be the same size. As already mentioned, neither do they have to be a uniform color. With some experimentation and a few simple rules of thumb, these important features can make worksheet data visible like never before. Various color schemes can be adopted so that things can be spotted instantly by their color. Worksheets themselves can be made into attractive presentations rather than just a place where data is stored.

Building Databases

Like most spreadsheets today, Wingz allows row-oriented databases to be built that afford rapid, easy editing, and high visibility of the data. Various macros and programs can be used to work with the records in a database. The most important thing in designing spreadsheet databases is to be able to make the formulas, macros, and programs independent of the number of record rows. You should be able to add and subtract records at will without affecting how any of the management utilities operate. Wingz provides an advanced query capability for searching database records. For example, there is even the ability to specify which fields NOT to include in a search. In performing qualified searches through Wingz records, you have the choice of having the found information highlighted or copied into a separate range of cells.

The Power of Matrices

A matrix is an array of cells that can be operated upon as a whole. Square matrices are those with an equal number of rows and columns. Wingz is capable of working with extremely large matrices. I have been able to create and manipulate square matrices in Wingz as large as 96 rows by 96 columns. Even larger ones are possible. Matrices of this magnitude can be used for various purposes, such as solving systems of 90 or 100 equations. The matrices can be set up so that plugging in the coefficient cells that represent the equations automatically plugs the matrices with the proper values and solves the equations.

Designing Business Models That Evolve

As with most spreadsheets, the best use of a tool like Wingz in business is to build accurate numerical models of a business. It is impossible to do this all at once. The ideal way to design worksheet models is in such a way that they can be continually updated to be increasingly accurate. One of the biggest obstacles to doing this is the format for cell formulas. Spreadsheets do not have an easy way of updating formulas to make them more accurate. However, by using foresight it is possible. One way that worksheet models can be designed to allow for easy and even automatic revision is by devoting cells to hold the coefficients of formulas, and then writing the formulas by reference to those cells, rather than constant numbers. Then the formulas can be updated by simply changing the value of the coefficient cells. You can even devise procedures for doing this automatically.

Forecasting Sales and Cash Flow

A good way to get the most out of Wingz is by using it with some of the tested forecasting techniques, like Multiple Regression, Box-Jenkins, Time-Series, the Census X-11 Method, and the Foran system. Whenever possible, try to build generic worksheets that can be easily adapted, progressively refined, and reused. This is the real meat and potatoes of using advanced spreadsheets like Wingz. Many of the new generation of spreadsheets add features geared primarily toward presentation. This presumes that there is something significant on which to bestow such lavish embellishments. It's here that you discover the real power of Wingz: doing the thing that modern spreadsheets do best.

Advanced Modeling

In advanced modeling, you make the attempt to build a representation of a business, and the industry it's in, which provides some ability to predict when something new and of importance is going to happen. In statistical modeling, usually various indicators are selected that have shown themselves to be useful in forecasting changes in market trends. Often these indicators have no causal relationship to anything that affects the business. The relationship is a one of pure numerical correlation. Methods are introduced for using knowledge about a particular industry and a particular business to do more than just extrapolate previous trends. And advanced modeling attempts to do more than just project from previous statistics. It attempts to predict from a model of how things actually operate. Although these predictions are naturally quite difficult, the powerful resources of a spreadsheet like Wingz make such goals possible to attempt.

Introducing Hyperscript

The Hyperscript language is the third thing, after the powerful 3-D graphics and the multicolor spreadsheets, that makes Wingz utterly unique. This is a full-fledged programming language that also has a number of development tools to assist programmers. Hyperscript is the most powerful language provided with a spreadsheet program that I have ever seen. Besides allowing standard scripts for automating routine tasks, Hyperscript also allows for preparing four specialized kinds of scripts: field scripts, control scripts, button scripts, and sheet scripts. These scripts are attached to the different objects for which they are named and handle user-generated events. Besides executing scripts from script files, there are two other ways of executing Hyperscript commands: from the Entry Bar and via Wingz menus. The Entry Bar is useful for interactive control of work sessions, and for trying out ideas prior to encoding them in scripts. And I also shouldn't fail to mention Hyperscript's support for advanced control structures and recursive programming.

Making a Hyperscript Application

The process of creating a Hyperscript application involves editing, debugging, and compiling scripts and then attaching them to worksheets, text fields, or controls. Scripts are prepared in a special editor called a script window, used specifically for that purpose. Syntax error detection is performed when a script is compiled. For fixing errors in logic, traditional debugging practices are needed, such as inserting messages at key points and the use of commenting to isolate trouble points. Generally speaking, any menu command and any formula function can be accessed from within Hyperscript. This language also allows user-defined functions to be developed. Once a new function has been written it acts like any other Hyperscript function. Include, or rather, GET SCRIPT statements allow you to reference functions defined elsewhere, in other script files. Utilizing this aspect of Hyperscript properly allows you to fashion the language as you see fit. With an open-ended language for an open-ended product, any application built with it is obviously going to be open-ended as well.

User Interface Programming

The Hyperscript language provides facilities for complete control of an application's user interface, including adding new menu items, new menus, and even new menu bars. A sample Hyperscript application is provided with Wingz that shows how the entire user interface of Wingz itself would be written in Hyperscript. Hierarchical or cascading menus are rather simple to program using the 'submenu' keyword. You can also add custom popup menus to a worksheet that are not attached to any menu bar. The ADD POPUP MENU command allows you to specify the range on a worksheet where you want the popup menu to appear.

Custom Graphics Programming

Very interesting and powerful graphics can be created with the Hyperscript DRAW command. Custom 2-D and 3-D drawings can be developed and assigned for convenience to special buttons or added as commands to menus. These custom drawings can include spline curves, partial arcs, arrowheads, special symbols, and 3-D shadowing. Larger graphics applications can also be produced that give interactive control to the user, allowing partial charts to be made period by period, allowing the user to interrupt at any point and alter worksheet parameters. In principle, given the external function capability covered next, just about any type of graphics program can be produced. Hyperscript offers an open-ended system that is a function of the coding and design skills of user-developers.

External Data, Functions, and Applications

Advanced Wingz applications can be built by accessing Dynamic Link Libraries (DLLs). Because of the special calling conventions, these DLLs have to be developed specifically for that purpose. A DLL provides a modular way of reusing code by several applications that can be loaded in Windows at once. Each program does not have to have its own compiled copies of the code. The one copy of code in the DLL can serve all of them at once. In general, script languages can call upon the functions provided in DLLs quite readily and use functionality provided there. An example of a DLL that comes with Windows 3.0 is PBRUSH.DLL, which provides a code used by the Paintbrush accessory program.

Limitations

Since the overall conclusions of this review have never been kept a mystery, the best way to end it would probably be to talk about the shortcomings of this product, if I can find any. And, of course, I can. One thing that comes to mind is the limited goal-seeking functions. Wingz has a GOAL function, but it is a rather low-level one that has to be fed a guess and then iterates up to twenty times to do its best. Personally, I prefer the way this is done in Excel, Quattro Pro, and especially 123/G. But, some will argue, that's what Hyperscript is for. Wrong. Most users don't know how to write this sort of thing, and it should probably be written in assembler for speed.

Another thing Excel users might miss is matrix operations that can be easily entered right in formulas. Wingz is like Quattro Pro, in that the matrix operations are performed interactively from menus. Those who have used the Excel matrix functions in formulas are going to have some work ahead of them converting.

As far as Hyperscript goes, one thing I'd like to see added in a future release is a set of commands for both executing other Windows programs and delivering commands to them. Hyperscript would then become a command language not just for Wingz, but for Windows in general. And last but not least on my little wish list would be some way of interfacing with anybody's DLLs for Windows 3.0, though this may not be possible. As it is, you need to write your own with special calling formats. What a world would be opened if all DLLs were accessible to Hyperscript.

■ A SESSION WITH WINDOWS 3.0

I've decided that the default color scheme has got to go on my Windows 3.0 desktop, so without really leaving my word processor I call up the Task Switch control, transfer to the Program Manager, and from there launch into the Control Panel. As I do, the windows start to stack up over my word processor, but still leave an area to which I can immediately return with a mouse click whenever I want to. I expand the Crayon box Colors icon and just as the Windows screen mockup appears, I click this time on the Color Palette >> Control bar and an adjacent window opens with a paint box of colors to choose from. I want to make the top menu bar of windows a deep green, so I click on that part of the window mockup and then click on the color green I want. That's it. The top bar is now green on the mockup. I click on the top menu title and then on bright yellow, and this color changes. The menu text should be a sharp, bright, and highly visible color, so I'll pick crimson. I do the same for the scroll bar and it becomes a light green. I find this very pleasing to the eye and so I go to the File menu and save the color scheme to hard disk.

The next thing I want to do is try out the PrintScreen hotkey on some non-Windows graphics programs. I go back to the Program Manager and in the non-Windows group I select the Autosketch icon. This will launch the Autodesk program Autosketch and I will load the locomotive design drawing that comes up with a blue background. It finishes redrawing, I press Shift-Printscreen, and the monitor winks, so I know that back in the Windows 3.0 Clipboard I'll have something to look at. So I exit Autosketch and the Windows desktop resumes its place on the screen. I open the Paintbrush program and first select the View menu to get the Palette and Toolbox out of the way so I can see the whole image on my screen. Then I select Paste on the Edit menu and after a few studious blinks of the cursor, I have the locomotive blueprint imported to the Windows environment where I will save it as a bitmap.

Now I'll try out this picture as a desktop background. It brings back memories of my father's contracting business, with blueprints often covering whole tables. Still, it's not really what I want, so I call up another program with graphics, Music Printer Plus, which is a program for printing and playing back music in a MIDI (Music Instrument Digital Interface) studio. I load the score for a small band arrangement of a song of mine called "Forever" and I see the music score notation for this music. Fine! Another Shift-Printscreen and once again the monitor winks at me. I exit the program, bring up Paintbrush again, and paste the contents of the Clipboard. Sure enough, there is my music score. With it now in a program intended for graphics design, I can hardly resist putting some different colors on the page of music, so I do. I've often wondered what music manuscripts would be like if more color were used. Now I know. This image looks pretty good, so I save it as a bitmap file. Then I go into the Control Panel's Desktop facility and select this multicolor music score as my desktop background.

The next thing I want to try out is going the other way: pasting information from the Clipboard into a non-Windows application. First I bring up the Ctalk VIEWS Browser, an object-oriented programming tool that is very useful, but has a rather marginal editor. I want to find some code that is like what I want to write, so that I can edit it quickly into what I need. I browse about in the VIEWS Browser for a while, then I find what I'm looking for, highlight it with the mouse, and copy it to the Clipboard. Then I call up the Programmer's Workbench. First I hit ALT-ESC to collapse it down to a DOS icon. Then I pop up the Control menu from this icon and select first Edit and then Paste from the sprouted submenu. I then expand the icon back to the fullscreen program and there is the code pasted in the editor where it should be. I save my work and end the session with Windows 3.0, satisfied that it does what the documentation claims it can do.

2

OBJECT-ORIENTED PROGRAMMING: WHAT IS IT?

■ INTRODUCTION

Although this book is about Windows programming from the object-oriented point of view, it is important to look at object-oriented programming (OOP) in its own right first, before considering its connection with Windows development. In this way, hopefully a more balanced perspective will result, one that will provide a somewhat more objective background for what follows. The assumption made in this chapter is that the reader has no previous exposure to object-oriented systems, but has some general background in programming.

In my view of it, OOP represents the most recent stage in the development of programming technology. Just as the structured programming model of Algol and Pascal represented an advance over the earlier block-structured programming of FORTRAN, so OOP is the latest stage in this evolutionary progression. As with all advances in technology, sooner or later most professionals recognize that there is something very "correct" about OOP. That is why it has already taken up a permanent place in the software development industry.

■ PROGRAMMING PARADIGMS

To some, it may come as a bit of a surprise that there are such things as different programming paradigms. A programming paradigm is a basic model for approaching the way programs are written. Most programmers are familiar with just one paradigm, that of procedural programming. But there are now many others. First of all, there is the object-oriented paradigm, which is what we are concerned with here. But, in addition, there are the rule-based programming, logic programming, parallel programming, visual programming, constraint-based, data flow, neural net, rehearsal, and other programming paradigms as well.

Why are there many programming paradigms? Partly because programming computers is still a relatively new discipline, and partly because there are still many different types of things people want to be able to do with them. It is also because the current type of digital computer in popular use is just one type of machine architecture among many. Currently, there is a considerable amount of experimentation with alternative machine architectures that are considered to be improvements in one respect or another. With many of them, an alternative programming paradigm is either required or intended. Because of the generality of all digital computers, just about any paradigm can be simulated with greater or lesser efficiency. The most successful will be the best mix of hardware and software paradigms for speed and ease of use.

■ THE OBJECT-ORIENTED PARADIGM

If you ask the question "What is object-oriented programming?" you had better be prepared for rather different answers depending upon who you ask. As with many terms that have become a "buzz word," people are apt to use them to describe whatever their current projects may be, often with surprisingly little justification. When it is a question of object-oriented programming methodology rather that products and tools, then the emphasis will tend to be on what programmers find most interesting or useful about object-oriented systems. Object-oriented programming, then, can be many different things to many different people. How shall we understand it here?

Before proceeding any further, it will help to eliminate any confusion in terminology, for there is at least one other use of the terms "object-oriented" besides the one that will be used in this book. A particular type of graphics application program is referred to as "object-oriented." Generally speaking, this is a way of contrasting these applications with pixel-based or screen-oriented graphics programs. The main idea is that the "object-oriented" type of graphics program stores images so that the component objects that make up a complete picture retain their individual identity. This means that it is always possible to perform various changes on an object by object basis with these programs. More often, computer graphics images are stored on a pixel by pixel basis, simply as screen information. As it is used in this book, the phrase "object-oriented" has an entirely different meaning, as will soon become clear. In the sense I am using it, "object-oriented" does not refer merely to graphics programs, and refers to a style of programming or programming tool, rather then specifically to a type of application. It is true that the type of graphics program in question is particularly easy to write with OOP techniques. However, it is also true that such applications can be written without the programming paradigm I will be discussing, and also that pixel or screen-oriented graphics programs can be written with object-oriented tools and methods. In this book, the only sense in which I will refer to application programs as being "object-oriented" is when they have been written in the object-oriented paradigm.

The preliminary definition of object-oriented programming that will be adopted here is one intended to allow the reader to proceed with sufficient clarity through the current introduction. It will be expanded upon at a later point. The initial definition we will adopt for now is:

Object-oriented programming (OOP) is a type of programming that provides a way of modularizing programs by establishing partitioned memory areas for both data and procedures that can be used as templates for spawning copies of such modules on demand.

Let's pause for a moment to consider exactly what this means. According to this definition, an object is regarded as a partitioned area of computer memory. This should provide an opportunity to dispel some misconceptions. Many people take the phrase "object-oriented" literally to mean that this is a type of programming that is concerned with objects in the world, as opposed to the state of the computer being programmed. There is some truth to this, but it is not the essential thing that makes OOP what it is.

What is essential is that a method of partitioning the memory of a computer is adopted, which allows each of these modules or objects to function relatively independently of one another. There are various consequences of this, most of which are advantageous to the programmer. However, most programmers tend to emphasize primarily those advantages that they find most interesting, or with which they are most impressed.

What exactly is meant by partitioning the memory of the computer? This means to provide a system of dividing the memory of the computer into areas that have a certain functional independence. The memory partitions are independent in the sense that they may be used in a variety of different programs without modification, and with complete assurance that none of the memory locations will be overwritten or in any way function differently because of their presence in a different environment.

Our definition states that the partitioned areas of memory are not just those that store data, but those that store code in the form of executable procedures. This partitioning is essential to keep the object protected. For if any procedure were allowed admission to the memory locations of an object, then it would be possible for unknown things to happen to the data stored in the object. This would clearly interfere with its functionality. For this reason, the active processes of an object-oriented system are defined as local functions or procedures, which are the only ones that may have access to the object's data. In this way, the object protects itself from having its data and functionality corrupted by unknown events external to it. The result of this is that once a functioning element of a program has been written correctly and completely debugged, it becomes functional in a way that no subsequent additions or modifications in any of the programs in which it is used can change.

Finally, the definition states that the partitioned memory structure can be used as a template for spawning further copies of the object. This means, for example, that once a window object has been defined, as many of these objects can be created as memory allows, without writing additional code to ensure that there are no interference problems. In stating that additional copies are made, I am referring only to the behavior of the objects. Everything behaves as though there are complete multiple copies in operation. Please note here, though, that no implication on how the objects are actually implemented is intended.

■ OBJECT-ORIENTED PROGRAMMING METAPHORS

Each programming paradigm has its own metaphors, which provide handles that can assist programmers in thinking about program design. Computer science itself is full of metaphors that have become the jargon of the field. Two excellent examples of this are the terms "memory" and "windows." Once we stop and think about it, these metaphors are actually rather remote from their origins. The memory and windows we encounter in computing have little resemblance to the things in our world after which they have been named. Nevertheless the terms have stuck and we use them indiscriminately, apparently without any great difficulty.

The metaphors used in describing programming models present a somewhat different situation in that to be of service, they must reflect a genuine model whose features actually have practical implications. The more accurate these metaphorical models, therefore, the better. What are some of the metaphors of OOP? As soon as we ask the question, we can see that many of the basic concepts, such as message passing and inheritance, have a metaphorical significance. However, at least in the case of these two metaphors, the analogy can be taken quite far with good results.

Some of the metaphors adopted to explain object-oriented systems, however, can be more remote and, therefore, less useful. In his book *Object-Oriented Programming,* Brad Cox uses the metaphors of software ICs and factories to try to explain the concepts of object-oriented systems. As I will argue later in more detail, although these metaphors have pedagogical value, they are not adequate to serve as more lasting metaphorical models of the components of object-oriented systems. Object-oriented systems have features that actually make them significantly more powerful technologically than ICs or factories. This is largely due to their extreme modularity. We cannot use off-the-shelf ICs to build other ICs, and the end products of factories generally do not resemble the factories that make them. However, it is an everyday matter in object-oriented programming to use existing objects to make still newer ones that inherit all the properties of their ancestors.

■ ACTIVE DATA

One very useful way of understanding objects is as an attempt at providing a form of active data. A sense in which it is true to say that an object represents active data is that the paradigm for performing operations in an object-oriented system is to send messages to objects telling them what we would like them to do. So, for example, if we want to print a string on the screen, then we send a message to the string to print itself. An object that is a string is not just a passive piece of textual data. It is, in a sense, an active entity that knows how to perform various operations on itself correctly. For a lot of reasons, it makes quite a bit of sense to package the operations for various types of objects right with the objects.

One of the most basic distinctions in programming is that of data and procedures. To some degree, this reflects the hardware difference between memory chips and processors.

The basic model of a program according to this design of computers is that data is stored in memory chips and the instructions of processors are used to manipulate the data. In this model, therefore, data is essentially passive and instructions are the active elements that operate on the passive element. Object-oriented programming (OOP) is part of a movement to define the programming model somewhat differently. An object is both code and data. It is a form of active data.

■ MESSAGE PASSING

One of the main models in OOP for allowing object modules to interact is the message-passing model. Objects are seen as communicating by passing messages that they can either accept or reject. Generally an object accepts messages it recognizes and ignores those it does not. In this way, the types of interactions between objects are carefully controlled. Because all interactions follow this protocol, there is no opportunity for code external to an object to interfere with its functioning in unpredictable and un-desirable ways.

At the very minimum, sending a message involves specifying the name of an object and the name of the message to be sent to that object. Often there will also be arguments that will have to be specified. The arguments may be the names of variables known only to the type of object that recognizes the message, or they may be global variables known to all objects. They may not be variables known privately by another unrelated type of object.

As mentioned above, message passing produces the appearance of active data. You can send a message to an object to write itself to disk, display itself on the monitor, delete itself, and so on. Is this only an appearance, or is there more substance to the connection between active data and message passing? This is a difficult question and requires more background than I have provided so far to answer adequately. Let us just say for the moment that message passing has the effect of making objects behave as active data from outside them, but not from inside. From within an object we have the same dichotomy between passive data and active procedures that is found in conventional programming.

What difference does it make whether or not a system uses message passing? Again, a final answer to this question is not possible here. However, the general answer is that message passing allows for advanced programming techniques that can exploit the partitioned functionality of objects that respond to messages. Although there are ways of getting many of the same results without message passing, it is generally more difficult and requires greater knowledge and skill on the part of the programmer. On the whole, objects in message-passing systems have a very special kind of autonomy that is unique in programming. In a certain sense each object behaves as a little specialized computer that communicates with other specialized computers. Although this is, of course, an-other metaphor, it is a fruitful metaphor that is worth pursuing. As we will see later on in this book, the message-passing model suggests many interesting and powerful algorithms that might not occur to programmers and software designers without this programming model.

■ CLASSES, INSTANTIATION, AND INHERITANCE

One of the most basic concepts in OOP is that of a class. As is it is understood in this context, a class is a template for creating actual functioning objects of a given type. In many object-oriented systems a class is an object in its own right, but one with very limited capabilities. One way of putting it would be to say that while a class provides the blueprint or genetic code for creating cows, it is the actual cow instance that gives milk and not the cow class.

We say that a class is instantiated when it has actually been used to stamp out one or more objects of its type. Appropriately, the objects that have been created of a given class are called instances of that class. What really gives practical justification to the class structure is the facility for inheritance. This is the ability to create classes that will automatically model themselves on other classes. When a class B has been defined so as to model itself on class A, we say that B is a subclass of A. Reciprocally, we also say that A is a superclass of B. This is to say that B inherits all of A's behavior.

Having one class inherit the behavior of another would be pointless if that were all that is involved. The point of creating a subclass is to add some additional behavior besides what is inherited. Usually the subclass is outfitted with behavior that allows it to act as a more specialized version of its superclass. Some object-oriented systems also have what is called multiple inheritance. This means that they may have more than one superclass. In such systems, sometimes we will create a new class so that it can inherit from two or more superclasses. Other times we will provide the additional behavior by hand coding. In either case, the result is a class that can stamp out objects with a somewhat different behavior.

Through this process of defining subclasses, an object-oriented system comes to have what is called a class hierarchy. This hierarchy is a tree or network of classes that starts with the most general, uppermost branches and descends to the bottom leaves, which are the most specific. One of the main things that defines the power of an object-oriented environment is the class hierarchy and its capabilities. Programmers extend an object-oriented language by expanding its class hierarchy and the vocabulary of messages exchanged by various objects.

The active element of objects, the messages, are also known as methods and are like functions that are local to a particular object. The names of these methods are often called selectors. They have this designation because they allow the system to select which code is to be executed when called by name.

One of the great advantages of object-oriented systems is that the protocol for handling various objects stays essentially the same as the language becomes extended. This means that there is an opportunity for allowing large systems that are developed by more than one programmer to be managed efficiently. This is so because it is possible to keep the communication and documentation of new features between programmers at a minimum.

One practice that facilitates this is often called overloading. Overloading is the convention of giving methods that do the same thing for different classes of objects the exact same selector name. In most strictly typed languages, it is necessary to name functions differently that perform the same function for different datatypes. So, for example, we might have one function called divideInteger and another called divideReal for performing the operation of division for integers and real numbers, respectively. In systems where there are a large number of classes, this could result in the system being very hard to use because the programmer has to continually look up the names of functions. With overloading, the method is called simply divide for all classes of numbers, even though the code that implements the divide method may vary from class to class. This way, the programmer or user has a uniform protocol for classes in a large range of operations that makes the system much easier to use. The programmer does not have to look at the code written by other programmers to know how to use that code to write new routines that utilize it.

■ TYPES OF OBJECT-ORIENTED SYSTEMS

There are several different ways to distinguish between various types of object-oriented systems. The most basic difference is between pure and hybrid systems. A pure object-oriented system is one in which everything is an object. An example of this is Smalltalk. In this type of system even classes are objects that are instances of a class. At first this may appear confusing, but there is nothing at all paradoxical about it. It is in fact a direct result of the desire for total consistency in the system. Just as objects are created from a class that serves as their model or template, classes themselves are objects that are created according to the blueprint laid out in a specific class. Usually this is called the metaclass.

The more inquisitive and logically minded reader will undoubtedly have sensed a familiar kind of conceptual hurdle here. The question may have come to mind that if classes always have to be instances of another class, how does the original class come into being. The answer is that we are not dealing with just concepts here. An object-oriented system is a practical system that is designed for certain tangible ends, not to create a purely logical artifact of the mind. The designers of pure object-oriented systems decided to make classes all instances of another class because this was the most coherent and consistent for such a system to operate. If the metaclass that serves as the template for all other classes is not itself an instance of a class, then this is not a flaw in the system. What we have is a working system that has been able to carry the object-oriented paradigm as far as it is conceivable to carry it.

A hybrid system is one in which objects coexist within a conventional programming language. Examples of this include, for instance, various object-oriented extensions to C and LISP, which will be considered in some detail in a later chapter. Because they must coexist with already existing programming languages, the elements in hybrid systems can obviously not all be objects. Whether or not encapsulation or memory protection can exist in a hybrid system depends on the design and implementation of the host language. Usually there will be ways that protection can be broken.

Another way of classifying object-oriented systems is by the type of inheritance scheme used. The two main types are those that have single or multiple inheritance. As was mentioned previously, multiple-inheritance systems are those that allow a class to inherit from more than one superclass. Multiple inheritance is still a relatively new feature of object-oriented systems, and many implementations still do not have this feature.

The main issue that prevents multiple inheritance from becoming as straightforward as one might wish is the possibility of conflicts between the names of variables and names in the different classes that are to be inherited. Although this is a rare situation, it is one that has to be handled in a rigorous manner. As yet there is no standard method of handling it with which all are in agreement.

A final distinction between different types of object systems is between those that have actual concurrent processing and those that do not. In a concurrent message-passing system, for example, the messages that are exchanged between objects can occur in parallel rather than waiting for their turn as in sequential processing systems.

Table 2.1 lists the five criteria that measure the degree to which a system is object-oriented.

■ HOW OBJECT-ORIENTED SYSTEMS WORK

For some applications, it is possible for a programmer to ignore any consideration of how an object-oriented system is implemented and how it really works. For many artificial intelligence applications, this is a luxury we cannot afford. It is true that one of the goals of object-oriented systems is to allow programmers to use code without the need to know the details of its implementation. But many goals of today's most progressive software projects are of the sort that push the capabilities of a programming system to its limits and beyond. For this reason, I will end this chapter with a general discussion of the basic mechanisms used to provide most object-oriented systems with their characteristic behavior.

Table 2.1 Degrees of Object-Oriented Systems.

Criteria or Level

1. Classes with Multiple Instances
2. Encapsulated Functions and Data
3. Run-time Binding
4. Multiple Inheritance
5. Message Combination

What actually happens when a message is sent to an object? In most object-oriented systems, objects generally have both a shared part and a private part. There is no need for the parts of an object that are always the same to be copied. This would be a waste of memory resources. Generally, the parts of an object that are the same for all objects of this type are stored at the class level. This often turns out to be all the code for methods as well as the data for class variables that comprises the shared part of objects. When a message is sent, therefore, it is handled by a routine that attempts to look this up in the area of memory owned by the class. The instance variables and their values are private, however. Each object actually stores its own instance variables. The class provides the information of which instance variables to create, but their actual storage is done by the instance itself. If the data or code being sought is inherited from another class, then it is only stored once, at the highest level. Routines that access it are redirected up the hierarchy until they reach the class from which all others have inherited.

■ USING AN OBJECT-ORIENTED SYSTEM

Largely due to the implementation of Smalltalk, the first full-fledged object-oriented language, systems of this type are known for the special user interface facilities that assist programmers. The multiwindow mouse-oriented environment that has become popular for all types of user applications on today's personal work stations was originally closely associated with the first object-oriented systems. Some of the unique features and requirements of object-oriented programming make the use of tools that make programs highly visible to the programmer highly desirable. So, for example, one of the tools that has come to be associated with object-oriented systems is the Browser. As the name suggests, a Browser is a facility that allows the programmer to peruse at will some aspect of the programming environment. For example, in Smalltalk, there is the System Browser, which allows the programmer to get first an overview of the Class Hierarchy of the current system and then to move down into some aspect of the hierarchy to inspect or edit its contents.

Object-oriented systems provide many desirable capabilities, but they do so only provided that the programmer knows how to utilize them. There are a number of responsibilities of programmers that are unique to object-oriented systems. First of all, the programmer has to know the basic operations are performed, such as defining classes, creating objects, and performing operations. In addition, the programmer has to know what methods are available to what classes of objects. Often there are many useful classes and methods present in an object-oriented system. However, programmers will not benefit from this unless they know what is there and how it may be used.

■ WHY OBJECT-ORIENTED PROGRAMMING?

There are various reasons why programmers find the object-oriented approach important and even indispensable. To one programmer, it might be the possibility of eliminating redundant code that is most appealing. To another, it might be the protection that objects have from being invaded by code in other parts of the program. To still another, it might be the time savings involved in being able to build programs out of standard working parts that communicate with one another, rather than having to start writing code from scratch. Finally, there are programmers who find the most appealing thing is the ability to have as many instances of an object as they like copresent without any interference. Most object-oriented systems provide the facilities for allowing programs to have all of these features. Which of them is the most important will depend on the requirements of a project as well as the preferences of those who undertake it. As your knowledge and experience with object-oriented systems increases, you might find that your preference shifts from one of these features to another. But this is not of very great importance, since, in theory at least, it is possible for programs to reap all of these advantages without any compromises.

When programmers stopped using just ones (1) and zeros (0) to program computers and began to use assemblers that could recognize mnemonic symbols that stood for the actual binary machine instructions executed, there was little chance that the old method would survive. Advances in programming technology have become increasingly more subtle since that time, so that important breakthroughs are not always immediately recognized by all. The development of compiled high-level languages led to just as wide an adoption as the assemblers before them. However, compilers did not replace assemblers. It would be more accurate to think of them as the next layer of software erected between the machine and the programmer, which made them still easier to program.

■ SOME CONCLUSIONS

Object-oriented programming (OOP) is not a direction that is entirely new and without precedent in computer science. It simply takes recent developments in programming languages to their next logical step, for increased clarity, modularity, and programming efficiency. From one point of view, OOP can be seen as the programming paradigm that takes structured programming to its natural logical conclusion. In structured programming, variables may be local to a particular procedure and these procedures typically pass arguments like strings and numbers between them. With object-oriented systems all this is taken quite a bit further. Variables are no longer local just to procedures. The main building blocks are now objects—protected areas of system memory—which can have both local variables and local procedures. Moreover, the building blocks do not communicate with one another just by passing arguments. The procedures themselves, usually called methods, which are local to objects, are actually the messages that are sent and received by objects. In this respect, objects resemble smaller computers within the host computer, each with their own data and code areas.

In most object-oriented systems there are at least two different types of objects: classes and instances. Classes may have a logical relation between one another in such a way that one class might be the subclass or superclass of another. Generally speaking, the superclass is the more abstract class and the subclass would be the more specific one. So, for example, if we create the class Furniture, then we can also create the class Chair as the subclass of furniture, and DeskChair as a subclass of Chair. In this example, Furniture would be the superclass of Chair, which is in turn the superclass of DeskChair.

There are at least three immediate advantages of object-oriented systems. One very appealing one is that once you have written the code for a class, you can have as many instances of that class present in the system at the same time as memory will allow. A class is simply a template on which each instance is modeled and is provided with its own area of memory that cannot be accessed by any other object except by using the object's own local methods. So, for example, this means that in an object-oriented system you can have as many graphics pens, windows, editors, interpreters, and so on as you like copresent without any fear that they will interfere with one another. The second advantage is that through the mechanism of inheritance, subclasses automatically share all the variables and methods of their superclasses. This means that greater specializations of functions can be written just by adding the part that is unique while the rest is inherited automatically. The third immediate advantage is that it is possible to provide a uniform interface over the widest possible range of object types. This is because the same name can be used for methods of different objects that have to be implemented differently, while the differences remain invisible to the user. So, for example, we might create different classes for a variety of different geometric polyhedra. Then for each separate class we would define the methods volume and surface-area. The actual formulas and their implementations would vary, but the calling names would all be the same. So, for example, you could say Tetrahedron-1 volume or Cube-3 volume, and in each case methods would be invoked that returned the value of the object's volume.

Some say that the key advantage of OOP is the ability to reuse code for many different programs. But, by itself, this is not significantly different from library functions. A more substantial difference is the improved ability to handle complexity in a transparent manner. A key advantage of OOP that is not necessarily immediately obvious, but which experienced programmers who have worked with these systems will verify, is that object-oriented languages can give you more leverage in working on very large programs. This does not come automatically, though. It is not guaranteed. Factoring a large program into the right parts is a large part of the battle. It is equally necessary to learn the right techniques for managing the code and making life easy for the members of a programming team. Object-oriented systems are usually rather diffuse, with parts of applications being dispersed among a number of classes and subclasses. To program efficiently with such a system, it is essential to have the proper tools and an effective method for keeping the application well-focused and well-organized.

It is important to point out that OOP should not be regarded as something that is easy to pick up extremely rapidly, since it is a very different paradigm from what most programmers are accustomed to. As programming approaches go, it is a rather knowledge intensive one. In other words, the readily available modular code is only useful providing that programmers know what they have available to them and how it may be best used. Many programmers resist learning new languages, not to speak of new programming paradigms, so it is important to spell out again in clear-cut, pragmatic terms, just what the real advantages are to programming with objects. As I see it, there are four main ones:

1. Standard calling conventions for a broad range of operations that exhibit differences in behaviorlike variations on a theme.

2. A means of managing very large programming projects by breaking up large problems into smaller, independently functioning, highly visible parts.

3. A truly modular programming environment where redundancies in coding are kept at an absolute minimum.

4. The ability to spawn multiple instances of a given function or object from the same code without the codes for the instances interfering with one another.

▪ ADDITIONAL PROGRAMMING RESPONSIBILITIES

Implicit in our discussion so far has been the fact that the object-oriented programmer has additional responsibilities that the conventional programmer does not always need to be concerned with. What are these additional responsibilities? First of all there is the task of modular object-oriented design. Considerable modularity is possible in the design of programs that use the ordinary procedural paradigm. With object-oriented systems, far more modularity is possible, and designing systems with this greatly increased modularity has a more specific focus. In object-oriented programming, you proceed far more with the whole system in view. Ideally, when a programmer writes an object-oriented routine, he or she is writing it in as generic a way as possible. The code should be written so that it will be usable in as many similar cases as possible.

The last statement is important, but I haven't spelled out some of the things that it implies. If you are new to OOP, some of it may not be completely comprehensible now, but I will give a first explanation here. If you don't get it this first time there will be other opportunities. I mentioned earlier that by using the inheritance feature of object-oriented systems, we can make more specialized versions of existing classes that inherit everything from the generic ancestor classes. This is one of the keys to the modularity of object-oriented programming. In designing a program, if you think a little bit about all similar programs you can begin to write code that is a little more generic. Let's take an example to bring out what I mean.

Let's say we are writing a program that is to be used by utter computer novices, and so has to be as user friendly as possible. With an object-oriented system, we have the flexibility of writing a simplified version of a program first, and then gradually adding the more sophisticated features later. We'll just consider a small part of this program, the part that reads and writes disk files. In the first cut of the program, we design a class called FILE, which has methods like readFile and writeFile for reading and writing files. They work fine, but provide no additional protection for unsophisticated users. Now when we start on the finished version, which will provide the additional protection, we don't have to rewrite readFile and writeFile. What we do is create a subclass of

FILE called SAFEFILE, which has its own versions of these two methods. What we do is first write methods that check the size of the buffer we want to write to disk and the room left both in system memory and on the destination disk. Then we write a new version of the writeFile method that first calls these methods and then calls the old writeFile from its parent. If the original writeFile was done well it will be usable for every situation that will ever come up in any program we have to write that involves writing files to disk. We never really rewrite it except to improve its efficiency. Whatever it lacks can be added in a modular way in the same way we have outlined here.

From what we have said, you can start to appreciate the significance of generic code. The FILE class that we wrote in the above example was really not written for the program we were writing. Ideally, it was written for all programs that we would ever write. The subclass of FILE that we wrote called SAFEFILE was written for the program, but in no sense is its code a captive of that program in the sense of being interwoven with its other code and variables. It's a functioning unit unto itself and can be installed in other programs similar to the way we install a new generator in an automobile. The generator does not need to know what kind of materials the car was made of or what octane gas we use. It does its job of generating electricity and if it was designed modularly enough, then it fits right in where the old one was located. With object-oriented software, we go one better than modular auto parts. We know in advance that the new parts will replace the old ones without a major problem because the new part is the old part's ancestor. It inherits everything we want it to about the old part and adds some new features of its own.

As you can probably see from this example, I was right in saying earlier that an object-oriented programmer has to think about the system as a whole while programming. This also implies that programmers need to know their system very well in order to program. Let's be a little more specific. The inventory of parts for building new programs in an object-oriented system is usually called a class library. This is what the programmer has to be very familiar with. You don't want to reinvent the wheel or write a lot of code that unnecessarily duplicates things that are already prewritten in your class library. But to avoid doing so you have to realize what is there and how it is used.

In practice, programmers who use the OOP paradigm do not need photographic memories. Like other programmers they need to rely on reference materials. However, an ingenious method has been devised for providing an online reference to an OOP system while at the same time providing an environment where one can design and edit programs. It is called a Browser and was first made popular with the Smalltalk programming language.

With a Browser for an object-oriented system, a programmer can get an excellent overview of a class library environment quite rapidly, then move in closer to get a more detailed understanding of the functioning of its objects, and then move on to begin designing and programming, without ever leaving it. It is the essential, premiere tool for object-oriented programming. One of the essentials for a browser of this type is a window in which all the classes in the library can be viewed by scrolling through a list. Typically when one of the classes is selected, all the local functions and variables of that class are displayed in other windows. Then, when a function is selected, the source code for that function is displayed in another pane of the window. Usually there are interactive facilities for adding or removing classes in the system. The result of this arrangement is a versatile tool that combines the ability to look up resources in the system and the ability to both design and code new programs. The Browser, as you can see, does far more than just allow one to browse. It is the key organizational tool that helps make both the programming system and particular programming projects visible.

3

OBJECT-ORIENTED C LANGUAGES AND TOOLS

"C++ is a young language, and there are many dark corners in it still for which there does not seem to be good solutions."—The Zortech C++ Compiler reference, p. 237.

This chapter is for the benefit of C programmers or those who are interested in using object-oriented programming (OOP) tools that have a strong similarity to C or are extensions of the C language. There are now a growing number of tools for programming in object-oriented C dialects for the Windows environment. Those who are considering using one of these tools will find quite a bit of helpful information here to give them an informed viewpoint on these increasingly popular programming tools and languages.

■ C++ 2.0: AN OVERVIEW

The C++ language is the object-oriented extension to C developed at AT&T by Bjarne Stroustrup. The central feature of the C++ architecture is that classes are everywhere regarded as user-defined types. If you recall, classes in object-oriented languages provide templates for working pieces of programs that allow many instances to be stamped out, as well as to provide generic code for other more specialized classes. As you can see, there is nothing in this that is inherently related to datatypes. Implementing classes in C++ formally as a way of providing user-defined types is a specific interpretation of objects that attempts to fit OOP specifically to the C language so as to provide a natural extension for it.

There are four storage class specifiers used in C++: auto, extern, register, and static. I will refrain subsequently from referring to them as "storage classes" because this just makes for confusion, since they are in no sense classes in the object-oriented sense. Table 3.1 lists the reserved words for the C++ language.

Table 3.1 C++ Reserved words.

asm	auto	break	case	catch	char
class	const	continue	default	delete	
do	double	else	enum	extern	
float	for	friend	goto	if	
inline	int	long	new	operator	
overload	private	protected	public	register	
return	short	signed	sizeof	static	
struct	switch	this	template	typedef	union
unsigned	virtual	void	while	volatile	

■ STRUCTS AND CLASSES

In C++ every struct or class can contain a collection of data objects, which can be basic datatypes, unions, or other structs and classes. Both structs and classes may also contain member functions. What does this come down to on the actual coding level? C++ simply uses the 'class' keyword to define new classes. The following declaration, for example, defines the 'set' class:

```
class set {
    struct set_member {
        int member;
        set_member* next;
        set_member(int m, set_member* n);
        };
};
```

Most often a class is defined as a subclass of another existing class. For example, we could write the following class definition:

```
class competitor : public business {
    // ...
};
```

This states that the competitor class is a subclass of the business class.

■ MULTIPLE INHERITANCE

One of the most powerful features of C++ is that classes can be derived from more than one class simultaneously. When declaring a class, a derivation list can be supplied of all the classes from which the new class will inherit encapsulated data and member functions. To define a class that inherits from more than one parent class, the notation for defining derived classes is extended. An example of such a definition is:

```
class competitor : public business, public adversary {
   // ...
};
```

This states that the competitor class derives from both the business and adversary classes.

■ MEMBER FUNCTIONS

Methods, called member functions in C++, are defined using the double colon (::). The syntax is the class name followed by the double colon and then the function name. For example,

```
set::setsize
set weekdays;
set workdays;
declares setsize as a member function of the class 'set'.
```

C++ also allows the creation of objects of type void**, which are essentially objects of unknown type.

■ PRIVACY AND PROTECTION

Unique to C++ among object-oriented languages are a variety of options for the kind and degree of encapsulation of object data. A member object can be declared as a friend, private, public, or protected. Normally member objects of a class are private. This means that only the member functions of that class have access to them. What is new with C++ is that member objects can also be declared as protected, which means that they would act the same as private members except that member functions of derived classes would also be permitted access to them.

■ FRIENDS

In C++, a friend is a function that is not a member function of a class but is still allowed access to the protected variables of that class. Why would this be useful? There are many situations where a function involves operations on objects of different classes, where there is no inheritance relation between these classes. An example might be a matrix and a vector. If an operation has to be performed on a vector and a matrix, then the easiest and most efficient way to do this would be to simply define the function as a member function of one of the classes, say matrix, but to also define it as a friend of the other class. In this way it would have access to all the elements necessary to perform the operation. That's a friend for you.

Creating actual instances of classes is simply a matter of declaring the item just as you would any other datatype. Declaring an object volatile amounts to telling the compiler that its value may change even without it being changed explicitly.

An important syntactic difference between C++ and C is that in C++ you can declare variables anywhere in a block of code, not just at the beginning of it. This is convenient because it means that you can locate the declaration of variables alongside the statements that use them. Another important difference between C++ and Ansi C is that the declaration:

void fun();

in C++ means that the function fun has no arguments at all, but in Ansi C it means that the function has an unknown number of arguments of unknown type. A better way to specify a function with no arguments is:

void fun(void)

Here there is no chance of ambiguity. The meaning is the same in both Ansi C and C++.

There are also some rules that have to be followed to avoid name collisions with compilers' internal representation. One basic one is that the underscore character (_) cannot be used as a leading or trailing character in any identifier names. So, for example, _wrong and wrong_ are both taboo.

■ OPERATOR AND FUNCTION OVERLOADING

Operator and function overloading is allowing functions and operators that use the same call name to operate on a variety of different datatypes or classes, even though separate codings may be required. This is something that statically typed languages that resolve types at compile time generally have an awkward time with. With list processing and interpretive languages like LISP, PROLOG, and Smalltalk, it is commonplace to have single functions capable of operating on many or all datatypes, even without the need to use different codings for each type. This is something that can definitely make it more enjoyable to program, because it is always possible to arrange things so that the function calls are very logical, appropriate, and easy to remember.

Operator overloading is a built-in feature of C++ in the sense that mathematical operators like + can be used for operations on integers, floating point numbers, and pointers. For defining new overloaded functions, the overload keyword is used to explicitly specify function names that are to be used with different datatypes. So, for example, if we wanted to declare a universal print function, we could write:

overload print(int), print(double), print(long), print(char);*

Another very useful feature of C++ is the opportunity to define functions that can take an unspecified number of arguments. This is a capability usually associated with languages like LISP. To do this, a simple ellipsis is used to represent an indefinite list of arguments. For example, a declaration could be made like:

int read(char ...);*

that could be used with any number of arguments in sequence.

■ PROTOTYPING

When you prototype a new function, you typically declare four things about it: 1) its name, 2) its return type, 3) its storage class, and 4) the number and type of the arguments that may be passed to it.

The function prototype or declaration typically takes the form:

storage-class type function(list of arguments) semicolon

A simple example of a C++ function prototype would be:

extern int multiply(int x, int y, ...);

In this declaration, the ellipsis (...) means that the function multiply can take more than just two arguments. There is a provision in function prototyping for declaring a default value for arguments. In this case, we could write:

extern int multiply(int x=2, int y=3, ...);

In this case, if the function call were made without any arguments as:

multiply();

then the value returned would be the product of the two default values or 6.

Static member functions in C++ are the same thing as class methods in OOP languages. They are functions that can be called without reference to any particular member of the class. The same is true of static data members, which are the same as class variables in other object-oriented languages.

■ VIRTUAL FUNCTIONS AND VIRTUAL CLASSES

Virtual functions are one of the more peculiar and difficult things to understand in C++. As it is, they offer a limited form of runtime binding. When a member function is declared as virtual, then that function can be redefined in any of its parent's derived classes. This does not differ from an overloaded function, you might think, because, in effect, they already allow functions to be redefined in other classes. However, there is an important difference. Overloaded functions are really just overloaded names, which the compiler "mangles" into different names. The overloaded functions really have no internal link to one another. They only appear to the programmer with the same name. Virtual functions actually use additional data structures to provide a link between the different versions of a function. They use the construction of indirect pointers to functions. This is where the changes at run time are permitted. For although everything in the code is rigidly compiled and linked, because of the pointers to pointers, changes at runtime are possible by altering data in memory. We have a name that points to another pointer, which points to a function. If the data in memory that contains the address of the second pointer is replaced by an address to a pointer for a different function, then a different function will execute at run time. Virtual functions provide a formalization of this mechanism. Another important difference between overloaded and virtual functions is that when a virtual function is redefined, it has to adhere to the form of the original function. It has to call the same number of arguments of the same type. This is, once again, due to the fact that the relationship between the functions is not in name only.

As they were conceived by Bjarne Stroustrup in the original version of C++, virtual functions were intended as an aid for writing interactive programs where the user does not have to know exactly what everything is in order to get results. As he expressed it then, "This style is extremely useful in interactive programs when objects of various types are treated in a uniform manner by the basic software. In a sense, the typical operation is for the user to point to some object and say 'Who are you? What are you?' or 'Do your stuff!' without providing type information. The program can and must figure that out for itself." (Stroustrup, p. 37)

Virtual classes really have nothing to do with virtual functions. They are the result of a need to be able to alter the default mechanism of multiple inheritance in C++. Ordinarily, if a class inherits from more than one class that have a common ancestor, that class will actually behave as though it contained multiple copies of the common ancestor's member functions and data. However, if that ancestor is declared as virtual, then only one copy of it is referenced in descendants, no matter how many times it indirectly appears in the class's derivation.

■ CONSTRUCTORS AND DESTRUCTORS

Although you declare an instance of a class the way you do any data structure, all instances also have to be initialized. You do this by calling a member function known as a constructor. These constructors have to be coded, and differ for each class of object, since the constructor is what really creates the data object. There are also destructors, which destroy objects by reallocating their memory and undefining them.

The C++ language does not provide very much built-in provision at all for input or output. This must be added by the developer, but standardization of I/O would seem to be a matter of crucial importance. There are three kinds of scope in C++: local, file, and class. Local scope applies to names that are declared in a block of code and are local to that block. Class scope refers to names that are declared within a class and are unknown outside of the operations that belong to that class. File scope refers to names that are declared outside of any block or class but are referenced in a file.

Creating an executable program from a C++ source file usually requires four steps: 1. preprocessing, 2. translating, 3. compiling, and 4. linking.

After all is said, the real issue for many programmers is how at home they can feel with coding in a language. What does a modest program in C++ look like, and how easy is it to read? To help answer this question, I've included a sample program, the notorious Eratosthenes seive benchmark program. The primes benchmark for C++ is given in Listing 1. Note that '//' is used for comments in C++ instead of the '/*' used in C.

```cpp
#include <stream.h>
class prime
{
    int  n;      // this is the "n'th" prime
    int  p;      // the prime itself
public:
    // constructor
    prime(int nn = 1, int pp = 2) { n = nn; p = pp; }
    // advance to next prime
    prime& operator++();
    // tells what the number of this prime is
    int n_th()    { return n; }
    // tells what the prime is
    int prm() { return p; }
};
// output a prime number
ostream& operator<<(ostream& s, prime &p)
{
    return s << p.prm();
}
// advance to next prime
prime& prime::operator++()
{
    ++n;      // n_th + 1 prime
    // special case for 2
    if(p == 2)
    {
        // the next prime is 3.
        ++p;
        return(*this);
```

```
    }
    // find the next odd prime.
    for(;;)
    {
        p += 2;
        int is_prime = 1;
        int loop_limit = (p / 2);
        for(int a = 3; a < loop_limit; ++a)
        {
            // is p not prime?
            if(((p / a) * a) == p)
            {
                is_prime = 0;
                break;
            }
        }
        // did we find a prime?
        if(is_prime)
            break;
        // else try again...
    }
    return(*this);
}
// A trivial main program that makes use of class "prime".
// print the first n_primes prime numbers
main()
{
    const int n_primes = 100;    // print 100 primes
    prime number;
    while(number.n_th() <= n_primes)
    {
        // Print the number of this prime, and the prime
itself.
        cout << number.n_th() << "\t" << number << "\n";
        // Advance to the next prime.
        ++number;
    }
}
```

■ THE ZORTECH COMPILER

This speedy versatile C++ compiler has the advantage of supporting MS Windows development. Unlike many of the other C++ systems this is a full-fledged compiler for C and C++, not just a preprocessor. An integrated editor allows compilation without exiting.

The Zortech compiler allows you to disable implicit function declaration tolerance. Its default operation is an approach called autoprototyping. This means that if a function is used that has not been prototyped, the compiler will produce a prototype according to the way it has been used.

Zortech C++ aspires to be more than just a programming language. It wants to be a programming environment. The full system includes an integrated editor, a debugger, and a library of C++ Tools classes.

■ MEMORY MODELS

The Zortech compiler supports five memory models: T, S, M, C, and L. Their specifications are given in Table 3.2 below. The default is the small memory model. The architecture is determined by the near and far addressing scheme. Near addresses can only refer to locations within the current segment, whereas far addresses can refer to addresses in any segment. Pointers to both functions and data can be either near or far in Zortech C++. The different combinations lead to these five memory models:

Table 3.2 Zortech C++ Memory Model.

Memory Model	Code Space	Data Space	Other Conditions
T	64K	64K	Code + Static + Global $< 64K$
S	64K	64K	
M	1MB	64K	
C	64K	1MB	
L	1MB	1MB	

Mixed memory models are also possible by using the near and far keywords.

The problem with the memory model approach is that if you have to change models as your program gets larger, all the data and code addresses will change. The drawback of the near and far keywords is that they are specific to the Intel architecture and therefore not portable.

■ THE MEMORY MAP OF PROGRAMS

The main memory map of programs in Zortech C++ is represented by the following major segments:

Code

..

Far Data

..

Near Data

..

Stack

..

Near Heap

..

Far Heap

■ THE C++ DEBUGGER

One of the rare debuggers for C++, Zortech C++ is a significant program unto itself that has a separate manual devoted to it. Like most debuggers today this one requires that special insertions be made to the code during compilation. It is compatible with the Microsoft Codeview debugger, but it accomplishes this compatibility by converting the Codeview insertions into others of its own format. When used with the Zortech C++ compiler, the debugger requires that the -g flag be used when compiling programs. Preparing multimodule programs for use with the debugger is sufficiently complex that it is a good idea to use the Make program for this purpose. Unlike the Microsoft Codeview debugger, which is a line oriented source debugger, the Zortech C++ debugger is a statement oriented debugger. This means that the smallest item it can handle is a complete statement rather than just a line of code.

The debugger's main screen is divided into three display areas. The first area is simply the top line menu bar. The second is the main display area composed of three different windows. The bottom line shows the commands that are available with Function keys. The debugger has two main operating modes, the Window Command mode and the Menu Command mode. The default is the window mode. These modes are mainly distinct as far as keystrokes are concerned. The program also supports the mouse, however, and the duality of modes is less noticeable to the mouse user.

Although the debugger starts up with three window display areas visible, fifteen different windows plus an additional help window are available if the need arises. As far as the three initially visible windows are concerned, the main one displays the source code or machine instructions and one of the smaller windows shows data, and the other the names of automatic variables. At any one time, a single window in the debugger has the exclusive focus of all input from the user. Table 3.3 shows the available windows in the Zortech C++ debugger and the function keys used to make them visible.

Besides the displays I have mentioned so far, there is also the program output screen, which shows whatever the test program is normally writing to the screen. Only when an executing program halts does the debug screen return. The two alternate modes in which the debugger can be used are source mode or assembly language mode.

The special features the debugger provides for debugging C++ programs include the Class window and a facility for "unmangling" overloaded function names. The Class window lists all the classes used by a program in alphabetical order. Initially only the

Table 3.3 Zortech C++ Debugger Windows.

The Help Window	F1
The Automatics Window	F2
The Files Window	F3
The Functions Window	F4
The Data Window	F5
The Trace Buffer Window	F6
The Conditionals Window	F7
The Expressions Window	F8
The Memory Window	F9
The Source Window	F10
The Register Window	Alt-F1
The Directory Window	Alt-F2
The Symbols Window	Alt-F3
The 8087 Window	Alt-F4
The Class Window	Alt-F5
The Buffers Window	Alt-F6

names of the classes are visible, but a class can be "expanded" so that an indented list of base classes for the class, a list of prototype functions, and a list of member functions, each indented a little deeper, are made visible. When you place the cursor over a member function and press ENTER, the source code for the function appears in the Source window. Pressing ALT-E at that point allows the source to be edited.

If a class in the Class window has been derived from one or more base classes, then the situation is a little more complicated. The variables inherited from these classes can be in the Automatics, Data, or Expressions windows, encapsulated in a base class member object, which may need expanding to show its contents.

One important feature of the debugger is its provision for "memory write protection." This does not mean that when this feature is turned on the debugger prevents writing to selected areas of memory, but rather it keeps track of such writing operations. The first write to a selected memory protect area is reported onscreen and all subsequent writes are recorded for analysis purposes. This facility is used in conjunction with the Memory window.

▪ ZORTECH TOOLS CLASSES

Bitvec	Gdynarr	Intvector
Slist	Node	Ce_handler
Gslist	Bintree	String_editor

Gqueue	Hash	Date_editor
Gstack	Ghsearch	Window_set
Iqueue	Bcd	Window
Istack	Gvma	Money
Dnode	Gvms	Event
Dlist	Rt_clock	Event_queue
Gdlist	Directory	
Dynarr	Filename	

The most interesting classes in the Zortech Tools are the Dlist, Dnode, Dnarr, Rt_clock, Event, and Event_queue. Node and Bintree are also interesting Classes.

The most controversial classes are those intended for virtual memory. Obviously, no one would want to pass judgment on these until seeing a working application that uses it. Although dynamic arrays are not as attractive as arrays that are growable during run time, they are certainly useful data structures to have.

■ CONCLUSIONS ABOUT C++

On the negative side, the weaknesses of C++, as I see it, are mainly two: 1) its syntax is not as clear as it could be for the main operations of object-oriented programming (OOP), and 2) it does not implement run-time binding and datatyping. With this said, I should mention immediately that C++ nevertheless provides one of the advantages of run-time resolving of types with its provisions for function overloading and virtual functions. However, there are still many other reasons for wanting run-time binding for programs. It seems to be essential for programs that will be required to effectively deal with situations that were not thoroughly and explicitly provided for in advance by the programmer.

C++ is an unusual but interesting attempt to provide a new type of object-oriented language. Of the criteria we listed for the levels of object-oriented systems, C++ has one that many other microcomputer OOPs lack, namely multiple inheritance. However, on the downside it also lacks some important levels such as runtime binding and method combination. One of the original things with C++ is the idea of protected members. Namely, that access is permitted to subclasses down the hierarchy. In my opinion this is an option that it is advantageous to include in an object-oriented system.

Some of the new terminology introduced by C++ is also helpful, such as the use of the term static for class variables and methods. This brings out the fact that class variables can be used as values that are constant while a program is running, but once again, I feel that changes during and even after run time are also important.

One thing on the wish list for C++ would be some proposed candidates for a standard Class Library, including perhaps such things as device-independent I/O. Also, a hierarchy of standard data structures would appear an essential thing to include as well. Generally speaking the Zortech Tools are an interesting contribution in this direction with some ideas that other object-oriented C dialects could benefit from. The converse is also true. Another thing on the wish list is a provision that could only come with run-time binding in C++, which would be class redefinition at run time, such as exists in the Common LISP Object System. There is still time for a more complete fusion of ideas before attempting to agree on a standard object-oriented extension for C. I think that the designers of all of these dialects would agree that while very interesting and impressive progress has been made in the object-oriented C category, it is still a young field that needs added experience and more advanced solutions before anything becomes cast in concrete.

■ OBJECTIVE-C

Objective-C from the StepStone Corporation was the first object-oriented C dialect to be implemented . This object-oriented C dialect was developed by C programmers who were looking primarily at the advantages OOP affords for handling conventional programming projects. In spite of this emphasis on the part of its developers, I believe that Objective-C holds considerable promise as a delivery environment for more advanced applications as well.

The current version represents a relatively mature implementation of the Objective-C dialect that reflects several years experience with problems that programmers typically encounter. Because of difficulties that arose with some of the classes in earlier versions of the foundation library, they have been continually revised. The current class hierarchy, therefore, is the result of several years of evolution.

The Objective-C compiler consists of two executable files, the driver program, OBJCC.EXE and the actual Objective-C program itself, OBJC.EXE. The driver program first calls the Microsoft CL.EXE program to check syntax, and then calls the Objective-C compiler. There is no need to specify libraries at link time, unless their paths cannot be found. The library references are imbedded in the .OBJ files by Objective-C.

One of the things that puts Objective-C potentially in the category of a suitable delivery environment for serious real world applications is its feature of dynamic run-time binding for all objects. It is able to accomplish this even though it compiles its own code into C for subsequent compilation by a C compiler.

An important difference between Objective-C and other object-oriented systems like Smalltalk is that it is really a hybrid language. So just as with object-oriented LISP systems, the programmer always has the option of writing code in conventional C. Another important difference between Objective-C and Smalltalk is the difference in the size of the class libraries. Smalltalk-80 comes with a substantial amount of code available for reuse in source code form. Objective-C, although it offers considerably more in this department than does C++, lags substantially behind Smalltalk, which is the senior member among object-oriented languages.

In certain respects, Objective-C is a rather conservative object-oriented language. That is to say, there are no substantial innovations in object-oriented concepts here that were not already in Smalltalk many years ago. On the other hand, not every powerful feature of Smalltalk is found in Objective-C either. If it can be considered as something of a hybrid of C and Smalltalk, then the more dominant parent by far is clearly C. Looking at it from the perspective of C, Objective-C has extended the C language by adding one new datatype, objects, and one new operation, message expressions.

The syntax of Objective-C is, for the most part, quite straightforward. To declare a new class, the equal sign (=) is used, and the colon (:) is used to declare its superclass. Other items in the class definition are set off by parentheses. All data declarations are set off in curly braces. So, for example, the following expression:

> = Array:Object { short capacity; }

declares Array as a subclass of Object with the instance variable 'capacity' declared as a short integer. There are two types of methods, class methods and instance methods just as in Smalltalk, and they are defined using the plus (+) and minus (-) signs respectively. Instances are usually created, as in Smalltalk, by sending the message (new) to the parent class. There are two main types of message expressions used in Objective-C, unary expressions and keyword expressions. There are no binary expressions like those used in Smalltalk. The expression

> id myarray = [ByteArray new:80];

creates a new instance of the class ByteArray sized at 80 units. The definition of the method (new) for the Object class is just

> + new { return (*_alloc)(self, 0); }

Here a built-in primitive is called on to do the job of allocating memory for an object. No further work is needed because the object is the simplest possible abstraction class. On the other hand, the 'new:' (pronounced "new colon") message for the Array class has this high-level Objective-C definition:

> + new:(int)nElements {
>   self = (*_alloc)(self, nElements *[self ndxVarSize]);
>   capacity = nElements; return self;}

All messages in Objective-C are set between square brackets. The expression [self ndxVarSize], therefore, is a message that the receiver object will be sent. The ndxVarSize message is an Array class method that is redefined:

> + (int)ndxVarSize { return (int) [self subclassResponsibility]; }

The subclassResponsibility method simply prints the message "Subclass should override this message," when called. The expression 'capacity = nElements' simply sets the capacity of the array to whatever argument is supplied to 'new:'.

■ CLASS HIERARCHY

Here is the basic class hierarchy of Objective-C as it might appear in a System Browser, if such a thing existed in Objective-C:

```
Object
    Array
        BytArray
        IdArray
        IntArray
            Assoc
            Cltn
                    OrdCltn
                Set
                        Bag
                        Dictionary
                    Stack
    AsciiFiler
    BalNode
        SortCltn
    IPSequence
        Sequence
    ObjGraph
    Point
    Rectangle
    String
    Unknown
```

In Objective-C, classes are also referred to as Factory Objects. This is to underscore the fact that a class is an object in its own right whose main function is to serve as a template for the creation of instances and subclasses. However, as you can see, there are no Class and Metaclass classes present. Classes in Objective-C are not instances of a metaclass object and are not created by sending messages to a metaclass as is true in Smalltalk and in Xerox LOOPS and many object-oriented LISPs. In itself, of course, this is not necessarily a bad thing and is simply another way of saying that Objective-C is a hybrid rather than a pure object-oriented language.

The library classes in Objective-C are arranged in roughly four broad categories: foundation classes, collection classes, and other datatype classes such as String and screen I/O classes. As you can see from the class hierarchy tables, in the new version of Objective-C, the AVL classes have been omitted, but a number of others have been added. The BalNode abstract class and its subclass SortCltn are now used instead. BalNode is generic code capable of supporting implementations of any binary tree. SortCltn, a class that handles sorted collections, is the replacement for AVLTree. Another important change is that the Sequence class is now implemented as a subclass of IPSequence. The latter implements sequencing quickly through any kind of collection by running in place over its contents. In order to accommodate the technique used by the IPSequence class, the 'contents' method was added to the collection classes, which returns the pointer to the instance of IdArray that the receiver is using to store the members of its collection. The AsciiFiler class is a new class that gathers all the file operations and is able to support the transfer of source files between machines of different architectures on the same network.

Another interesting class is ObjGraph. This is used to create a graph of a class hierarchy, meaning that of all the classes from which it inherits. The manual provides an example of the use of ObjGraph by implementing a method called 'broadcast,' which takes a method name or selector as an argument and sends this method to all the objects that can be reached by the receiver. To accommodate this new way of creating graphs, the 'asGraph' method of the Object class was rewritten.

Above I demonstrated some rudimentary operations with the Array class. Arrays are implemented differently in Objective-C than in other object-oriented languages. In Smalltalk, the Array class is a descendant of the Collection class, though not a direct descendant. In Objective-C, Array is a formal or abstract class that is the direct descendant of Object, the root class. This is obviously for efficiency purposes, since C already has an implementation of arrays. A new Array class feature is the implementation of indexed instance variables instead of named instance variables. Arrays are fixed in size. Unlike the more sophisticated collection classes we will encounter later on, they cannot be increased in size when the number of elements reaches the maximum that was defined for a given array. The subclasses of Array handle arrays comprising the various C datatypes. As with most object-oriented languages, the Array class does not provide a facility for defining the dimension of arrays. To create multidimensional arrays, special subclasses of Array must be defined.

As we saw, array classes in Objective-C have a fixed capacity. Once an array instance of a certain capacity is created, its size cannot be changed. This is not true, however, of collection classes. They are designed as "growable" classes that can later have more elements than specified by their initial capacity.

The method that allows this in the Cltn class, 'expand,' is written:

```
expand { contents = [contents capacity: capacity += capacity];
    return self; }
```

This is a transparent high-level Objective-C method definition that resets the value of the 'contents' variable and uses a simple increment operation to double its capacity.

Objects in Objective-C are designed to reside in a single address space and to be identified exclusively by this address in system memory. This means that systems cannot generally be built with Objective-C where objects need to reside on disk or at other locations on a network. All objects in Objective-C have to reside in the host computer's memory.

Because Objective-C is a hybrid language, it allows "cheating." This means that, unlike a pure object-oriented language such as Smalltalk, it allows access to the protected memory of objects with C code that can access that memory directly. Needless to say, this is a good way to get into some deep trouble, defeating the whole idea of the encapsulation, which is one of the main points of an object-oriented system, unless a programmer understands the implications of such actions fully. But the main gambit of a system like Objective-C is to take that risk for the sake of greater performance.

■ COLLECTION DATA STRUCTURES

As with Smalltalk and most other object-oriented languages, the centerpiece of Objective-C for creating data structures is the group of Collection classes. This part of the hierarchy has the following member classes:

Cltn
    OrdCLtn
    Stack
    Set
      Dictionary
      Bag
  BalNode
    SortCltn

The Cltn class is an abstract or formal class whose variables and methods are there to be inherited by its various descendants who do all the actual work in programs. It is only the subclasses of Cltn that are meant to actually have instances. The methods for collections are divided into about a dozen categories: instance creation, adding, removing, sequencing, 'elements perform', conversion, printing, freeing, copying, interrogation, comparison, and private methods. To understand them it is necessary to know a little about how collections work. The collection data structures themselves are not used to store the elements themselves, but pointers to the instances of the IdArray class that actually holds the members. The interrogation methods can be used in an application to query collections much as database queries and searches are performed in conventional programming systems. So, for example, the 'find' method searches for objects by name and returns them, if they are present.

The 'elements perform' methods are those that can map operations onto each element of a collection in turn. They do this by actually sending a message to each of the objects that are elements of the collection. One complexity is that different methods require different numbers of arguments, and Objective-C does not support functions with an optional number of arguments. The solution is that different 'elementsPerform' methods must be implemented that accept different numbers of arguments. Versions are supplied that support up to three arguments. For more than this, it is no great problem to use these methods for implementing those that can accept more than three arguments.

As the name reveals, ordered collections are those whose elements are kept in order. Often more specialized subclasses of the OrdCltn class are used for handling queues and stacks. In ordered collections no nil entries are permitted. So whenever elements are removed from ordered collections, their contents are automatically compressed to take up the space created by the vacated element. Because of the nature of ordered collections, methods for adding elements to them specify a specific location at which to add them. These methods include addFirst, addLast, insert:before, and insert:after, which do the operations you would expect them to.

Stack implements collections that can keep entries in the last-in first-out order. In addition to the 'push:' and 'pop:' methods for accessing the contents of a stack, Objective-C stacks provide the 'at:' and 'removeAt:' methods for random access of stack elements. Stack manipulation methods include those that modify the order of stack elements such as 'swap' as well as those like 'topElement' and 'lastElement', which provide information without making any modification to the stack.

Sets are collections that are only permitted to have one of each element. No duplicate elements are allowed. One application of Sets that is particularly efficient is the creation of symbol tables. The Set class is implemented so that sets may contain any type of object. Several different types of object may even be collected in the same set. This means that to add new methods to a set an exhaustive search must be made of all existing elements in it. The Set class in Objective-C supports a hashing facility, so that with the 'hash' message a set will place all objects it contains in a hash table for increased efficiency. An important limitation of Sets as they are designed here, though, is that they are not designed to be change dynamically. If the objects in an Objective-C Set are modified, then the accessing facilities will no longer work correctly.

Dictionary class is a descendant of Set because dictionaries are implemented as a set of associations. In this case, you want to allow duplicate values, but each of the keys has to be unique. This is done by means of designing dictionaries to have a close relationship with the Assoc class. Associations store links between keys and values in such a way that these pairs can be stored in dictionaries and accessed by the key. Associations perform comparisons and equality testing by passing on messages to key objects. In addition to the methods inherited from Set and the other ancestor classes, Dictionary implements six new messages of its own: the class method 'with:' for initializing new dictionaries, and five methods for indexed access: 'atKey:', 'atKey:put:', 'values', 'includesAssociation:', and 'includesKey:'.

As we saw previously, the SortCltn class replaces the earlier AVLTree class in Objective-C. A sorted collection is one whose member elements always remain sorted. When an object is added, it must be inserted in the appropriate place right away. How the elements are ordered depends on what has been chosen as the value of the 'cmpSel' instance variable. The default is the 'compare' selector. Other options for its value are 'invertCompare' and 'dictCompare'. These are the names of methods. 'Compare' and 'invertCompare' are implemented in the Object or root class. The 'dictCompare' method is implemented in the String class. Although SortCltn is not a subclass of Cltn, it acts as though it were. Its defined operations are 'plug compatible' with it, as the manual describes it.

Another instance variable that alters the behavior of instances of the SortCltn class is the 'addDupAction' variable. It can take on four different values: ADD, REJECT, MERGE, or REPLACE. These different value options select different ways that duplicate elements are handled. If the ADD value is chosen, duplicates are permitted. In order to preserve the sorted ordering, any duplicate elements must always be the immediate successors of the elements they duplicate. With the REJECT option, duplicates are forbidden. As the name suggests, the MERGE option specifies that any duplicates will be merged using the 'merge' method of the member's class.

■ GRAPHICS

Objective-C provides the two rudimentary "graphics" classes, Point and Rectangle. As such, this is a far cry from a full object-oriented graphics system, but the construction of these classes is still quite informative. There are two main instance variables for a Point, xLoc and yLoc. Instance methods include all those it inherits from the Object class, as well as those for setting and accessing the values of the two coordinates, those for moving the coordinate, and even those for performing simple math operations on the coordinate values.

To make use of instances of the Point class for making actual drawings, object-oriented systems generally have something like the Pen class used in Smalltalk and Actor, which implements the basic turtle graphics functions. In these systems, Pen is a descendant of the BitBlt class, which implements bit block transfers. These classes do not come with the Objective-C system, so to actually use the Point and Rectangle classes, the equivalents of BitBlt and Pen would have to be implemented.

Below is a short demo function in Objective-C (Listing 2) and the actual listing in C (Listing 3) generated by the compiler. The C output has been reformatted in a less compressed form for easier reading.

Listing 2. Short Objective-C Demo Program.

```
= DemoPoint : Object ( Practice) {int xLoc,yLoc; }
+ create {return [ [ super new ] initialize] ; }
- initialize { xLoc = 100; yLoc = 100; return self; }
- print { printf ("This point's coordinates are (%d@%d ) \n" , xLoc, yLoc) ; }
=:
```

Listing 3. C code Output of Objective-C Compiler.

```
#line 2 "demo.c"
typedef struct _PRIVATE * id; id _msg(), _msgSuper();
#line 1 "demo.m"
#line 5 "demo.c"
```

```
struct _PRIVATE
{
struct _SHARED *isa;
int xLoc;int yLoc;
};
extern id DemoPoint, Object;
struct _SHARED
{
struct _SHARED *isa, *clsSuper;char *clsName;
char *clsTypes;short clsSizInstance;short clsSizDict;
struct _SLT *clsDispTable;
};
extern struct _SHARED  _DemoPoint, __DemoPoint;
extern char *Practice[];
#line 1 "demo.m"
#line 3 "demo.m"
/* create=Practice[0] */
static id _1_DemoPoint(self,_cmd)id self;char *_cmd;
{
return__msg(_msgSuper(__DemoPoint.clsSuper,Practice[1]
/*new*/),Practice[2] /*initialize*/);
}
#line 5 "demo.m"
/* initialize=Practice[2] */
static id _2_DemoPoint(self,_cmd)id self;char *_cmd;
{
self->xLoc = 100;self->yLoc = 100;return self;
}
#line 7 "demo.m"
/* print=Practice[3] */
static id _3_DemoPoint(self,_cmd)id self;
char *_cmd;
{
printf("This point's coordinates are (%d@%d ) \n",
sel >xLoc,self->yLoc);
}
#line 16 "demo.c"
extern struct _SHARED  _Object, __Object;
struct __SLT
{
char **__cmd;id (*__imp)();
};
static struct __SLT _clsDispatchTbl[1]=
{
&Practice[0], (id (*)())_1_DemoPoint, /* create */
```

```
};
static struct __SLT  _nstDispatchTbl[2]=
{
&Practice[2], (id (*)())_2_DemoPoint, /* initialize */
&Practice[3], (id (*)())_3_DemoPoint, /* print */
};
static char _bufClsName[]= "_DemoPoint";
struct _SHARED __DemoPoint=
{
&__Object,
&__Object,&_bufClsName[0], 0,sizeof(struct _SHARED), 1,
(struct _SLT *)_clsDispatchTbl
};
struct _SHARED _DemoPoint=
{
&__DemoPoint, &_Object,&_bufClsName[1],
"#ii",sizeof(struct _PRIVATE), 2,
(struct _SLT *)_nstDispatchTbl
};
line 8 demo.m"
```

■ SYMBOLIC DEBUGGING

One very convenient feature of the MS-DOS version of Objective-C is that you can use the Microsoft Codeview debugger as a source-level debugger even for the Objective-C syntax. To be able to work with Objective-C source in Codeview, it is necessary to use the -g option initially when compiling the application. Once done, you can bring up CodeView with Objective-C source displayed and are able to set break points in the source for interrupting execution, enter expressions for evaluation, and so on. However, the values of objects cannot be inspected directly. To do so, you must obtain access on the lower level by first using CodeView to find the addesses of objects whose values are sought. You then have to know the structure of the information stored there as represented in HEX. Only by applying CodeView commands to thirty-two bit pointers in HEX can you inspect the values. So, as you can see, there are substantial limitations to how much of the debugging occurs at the source level.

■ DISCUSSION

One question that inevitably comes up with a system like Objective-C is just how well it stacks up against a more traditional object-oriented system like Smalltalk. Certainly, if you are using it on an MS-DOS machine without the benefit of an interpreter there are some decided limitations to your ability to gain knowledge of the system through exploring it interactively. In a Smalltalk system, besides the convenience of the browsers and other window-oriented facilities, you can also use various built-in methods to help you explore the system and to provide you with information interactively that you need for writing your program. With Objective-C on an MS-DOS machine, you have to rely on written documentation. Fortunately this documentation is extremely well written, and the difference is essentially one of convenience. As with any programming language, it is possible to write various utilities, such as cross-reference programs and others that can assist you.

Another issue is the size of the foundation class library that comes with the system. Here, Objective-C lies about midway between C++ and more fully developed environments like Smalltalk and Actor. One thing that compensates somewhat for this is the ability to use existing C code and libraries to build up a custom class library relatively quickly. However, this possibility also exists in some cases for other languages too. Also, keep in mind too that the run-time image of Objective-C may not always be compatible with all C programming systems and libraries available for Microsoft C. Unfortunately, this was the case with the Microsoft Windows programming environment. There was apparently a conflict between its runtime requirements and those of Objective-C that made it impossible to use the two together. With the new version, however, this limitation has been fortunately overcome.

A major difference between Objective-C and other object-oriented languages like Smalltalk and Actor is the absence of the block construct. In these languages, a block of code is implemented as an unnamed object that allows evaluation to be deferred. Block objects are an extremely powerful construct that allow an additional degree of modularity in defining methods. Research is being conducted on adding the block construct to Objective-C, but it has not as yet been announced as a feature for a future release.

The field of object-oriented programming is besieged with metaphors. These metaphors can be a mixed blessing. There is no doubt that they perform a useful function in introducing the basic notions of this programming paradigm. But they also can be the source of misconceptions. So it is important at some point to give them a hard shake to see what fruit they really bear.

In what sense is it really appropriate to compare classes with factories? It is only the products of a class, its instances, that really do anything. Like a factory, the class is designed to produce a specific product. But does a factory ever resemble its products? Is a class designed purposely to produce massive numbers of instances efficiently? This tells us right away that a class is more like a mold or template used in a factory rather than the factory itself. However, they are most unique in that they are molds that can also be used to produce other molds as well. In this sense they are more flexible than either factories or manufacturing molds.

What about the Software-IC metaphor? The idea behind it is that just as functional hardware modules can be reused in many different circuit boards, so can classes in a software design. But in just what sense are classes reusable? Aren't library functions also reused in many different applications that their original authors never foresaw? It is important to recognize that classes are reusable in ways that neither library functions or hardware ICs (Integrated Circuits) are. You cannot generally use off-the-shelf chips to construct new chips. But you can clearly build new library functions and classes out of existing ones. The real difference between classes and library functions is that classes are much larger and more complex units and are used in very different ways. A class usually has many library functions and data objects contained in it that will belong together in any application in which they are used. Library functions and hardware ICs both fall far short of this generic functionality.

One of the best features of the Objective-C language is its syntax. It is far more readable than C++ or C. Many people have criticized C for its poor readability. Here, I think, is one area where Objective-C represents a clear-cut advance over its mother tongue. Another is that you get many of the advantages of C but on a much higher level, with so many data structures and functions provided as standard features of the language. In principle, Objective-C allows some fairly large, high-level applications to be written without the danger that much of them will depend on machine-specific library routines or custom code that becomes obscure with the passsage of time. Finally, Objective-C implements dynamic binding in a C-compiler environment. This means that objects are created at run time rather than at compile time. This is clearly one of the features that complete object-oriented languages have in common. It is very difficult to imagine writing programs that can respond to novel situations when everything has been defined statically when the program was compiled. This, aside from the more readable syntax, is what really differentiates Objective-C from C++.

The release of Objective-C that I used for my evaluation was the version 4.0 implementation ported to the IBM PC/AT. The language is also running on Vaxes, Sun workstations, and the HP 9000. The MS-DOS version of Objective-C comes on high-density disks and includes the compiler, libraries, and the main classes also in source form. At this point, the only C compiler on PCs supported is version 5.1 of the Microsoft C compiler. Support for version 6.0 is planned.

■ CTALK

As its name reflects, Ctalk is an object-oriented programming tool that effectively operates as a hybrid of the C and Smalltalk programming languages. What enables it to do this more effectively than other similar attempts is an ingenious method of incorporating a Smalltalk-like browser in the C-programming environment. The Ctalk VIEWS browser is used interactively as is the Smalltalk browser in spite of the fact that C is a compiled, rather than interpreted language. Besides the browser, Ctalk also incorporates other essential features of a true object-oriented language, such as inheritance, encapsulation, and run-time binding. In all, there are three main programs in the Ctalk system. Besides the browser, there are the preprocessor compiler and the Make utility. To get an idea of the advantages presented by programming with a tool like Ctalk, I will first describe the innovative browser, which forms the real center about which this programming tool revolves.

It is surprising how similar the Ctalk browser is to the Smalltalk facility after which it was modeled. Like its parent, the Ctalk browser acts as a combination editor and application manager that allows object-oriented systems to be developed incrementally and interactively. That's quite an important achievement for a C-based object-oriented tool.

The browser exists as a stand-alone program that is called up as any stand-alone application is. However, as will be seen, it is a program that provides an extremely powerful facility for integrating virtually the entire Ctalk system. Not only does the program allow you to familiarize yourself with the environment through interactive browsing, but it can be used for doing many of the programming chores interactively, including creating a Make file for batch processing the compilation and linking operations.

The Ctalk browser is divided into a number of panes that operate like tiled windows, in that these apertures cannot be overlapped or resized. At the upper left is the pane that displays the class hierarchy. Just as with a Smalltalk browser, when a class is selected, its methods are shown in the upper right window pane. Then, in turn, a method can be selected and its code is made available for editing in the bottom text pane. Alternatively, any text file can be loaded into the browser and displayed in the lower text pane to be edited. Thus, the browser fills the dual purpose of a small, simple editor and a tool specially equipped for handling Ctalk objects.

To operate the browser, various popup menus are available in different pane areas. These popups can be activated either by mouse or key commands. Included in the browser facilities is a shell that allows you to issue commands to the operating system from within the browser, or alternatively, to temporarily exit to the operating system for doing various chores, and return to the browser just as you left it. This kind of shell has become so widespread that it is now really conspicuous when it is absent.

There is an important difference between the Ctalk browser and a Smalltalk browser that is due to the fact that the former is a stand-alone application in a compiled environment and the latter is part of an interactive system in which everything is copresent. When the Ctalk browser is first loaded, since it does not have the classes as part of itself, it looks for all the class definitions that exist in the current directory on disk and compiles them into its database so that it can provide interactive access to them.

However, once everything has been loaded into the browser, many functions needed for writing applications can be done interactively, so that the browser actually generates the code. Such functions include specifying a new application, loading existing classes, defining new classes and their methods, and saving all work.

Not everything was "ideal" yet in the version of the browser I tested. For example, the ability to load text files into the editor is confined to rather small files. If the file you load into the browser editor is larger than the maximum size, only the amount that fits will be loaded, and no error message is given. This can be dangerous for the unwary, because if you were to make a small change and save such a file, this could result in a substantial loss of data. For this reason, I would say that the browser is useful primarily for using the "build" facilities that allow you to create various small files that will form modules in a complete system. For editing relatively large files, another editor must be used.

■ CTALK SYNTAX

The syntax of Ctalk is slightly different from other object-oriented C dialects, but once a few conventions are mastered it becomes relatively straightforward to read and write, if you already know C. The main convention concerning Ctalk messages is that they are always flanked by two "at" (@) symbols on either side. So, for example, if we want to create a new instance of a class such as Rectangle, then the message would look like this:

@Rectangle new_ &rect@;

Here, the ampersand character is used for pointer notation exactly as in C.

One of the most powerful features of Ctalk is the ability to map one message to another. This means that the selector, or name of a message, can be passed as an argument to another message. The syntax for doing this is a variable assignment statement with the name of the message selector enclosed by backquote characters.

To actually send a message, which references another message that has been stored as a variable, special messages are provided as methods of the Object class that are inherited by all other objects. These methods are 'perform_', 'perform_with_', and 'perform_with_with_'.

So, for example, if we have defined the variable 'gval' as follows:

id gval;
gval = 'getValue';

and an object,

id obj;
int gval;

the 'id' statement is a Ctalk class id declaration. In Ctalk programs you must make external declarations for each class id that is referenced.

Then the 'getValue' message could be mapped by the expression:

@obj perform_ gval with &val@;

Here it is assumed that val is a slot in obj, and that the 'getValue' message takes this as an argument.

As with most object-oriented languages, the pseudovariables 'self' and 'super' are used to reference objects within a message. The 'self' pseudovariable references the object to which the message is sent. The 'super' pseudovariable references the superclass of a class. To access the instance variable of the object to which a message is sent, the following notation is used:

self-> width

assuming that 'width' is the name of an instance variable for the object in question.

Another Ctalk syntax convention involves the use of the underscore character. Whenever an underscore follows a message selector name, this indicates that an argument is to follow. From a practical point of view, one of the more important things about an object-oriented C system is the size of its built-in foundation classes, so we'll look at this next.

■ CTALK FOUNDATION CLASSES

Table 3.4 lists the foundation classes for Ctalk.

The Container class is an abstract or formal class that is used for creating subclasses, which provide dynamic data storage elements. This means that a subclass of Container can allow instances to be created that have either fixed or variable sized data elements, as well as sequential or nonsequential access methods. So, for example, if the 'expand' message is sent to an object, the object is doubled in size. For more precise size expansion, the expandBy_ method is used, which takes an argument that specifies the number of additional data elements the expanded object will contain. The putRecSize_

Table 3.4 Ctalk Foundation Classes.

Object
Assoc
Container
Buffer
Stream
ByteArray
Collection
OrdCollect
Stack
Set
Dictionary
IntArray
String

method similarly sets the size in bytes for each data element that the object contains. To access an indexed object, you use the at_ get_ nRecs_ method, which returns as many records as you specify, starting at the specified index number. Nearly all of these foundation classes are various subclasses of the Container class for implementing various different types of data structures. Usually a dynamic data structure is defined much farther down the class hierarchy in an object-oriented system. This is a fairly innovative way of approaching the matter that has a lot to be said for it.

The Buffer class is intended to provide a simple means of storing and maintaining large blocks of data in either byte or word formats. An immediate extension to this class that suggests itself is to add an instance variable that indicates whether a given Buffer object is a byte or word buffer. General read and write routines could then be written that first send a message to a buffer to see if it is in byte or word format. In this way, a program need not be specific to one type of buffer or the other.

The Stream class is implemented as a subclass of Buffer and includes one instance variable 'position' as a way of indexing the current stream position. The Collection classes provide for objects in which other objects are grouped. The subclasses of Collection itself vary according to whether access to elements is ordered or random, and whether the size is bounded or unbounded. So, for example, the OrdCollect class allows elements to be inserted and retrieved in sequential order, and for the size of the collection itself to be expanded automatically as new elements are added.

Text Window Classes

Some additional classes have been developed by CNS that provide support for the creation of text windows in the Ctalk environment. The additional classes as they are arranged hierarchically are listed in Table 3.5.

Let's look briefly at what some of these additional classes do. The Browser class provides some of the basic methods for creating a browser similar to the one included in the Ctalk system. Over twenty methods are supplied with this class. A sample main program is included for creating a test browser program. This code can produce a "test browser" that lacks various things that the real tool has, but shows many of the essentials of how the tool is created. For those who want to develop their own custom browser that they can continue to extend at will, this code will represent a flying head start in that direction.

The initialization routine first sends a message to the Screen Manager and tells it the type of screen to create. Then the Mouse object is told to create the specified type of cursor. Next an Ordered Collection object is created to serve as a window list. Then the Window object itself is created with the designated proportions and attributes, and finally an Event Manager is created. This is an excellent example of how Ctalk makes use of one of the main paradigms in object-oriented system design, that of employing one object as the manager of other objects. The only shortcoming of this approach is that it tends to bog down when the number of objects involved gets large.

Table 3.5 Additional Text Window Classes.

Browser

File

Menu

Mouse

Notifier

ScreenMgr

TxPoint

Window

ButtonWin

ItemWin

Scrollbar

StdWindow

ListWindow

HorListWin

PopUp

Response

TxtWindow

TxEditor

WinManager

■ RUN-TIME APPLICATIONS

Completing a Ctalk application is generally a five-step process. The first step is to write the necessary source code files in the C and Ctalk syntax, which is written in disk files with the .PRE file extension. The second step is to write a main routine in C that calls all the necessary modules. Once this is done, the third step can be taken, which is to run the proprocessor and compile all the Ctalk files into the corresponding C files. The fourth step is then to compile all the C files with a C compiler. Finally, the compiled .OBJ files are linked together to form the executable file for the application.

For those who wish, as mentioned earlier, there is a convenient way of collapsing some of these steps using the "Make" option in the Ctalk browser. To do so, you would select the "Make Spec" popup menu. The result of using this interactive procedure is the creation of a .MAK file, which can be used by a special auxiliary program that will automatically carry out the three steps of preprocessing, compilation, and linking as a batch process. And since the browser supports calling DOS commands, and exiting to DOS, it is not necessary to exit the browser to "make" the finished executable and even test it afterward.

■ CONCLUSIONS ABOUT CTALK

Ctalk succeeds very well in doing what it sets out to do, namely provide a language that is a true hybrid between C and Smalltalk. The browser puts it in a class all by itself among other similar attempts. One thing that should be pointed out is that a major difference between Smalltalk itself and all of the C hybrids that have appeared so far is the great difference in the number of foundation classes present. As it is sold Smalltalk is not just a bare-bones language, but amounts, in effect, to a language plus a large generic function library that is standard in this case by definition.

For this reason, the Window classes I have described are an important addition for the Ctalk system. The importance of these library classes can be appreciated when you recall that objects in an object-oriented system are working parts for programs rather than just stand-alone functions. In a sense, then, a system with a large class library is one with a substantial part of the programming already done. The downside is that the programmer has to learn these classes and how to use them. Although one of the advantages of the object-oriented approach is that this is all done generically, the learning curve still exists for class libraries.

One minor potential drawback of this type of system is that it is set up to work mainly with Ctalk source code in the browser. If a developer wants to sell class libraries in the object file format, it will not be possible to use them with the browser in the current design. Perhaps a way can be devised for loading key class information into the browser without divulging all the source code involved. This would allow the browser to be used even with object code class libraries. The main thing to emphasize is that Ctalk has all of the essential things of a true object-oriented language, and the browser has been done well enough to give the interactive feel of a Smalltalk environment while offering all the advantages of any C-based system.

■ VIEWS: AN OBJECT-ORIENTED C DEVELOPMENT TOOL FOR WINDOWS

In this section I will discuss the VIEWS development tool, a Windows-based environment for programming in any of the object-oriented C dialects we have been discussing. That is, there are versions of VIEWS currently available for C++ version 2.0, for Objective-C, and for Ctalk. No matter which one of these dialects you find most appealing for your own purposes, you have the opportunity of using it for Windows development with the VIEWS environment.

With all the MS Windows development tools that are appearing, it's tempting to consider alternatives to the bare-bones Software Development Kit (SDK) approach. One way to narrow down the list of possibilities quickly is to limit the choice to true object-oriented systems that are suitable for real-world projects. VIEWS is such a tool. If there are others that satisfy this condition they are few and far between. The programming language is the Ctalk dialect of object-oriented C, certainly one of the most readable and usable of the alternatives.

At the very first look, MS Windows itself appears to be an object-oriented system. The different types of windows are broken down into classes, and everything happens by messages being sent. Isn't this all that's required for an OOP environment? Apparently not, because Windows programmers enjoy few, if any, of the benefits of OOP systems. One such benefit is the virtual elimination of redundant coding. Programmers using just the SDK get nearly the opposite: pages of convoluted C code that seems the very definition of redundancy. What other advantages are there with an OOP? Clearly demarcated program design that leads right to the precise coding modules to be implemented. In contrast, Windows programs tend to be an apparently endless concatenation of case statements, with no sure method of determining whether or not their logic is flawed or flawless. For these reasons alone, a tool like Ctalk VIEWS should attract the attention of serious Windows developers.

■ THE C++ VIEWS BROWSER

If for no other reason, VIEWS would be worth examining just for the fact that it has a programming environment, one that is utterly unique among compiled languages. VIEWS has a browser that strongly resembles those used with Smalltalk, the oldest general purpose OOP language. The browsers vary somewhat for the different object-oriented C dialects VIEWS supports. In this section I will be focusing on just one of them, the browser used with C++.

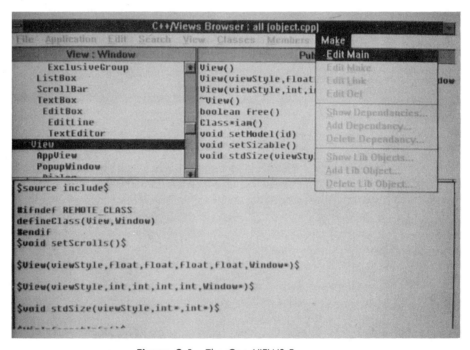

Figure 3.1 The C++ VIEWS Browser.

One of the most important things to know about this browser is that it offers a tremendous amount of control over what can be viewed and edited at a given time. It also makes full use of the Windows environment for providing interactive tools for making just about any choice one is likely to be faced with in developing C++ programs. The browser is set up, as it should be, so that you have an overview of all of the classes that may be relevant to your application. The Classes menu provides options for adding a subclass to a selected class, removing a subclass, saving and loading classes, and even swapping classes out to disk to save memory. Another important menu is the Make menu. Figure 3.1 shows the C++ VIEWS Browser with the Make menu selected.

The VIEWS browser is designed to be used with .ENV or environment files. An environment file records a class hierarchy composed of a set of classes that make up an application. The Application option of the main menu is used for loading and saving environment files. When the VIEWS browser is first invoked, there are no .ENV files loaded, and the only options that appear on the main menu bar are File and Application. To get a complete overview of the entire system of classes in the VIEWS development environment, the ALL.ENV file is loaded. Generally, environment files are prepared that include only the classes used in a given application.

When VIEWS displays class files, it typically removes certain sections of them and replaces them with tags set off by the $ characters. These tags represent the sections they replace and may be moved about by cutting and pasting.

The View menu contains various options for limiting or specifying which aspects of a member or class are shown in the text editor pane and which class members are shown in the member list pane. When an .ENV file is first loaded, nothing is displayed in the various panes of the browser. To display something, you must first select a class from the class hierarchy list in the top left pane. For the browser to display anything about the selected class, you must choose either the Header or Source option from the View menu. In the one case the header file for the class is loaded, and in the other its source text is displayed for editing. The remaining options of the View menu: Public, Protected, Private, Variables, Methods, Friends, and All determine which type of members are displayed in the member list pane. So, for example, by choosing either the Variables or Methods options you can limit the type of class member displayed in the member list pane to either variables or members.

The Members menu shows only the Add option until some member has actually been selected. At that point, a large variety of options become available. In contrast to the View options, these options actually change the selected member so as to be the type of member that the options name describes. So, for example, selecting Virtual makes the selected member a virtual member.

The options of the Make menu handle the preparation of all the different types of files needed for a complete application. This menu is divided into three different sections. The top section of the Make menu allows you to select what will be displayed for editing in the lower editing pane, the main file, make file, link file, or definition file. The middle section is for managing dependency or include files. You can select either showing, adding, or deleting them. Finally, the third section of the Make menu is for managing class library object files. Selecting Show from this menu opens a scrollable list box of library objects assumed by the current environment file.

■ THE MVC USER INTERFACE MODEL

The VIEWS architecture for organizing the Windows interface into object classes is based on the popular MVC (Model-View-Control) paradigm. The components of this paradigm are:

Model—The Application Layer

View—The Presentation Layer

Controller—The Interaction Layer

The basic strategy involved with the MVC paradigm is to keep a program's operation partitioned into three independently functioning modules: the application layer where the main data and operations are contained; the presentation layer where various views on the application layer can be obtained; and the interaction layer, which interprets user input and focuses it on the other two layers. This is one of the classic models in object-oriented user interface design. An example of the MVC model is provided by the Browser class. The model of objects of the Browser class contains a hierarchy of classes and methods stored in an instance of the Ordered Collection class.

■ THE APPVIEW CLASS

The Notifier is the focal center of the VIEWS MVC user interface model. Notifier is a class with no instances that handles its message-passing chores exclusively with class methods. Its name conveys what Notifier does. It has the responsibility of letting the different parts of an application know about the changes that occur while a program is in use. Notifier can handle six different types of interactive events:

1. Mouse moving and clicking

2. The keyboard focus changes

3. Keyboard input

4. Window exposures

5. Window resize and relocation

6. Miscellaneous environment changes

There are corresponding methods in the Window class to handle each of these type of events. The Notifier sends a message of the appropriate type to the window in which an event occurs. So, for example, if part of a window becomes uncovered by the movement of another window that had obscured it, the Notifier sends a message to that window to repaint itself on the screen in light of the new desktop configuration.

Keyboard focus refers to the situation where a particular window or sub-window temporarily becomes the exclusive focus for all events coming from the keyboard. Typically, when a window becomes highlighted after it has been selected, it is also the keyboard focus window. A window can be forced to assume the keyboard focus by sending it the 'takefocus' message. Besides event handling, the Notifier also provides various kinds of services to windows. If for any reason the shape of the cursor needs to change, the Notifier can handle that.

It's a common occurrence that some change has been made by a user in a work session and that change has to be registered immediately in the display of a particular window. In the MVC model, the way this situation is handled is by a sequence of messages being sent back and forth. The top view detects a change in the data model and sends an update message to the subview currently responsible for displaying that part of the model. All this message really says is that the former display is no longer valid. This results in an "exposure event," which in turn results in a 'paint' message being sent to the window in question. It is in the redrawing operation that the view sends a message to the model that results in the most up-to-date changes in the model being made available for display.

Views has seven different types of object class that are utilized for building the user interface part of programs:

1. Controller classes such as the Notifier class

2. The windows themselves

3. The Control windows or sub-windows

4. Views

5. Application views

6. Popup windows

7. Dialog boxes

When an event occurs in a window, the window has to respond either TRUE or FALSE. Answering TRUE means that it will consume the event. Answering FALSE results in the underlying windowing system taking an appropriate default action. When any application is launched, first its models and views are set up. Then the 'start' message is sent to the Notifier, and it begins processing and dispatching events. As a compromise aimed at portability, the Notifier class supports only the least common denominator mouse, that with a single button.

■ WHAT VIEWS WINDOWS DO

It may sound strange to say that there are parent and child windows, but these are the metaphors used to describe the dependence of one part of a screen's user interface on the other. In MS Windows, every window has to have a parent, and this is reflected in VIEWS by the fact that every instance of a subclass of Window has an ID that contains the name of its parent window. There is also an instance variable ID for an Ordered Collection instance that contains the handles of all the window's children.

Windows in VIEWS are broken down into two areas, called the client area and the nonclient area.

Unlike human children, when a window moves, its children automatically move with it. This means both laterally around the screen as well as up and down through the vertical layers of the screens state. If you cover a window, its children get covered up with it. If you select a child window, the entire parent of which it forms a part becomes the selected window. When a window has one or more children, it is usually given a minimum size so that its children will amount to something. So if a user resizes a window, it cannot be made so small that its children will vanish or become useless.

What actually allows windows to appear on the screen is the 'show' method, which is sent to the parent window and automatically propagated down to all its children. VIEWS window classes have simple methods for outputting text. More elaborate text and graphics output are provided by the Port class. ControlWindow is the abstract class for those child windows used as controls. Descendant objects of ControlWindow are designed to work in cooperation with another object, usually one in the View, AppView, PopupWindow, or Dialog class. So, for example, the Buttons class is a descendant class of ControlWindow. Button has the 'is Auto' instance variable, which is a boolean flag that when TRUE allows the button to immediately change its state when clicked on by the mouse.

The ready-to-use subclasses of Buttons include CheckBox, TriState, PushButton, and RadioButton. CheckBox supplies the small square areas that toggle a particular yes/no option and display an X in the box when the option is toggled on. TriState is the same basic thing, but also includes the third state when the button is disabled and 'greyed out' to show its state to the user. A PushButton is a different style, an elliptical shape that can contain its title inside it. A RadioButton is a small circle with a name beside it that is often used in groups.

■ THE VIEW CLASSES

The View class and its descendants are provided for programming the View layer of the MVC model. An abstract descendant of the Window class, View is intended to help in building the views and subviews specific to applications. View has an instance variable called 'model' for holding the ID of the application model object. Typically the View objects send messages to the model objects to extract from them the data to be displayed. As subclasses of Window, View and its descendants are actual visible windows complete with scrollbars and scrollable window views.

AppView, a direct subclass of View, is the more detailed base class intended for deriving the top level look of a program. Typically, the view layer of an application will include an object spawned from a subclass of AppView. Another subclass of View, Popup-Window has Dialog as its descendant, the class of objects that appear on the screen requesting a response from a user. They are not to be confused with popup menus, which are activated by the user and contain a list of options. There are several subclasses of Dialog that provide ready-to-use prototypes for different types of dialog popups. They include the FileSelect, Input, Report, YesNo, and YesNoCancel classes.

Popup dialogs are unique in the MS Windows environment because they temporarily suspend access to the rest of the interactive environment until they are attended to. This gives their implementation some subtleties that can be troublesome to novice Windows programmers.

■ CREATING DIALOGS WITH THE INTERFACE GENERATOR

VIEWS provides a shortcut for creating object-oriented code for dialogs as an alternative to coding them by hand. This method assumes that you have the MS Windows Dialog Editor program DIALOG.EXE that comes with the SDK. VIEWS provides an Interface Generator program CTIG.EXE that translates the output of the dialog editor into Ctalk VIEWS source code. The code produced is not ready to run as-is, but requires some touching up. What you have suffices only for creating the Dialog. You still have to write the callback methods that will interface with various other control objects. And you have to write the methods that handle the before and after conditions governing the Dialog's use. Unfortunately, CTIG.EXE is not an MS Windows program, so you are required to call the DOS shell so that you can execute this program in the old-fashioned command line manner.

Another interesting class is ControlView, which allows subclasses of ControlWindow—things like buttons, list boxes, text editors, and so on—to have titles and be resized and relocated. This, for example, allows a text editor that is part of a larger parent window to have its size altered by a user.

■ SETTING UP MENUS

The VIEWS Menu system is designed so that three classes of objects are needed to implement the customary Windows drop-down menu bar: Menu, PopupMenu, and MenuItem objects. The Menu class provides a collection of menu items that constitute the structure needed to construct the top level menu bar of an application. In VIEWS, a Menu object can only contain PopupMenu objects as menu items. Since Menu instances contain the ID of their parent window, a two-way link between window and menu bar exists. The append_ and remove_ methods are available in the Menu class for adding or removing items from the menu bar. Although they can be removed from any position, items can only be added at the end, which means to the right.

■ TEXT EDITING CLASSES

One of the most useful branches of the subclasses of ControlWindow looks like this:

```
ControlWindow
    EditBox
        EditLine
            TextEditor
```

EditBox is the top level edit control class. An instance of it gives you a basic window area for editing text with either vertical or horizontal scrollbars. The EditLine class is for providing objects that are needed when just a single line of text needs to be edited, as in a box for entering file names and directories. But with TextEditor the features we normally expect in an editor become available. TextEditor objects hold the text to be edited in instances of the String, Stream, or Filestream classes. The instance of TextEditor class maintains editing buffers, which it can use to replace the String or Steam text objects when editing is completed. TextEditor objects can also be responsible for providing ready-made pull-down menus suitable for generic text editing.

Here is a Ctalk routine that handles file I/O for VIEWS TextEditor objects:

```
id myEditor;
if (@myEditor isChanged@)
{
    if (@YesNo ask_
    "Text has been modified. Do you want to save changes?"
    of_ self@)
    @self editSave@;
}
```

EditBox and all its descendants contain methods for controlling the alignment of text in their windows. As everywhere in an object-oriented system, the programmer uses the base classes as generic starting points for developing more specialized versions suitable for the problems of a particular application.

■ TIMER

The Timer class allows any type of object to request that an instance of it time a particular event. There are, of course, a multitude of uses for such a timing mechanism. Two common uses are in running benchmarks and for use as a clock in discrete simulations. Timer objects can be created, which will send messages to other objects at regular intervals as long as they are alive, or they can wait for messages from client objects that alter their behavior. It can be told to temporarily suspend notifying other objects about the time and can later be told to resume notifying.

■ COMMUNICATIONS CLASS

VIEWS handles communications with the ComPort class. This contains facilities for both input and output on a computer's serial port. There is support for either polled or interrupt driven buffered serial I/O with all the necessary control of data flow, hardware handshaking, and port configuration. Two buffers are utilized by Comport, one for the receive buffer, and one for the transmit buffer. It is up to the programmer to select sizes of these buffers that will result in the most optimum performance for available data transmission rates. The ComPort is designed with the idea that it is to provide services to another object, which knows how to make use of these services in the context of an application.

■ GRAPHICS

VIEWS graphics capability is based on objects of the Port class. Methods are provided for drawing and painting rudimentary shapes, drawing lines, text fonts, and some general viewing transformations. The Port class is designed for portability, so that graphics routines written with it are hardware independent, with the exception of some aspect ratio issues. Port's openOn_ method has parameters that specify the BitMap and Window or Printer object to which the graphics output will be directed. There must always be a 'close' message after every openOn_ message with graphics output. The two messages go together like matched bookends, as it were. To make good with the intention of providing portable graphics, the Port class allows virtual coordinates to be constructed for controlling Port pen objects. Six different line types are available: solid, dash, dash-dot, dash-dot-dot, and null pattern. Filled objects can be drawn, with a choice of ten different fill patterns. There are two different operating modes to Port objects, local mode and virtual mode. In virtual mode, all drawing operations assume a virtual coordinate system that keeps code machine-independent. These need to be translated for particular hardware platforms. The local mode is for using the coordinate system specific to the local hardware on which VIEWS is currently running. The methods setVirtOn and setVirtOff are provided for toggling between these two modes.

■ THE APPLICATION STREAMLINER

The VIEWS application Streamliner utility is contained in the CTSW.EXE program, which is launched as an ordinary DOS command line program. It is a code optimizer, which is intended to produce a smaller, faster running program by stripping out dead code and performing static binding where permissible. All classes and methods that can never be accessed during use of the program are removed from the source, and only those procedures that absolutely need run-time binding are left with that capability. The result can be a program decreased in size by as much as 50 percent and with noticeably better performance.

■ CONCLUSIONS ABOUT VIEWS

As with most microcomputer implementations of object-oriented languages, the Ctalk dialect underlying VIEWS lacks multiple inheritance. One type of thing missing in the VIEWS programming environment is any special debugging tools for use at the object level. You have to debug at the C level using a program like Codeview. This somewhat defeats the idea of working at the object-oriented level in a C environment. One limitation that is really a by-product of the MS Windows environment is that VIEWS objects cannot be accessed directly from the C level. You cannot reference objects of the type Id from an ordinary C routine because of the way Windows sets up its pointers. However, despite these lacks, VIEWS still offers one of the more complete object-oriented development environments for programming Windows in an object-oriented C dialect.

4

WINDOWS 3.0 SOFTWARE DEVELOPMENT

This chapter will introduce you to the Windows 3.0 platform from the point of view of the developer. A wide range of topics are covered briefly in this overview with enough detail so that you can have ample familiarity with them to understand references to them throughout the remainder of the book. Included are: the new features of Windows 3.0, the basic working of the Windows GUI, the elements of user interfaces, the Microsoft Software Development Kit (SDK), the resource compiler, and the debuggers. A handy reference is also included at the end for Windows functions, messages, and structures that are new with Windows 3.0.

The major update to Windows marks an important milestone for software developers with their eyes on the desktop computer market. With so many of the important new applications now running on this interface platform, there are strong incentives for undertaking the not-too-trivial task of mastering the art of Windows programming. In this chapter I will survey the MS-Windows SDK and put the inner workings of the Windows system under the magnifying glass, so to speak. One by one, I'll look at the various support programs and other facilities that make up this toolkit for developers. Finally, I'll look at how Windows programs are constructed using the SDK and discuss some of the typical issues the Windows programmer faces.

■ WHAT'S NEW WITH THE WINDOWS 3.0 SDK?

For the benefit of those who have worked with earlier versions of the SDK I will present an overview of the changes and additions that have come with Version 3.0. I will also outline some of the new additions to the PDI itself.

First of all, there are some new kinds of objects in Windows. The new types of Windows objects include:

- Floating Popup Menus
- Hierarchical Menus
- Combo Boxes
- Definable Menu Checkmarks

Three new programs provided with the SDK are:

- A new graphics resource editor called SDKPaint
- The Profiler, which times all routines in a Windows program
- SWAP, the Swapping Analyzer

There are also many improvements to existing programs, such as:

- The Dialog Editor now allows custom controls to be added to dialog boxes, selecting standard controls from a palette or the Controls menu, improved support for header files, as well as support for the new combo box.
- The Font Editor now lets you change variable-width fonts to fixed-width fonts and many of the commands have been made easier to use with better feedback.
- The Resource Compiler has new resource script commands to support combo boxes, hierarchical menus, and popup menus.
- The HeapWalk program supports EMS memory.
- Codeview for Windows now supports debugging only in protected mode with improved performance, the ability to trace and break at any Windows message, but requires a second monochrome monitor with a 25-line display rather than just a serial terminal.
- Some of the new window class functions include UnRegisterClass, which frees memory by deleting a registered window class, and GetClassInfo, which gives documentation on the latter.

■ HOW THE WINDOWS SYSTEM WORKS

Now it's time to get under the hood somewhat and see just what makes the wheels turn in the Windows environment. As long as we just talk in generalities, that's not hard to figure out. It's Windows messages that make everything happen. But exactly how does that work? What messages are sent where? Windows has an overall system queue, and there is a specific input queue that goes to each Windows application. The message loop of each application receives input from its own application queue. Every time a user does anything, hits a key, moves or clicks the mouse, a message is sent and enters the input queue. The one exception to this is unqueued messages. Events that affect only a window can be sent directly to it without entering the input queue. They don't have to wait.

Although it is usually the user and the Windows environment itself that create messages, it is possible to write applications that initiate messages, which are inserted in the queues of other applications. It is even possible to write an application that allows users to construct any Windows message interactively and then send it.

The centerpiece of every Windows program is the *message loop,* which receives input messages from the input queue and sends them to their appropriate window. Every application has its own GetMessage loop, where, if the GetMessage function does not find any messages in its queue, it surrenders control to the Windows environment. But as soon as you select an application window, a message is sent and the GetMessage function finds its target. The application gets the input focus and GetMessage keeps looking.

■ FUNCTIONS THAT CREATE THINGS

Probably the most important kinds of messages programmers need to know about are the messages that allow objects to be created. It may not come as a surprise that in Windows the main things that are created are—windows! Table 4.1 lists the principal Windows functions for creating, destroying, and modifying windows, and the operations they perform.

■ WINDOW CLASSES

Before proceeding, it will be helpful to make some clarifications about terminology. I will use the phrase "MS window class" to refer to window classes in the MS-Windows system, as distinct from the term "class" by itself, which will always refer to the structure in an object-oriented programming (OOP) system. So, for example, if an OOP system has a class called Window, when I say "Window class" I will never be referring to the lower level Microsoft window class. This should avoid any ambiguity resulting from the two different ways that "class" might be used here.

There are currently three types of built-in Windows classes: system global classes, application global classes, and application local classes. System global classes are available to all applications at all times. They are created when Windows starts up. Table 4.2 provides a convenient outline of the salient items of class structure.

■ MESSAGES

A Windows input message conveys information about: 1) the system time, 2) the mouse position, 3) the mouse button pressed, 4) the keyboard state 5) the scan codes of pressed keys, and 6) the device that generated the message.

There are five different categories of Windows message:

1. Window messages
2. Button Control Messages

3. Combo Box Messages

4. Edit Control Messages

5. List Box Messages

These messages provide the efficient inner mechanism that allows many of the complex details of a user interface to be handled automatically without redundant recoding of every detail for each application. Typically, these messages carry information both on the types of events involved as well as quantitative parameters that specify the precise amounts. While Windows functions provide an interface for the programmer to tell Windows what is to be done, the Windows messages are what actually execute events on an ongoing basis.

Table 4.1 Windows Window Creation And Modification Functions.

CreateWindow	For creating overlapped, popup, and child windows
CreateWindowEx	For creating windows with extended styles
DestroyWindow	Removes a window from the system
DefWindowProc	For processing window messages which applications do not
AdjustWindowRect	For sizing a window to fit a given user area
AdjustWindowRectEx	Sizes windows with extended styles to fit given areas
GetWindowLong	For obtaining information about a window
GetWindowWord	For obtaining information about a window (alternate format)
SetWindowWord	Modifies a window attribute
SetWindowLong	Modifies a window attribute
DefDlgProc	For processing dialog messages which applications do not
DefFrameProc	For processing MDI (Multi-Document Interface) frame messages applications do not
DefMDIChildProc	For processing dialog child messages which applications do not
GetClassInfo	For obtaining information about a class
GetClassLong	For obtaining information about a WNDCLASS structure
GetClassName	Obtains a window-class name
GetClassWord	For obtaining information about a WNDCLASS structure
RegisterClass	For registering a window class
SetClassLong	Modifies a window class description
SetClassWord	Modifies a window class description
UnregisterClass	Removes a window class from the system

Table 4.2 Windows Window Class Structure.

Class Structure

Class name	Uniquely labels the window class
Window procedure address	Pointer to function that handles all messages to the class
Instance handle	The name of the application that registered the class
Class cursor	Determines the shape of the cursor when in class window
Class icon	Determines icon used when class of window is closed
Class background brush	Determines color and pattern of window class background
Class menu	Determines default menu for window class
Class styles	Determines space allocation, updating style, etc., for class
Class extra	Specifies extra memory to be allocated in class structure
Window extra	Specifies extra memory to be allocated in actual windows

Windows also provides a mechanism for avoiding message deadlocks. To understand how it works, you first have to realize how a message deadlock can occur in the first place. It might happen if a program task used the SendMessage function to send a message to another task and had to wait for the function to return because the second task surrendered control. This is not a perfect deadlock situation unless the second task surrenders control to the first. In that case both of the tasks need each other to take the initiative and neither of them can. In practice, though, in other situations, unless the task to which it surrendered control was expressly equipped to deal with this matter, there could still be trouble.

■ WINDOWS FUNCTION

There are certainly a large number of Windows functions provided with the Windows PDI. There are no fewer than eighteen different function groups concerned with window management alone. Windows functions are generally used with what are called *window styles*. Window styles are prefabricated parts that can be put together in various ways to make different types of window. The window styles are used to form a specification for the CreateWindow function when it is called on to create a window. The four main styles used in the standard Windows environment are: 1) overlapped windows, 2) owned windows, 3) popup windows, and 4) child windows (Table 4.3). The various categories of window messages are listed in Table 4.4.

Table 4.3 Window Style Keywords.

1. Overlapped windows	WS_OVERLAPPED
2. Owned windows	WS_OVERLAPPED with hWindParent named as its owner
3. Popup windows	WS_POPUP
4. Child windows	WS_CHILD

Table 4.4 Categories of Window Management Functions.

1. Message functions	10. Information functions
2. Window creation functions	11. System functions
3. Display and movement functions	12. Clipboard functions
4. Input functions	13. Error functions
5. Hardware functions	14. Caret functions
6. Painting functions	15. Cursor functions
7. Dialog box functions	16. Hook functions
8. Scrolling functions	17. Property functions
9. Menu functions	18. Rectangle functions

■ DISPLAY CONTEXTS

The display context system in Windows is a way of managing the computer's display so that it can be shared by several applications at one time. The four types of display contexts Windows has to work with are: common, class, private, and window. The window display context allows data to be written anywhere in the window. The others allow writing only to the window's client area. The type of display context is assigned when a window is created based on the specification in the window's class style.

■ ELEMENTS OF WINDOWS USER INTERFACES

In a completed Windows user interface there are typically numerous controls, each with a uniquely defined ID number, and when a user interacts with these controls, WM_COMMAND messages circulate to the windows and controls affected carrying the IDs of the controls that have been selected. Every Windows user interface forms a control loop like this that can be extended at will and encoded to determine what will happen when each type of control ID is reported. The WS_TABSTOP and WS_GROUP parameters set the control style for groups of buttons and dialog fields so that the control focus may be shifted either by the tab key or the arrow keys, respectively.

■ OWNER-DRAW CONTROLS

Normally, Windows assumes responsibility for redrawing the various types of controls. However, starting with Windows 3.0 there is a provision for styling controls as owner-drawn. This means that the control can be of a type whose owner window assumes the responsibility for redrawing. The advantage of this is that customized data can be stored in data structures, which allows some variation in the style of the control. Instead of Windows redrawing the control automatically in a standard way, the task is left for the owner window, which has access to specific information on how to draw the custom control.

■ ICONS

Icons are much more prevalent in Windows 3.0 than in earlier versions of the program. The icons are created from special bitmap files and statements in a resource script that provide access to the files. Windows icon files generally contain a set of different icons with different color and resolution attributes and leave it up to Windows to decide which best fits a given display device. The built-in icons supplied with Windows can be used in any application program. The built-in icons include the exclamation point, the question mark, the asterisk, and the stop sign. These are usually used for display purposes in dialogs. But icons have a much broader use in the Windows environment.

It is often useful to create class icons, that is, icons that will be used whenever objects of a particular Windows class are minimized, or collapsed on the screen. When class icons are specified, Windows takes over the job of automatically displaying them whenever the corresponding windows are minimized. The application programmer doesn't have to be concerned with it. Custom icons can be created with the SDKPaint utility provided with the MS Windows 3.0 SDK and its resource declarations entered using the resource compiler.

■ MENUS

The menus we are most familiar with are text oriented menus. But in a GUI like Windows, we also frequently encounter graphics oriented menus using icons, such as in the paintbox section of many drawing and painting programs. As with other controls in Windows, every menu has its own unique ID number that the programmer determines. Whenever a user selects a menu its ID number is transmitted by a Windows message that notifies an application of this user event. It is up to the application to supply instructions on what to do when each menu item is selected by a user. It is good programming practice to disable menu items and "grey" them when it is utterly inappropriate that they be used. This should be confined to situations when it is impossible or harmful for the menu item to be activated. This should not be used in situations when it is in any way possible that a user might be able to use a menu item. If there is room for any doubt at all, the menu item should not be disabled. Windows menu functions are listed in Table 4.5.

Table 4.5 Windows Menu Functions.

SetMenu(hWnd,hMenu)

AppendMenu

InsertMenu

GetSubMenu

ModifyMenu(hMenu, nPosition, wFlags, wIDNewItem, lpNewItem)

SetMenuItemBitmaps

▪ CONTROLS

In Windows, controls are child windows that respond to user interaction by sending notification messages that can be tested by program code and assigned to desired procedures. Having stated this, it should be immediately mentioned that there is an exception: that of static controls. Static controls are those that simply display a message without accepting user input and sending notification messages. On the Windows level, controls are created by specifying the appropriate parameters to the CreateWindow function. Windows uses the WM_COMMAND message to notify windows of the status of controls. The WM_COMMAND has two data parameters that it transmits: wp and lp. The wp parameter tells you the ID number of the control. The lp parameter tells you what type of control is transmitting, a menu, an accelerator key, or another control. In the sections that follow the various types of controls will be described.

▪ BUTTONS

As with all controls, buttons are actually separate child windows that are used basically the way simple on buttons function on hardware devices. In principle, they can be used to trigger any command or message and they can be of any size. The standard button types are pushbuttons, checkboxes, and radio buttons. Depending on the button style, its text label goes either on the button itself, or just to the right of it. Generally speaking, buttons do not have to have the input focus to be able to respond to mouse input. However, to use keyboard input the focus is required. Checkbox buttons are often used in groups, where one alternative is selected to the exclusion of the others. The same is true of radio buttons. Group boxes are assemblies of checkboxes or radio buttons. They are essentially rectangular boxes that enclose two or more controls that belong together functionally. In and of themselves, group boxes do not respond to user interaction. They do not produce notification messages of any kind.

▪ SCROLL BARS

In theory, scroll bars can be positioned anywhere in a window. They are essentially controls that allow users to interactively select a value from a continuous range of values. When a user moves the scroll-bar thumb with the mouse, notification messages are sent that allow the values to be sent and the visual appearance of the scroll bar to be updated. There are two different types of scroll bars, those that are part of a window's border, and those that are freestanding, as it were, and may or may not have anything to do with scrolling text. In the case of freestanding scroll-bar controls, it is totally the responsibility of the application to determine what happens when the scroll-bar thumb is moved. Windows provides the SetScrollRange function that determines the range of values that the scroll bar will be able to select. The application must then determine what will be done with the values that are sent when the scroll bar moves.

■ DIALOGS

Besides Menus, Dialogs are the other most important element in Windows user interfaces. It is very typical for a menu selection to result in the opening of a dialog. Dialogs or Dialog Boxes are popup windows that are generally used for rather short interaction events by users. This is usually to prompt the user for additional information or for a decision about options. Dialogs can be declared to run either modally or modelessly. Unlike running a dialog in modal fashion, running it modelessly does not temporarily disable its parent window. An example of a modeless dialog is in the Windows Write program where the Find command produces a dialog box that still allows a user to continue editing the main text. This could also be appropriate for a spelling corrector and other similar auxiliary tools.

A little reflection will convince you that there is a major difference in the way keys are handled in modeless as opposed to modal dialogs. In modeless dialogs, the keys must retain their former use, whereas in modal dialogs the role of the keys can be tightly controlled. Windows predefines the functionality for a small set of keys for use with dialogs. Windows dialog functions are listed in Table 4.6.

■ LIST BOXES

List boxes are divided into those that allow only single items to be selected and those that permit multiple selections. Another optional style of list box is the multicolumn one. In a single selection list box, when you make a selection, this automatically supersedes any other previous selection. Multiple selection list boxes allow more than one item to be highlighted. In a multicolumn list box, instead of vertically scrolling

Table 4.6 Windows Dialog Functions.

DialogBox	GetDlgItem
CreateDialog	SendDlgMessage
EndDialog	SetDlgItemText
IsDialogMessage	CreateDialogParam

when the items overflow its length, the list box will spill over by automatically snaking the items into additional columns of the box.

■ COMBO BOXES

Combo boxes are more elaborate list boxes. They also allow editing. There are three basic styles of combo box: simple, dropdown, and dropdown list. With simple combo boxes, the list box is always displayed below the edit field. Users can type in the edit field when the combo box has the input focus. With dropdown combo boxes, the list box is not initially displayed. Only the edit field is displayed with a small arrow to the right. The list box drops down when the arrow is selected with the mouse. The dropdown list combo box is identical to this, except that a user can select items from the list box simply by typing their first letter in the edit field.

■ FLOATING POPUP MENUS

It is now possible to create popup menus that are not bound to the top menu bar but do their popping up at the click of a mouse button on a multibutton mouse. This is an important user interface concept because it can be a real time-saver for users. They don't have to be continually dragging the mouse cursor up to the menu bar, but can get menu facilities wherever they happen to be working in a window.

■ GDI

The Windows GDI is designed with the purpose of allowing display independent code to be written, leaving it up to the device driver to make the translation to for specific display devices. The way this device independence is accomplished is by first creating output to an imaginary logical space and then mapping it to the real output displays, printers, plotters, and so on. In doing this, eight different mapping modes have been established.

Six of the eight mapping modes are constrained modes. The Isotropic and Anisotropic modes are partially constrained and unconstrained, respectively. In the constrained modes, logical units are mapped to actual physical units. For example, in the Low English mode they are mapped to units of .01 inch. In the nonconstrained modes, the window and viewport are used to derive horizontal and vertical scaling factors. Table 4.7 enumerates the GDI mapping modes.

The Windows GDI allows graphics output to be created by bitmaps, brushes, and pens. The GDI predefines just three pens: Black, Null, and White. These can be used by calling the GetStockObject function. Seven brushes are predefined: Black, Dark-Gray, Gray, Hollow, Light-Gray, Null, and White. There are six hatched brush patterns. The GDI also supplies twelve text formatting styles.

Table 4.7 GDI Mapping Modes.

Anisotropic		assignable
High English	1000	inch
High Metric	100	millimeter
Low English	100	inch
Low Metric	10	millimeter
Text	1	device pixel
Twips	1440	inch

Device Contexts and Information Contexts

A Windows device context is a particular linkage between an application program, a device driver, and the output device itself, for example, a laser printer. Another way of describing it would be as an output chain. An information context is like a device context minus its ability to perform the output.

There are a total of seventeen different types of Windows GDI functions, as listed in Table 4.8.

Metafiles are files that, instead of storing graphic images, store the commands that can create images. Window metafile functions are listed in Table 4.9. They do not have to be played back in their entirety, but have considerable flexibility in this respect.

Windows is designed to mediate situations in which the number of colors requested exceeds the number allowed by a display device. This can happen, for example, when more than one application is making use of the same logical palette.

∎ MULTI-DOCUMENT INTERFACE

The Multi-Document Interface has been a feature of earlier versions of Windows. As the name suggests, it is a standard for allowing single applications under Windows to present, manipulate, and manage more than one document during a session. This is done by providing each document in a child window while user control is still administered through a single parent window.

In Multi-Document applications, the main window acts as a frame window, and that is what it is called. By utilizing this interface, very little special data and code has to be devoted to maintaining it. Its management is carried out in a standard, automatic way by the Windows environment itself.

The first step in writing an application using the Multi-Document Interface occurs in the initialization phase. You must register two MS window classes, one for the frame window and one for the document windows. The registered structure of the document window class differs from ordinary child windows in a few different respects. An icon

Table 4.8 Categories of Function in the Windows GDI.

1. Device context functions	10. Ellipse and polygon functions
2. Drawing tool functions	11. Bitmap functions
3. Color palette functions	12. Text functions
4. Drawing attribute functions	13. Font functions
5. Mapping functions	14. Metafile functions
6. Coordinate functions	15. Printer control functions
7. Region functions	16. Printer escape functions
8. Clipping functions	17. Environment functions
9. Line output functions	

Table 4.9 Windows MetaFile Functions.

CreateMetaFile	EnumMetaFile
CopyMetaFile	PlayMetaFileRecord
GetMetaFile	AnimatePalette
DeleteMetaFile	SetDlBitsToDevice

should be provided for the document window because a user can minimize this child window just as they would a main window. The name for this MS window class should be NULL, because they are not allowed to have their own menus. There should also be extra memory reserved for the window class for doing things like storing the name of a disk file to be associated with each document.

■ DYNAMIC LINK LIBRARIES

A new requirement with Version 3.0 is that the Resource Compiler must be run on all dynamic link libraries, if for nothing else than to provide it with the 3.0 version stamp. This is not to win a Good Housekeeping seal of approval. It is needed to prevent the warning message on startup that alerts users so that, in the case of problems, they have an idea of what might have been the cause. The presence of the version stamp is an indication that the developers, and their work, are aware of the conditions for running in the new Windows environment. Dynamic link libraries, from Version 3.0 and on, also have to use the .DLL file extension instead of the .EXE extension in earlier versions. This is so that users will not confuse them with executable Windows applications. Handling these dynamic link libraries is now much easier for developers, for instead of having to hand code the entry points in machine language, Windows provides a standard routine for establishing entry points.

DLLs Require Both Initialization and Termination Procedures

Version 3.0 dynamic link libraries also have to include a Windows exit procedure named WEP. This is the message that is sent to notify the dynamic link libraries that they are being unloaded. Dynamic link libraries now may also be designated private, which allows them to be moved up to high memory, freeing up the main memory space for other uses.

For compatibility with Windows 3.0 DLLs also have to be compiled with the resource compiler. One of the unfortunate things here is the -p option, which designates the DLL as private. This defeats the very idea of a DLL, in an important sense. For if everyone marks their DLLs as private, then there will still be quite a bit of redundant code running and memory wasted to run it. It is quite clear that those who advertise that their DLLs are not private will enjoy an important advantage in the marketplace.

■ DYNAMIC DATA EXCHANGE

The Dynamic Data Exchange (DDE) is one method among several for exchanging information between separate Windows applications. What the Windows DDE provides is essentially a message protocol. The way this protocol works is by either sending the data directly using DDE messages, or by passing the handles for shared global memory blocks. Typical applications for which the DDE can be used are:

1. Links to real-time data sources like process control sensors, stock updates, and so on.

2. Using compound documents, that is, those composed of a variety of different files.

3. Linking spreadsheets and databases for data sharing.

4. Information exchange between different computers running Windows.

■ DEVICE-INDEPENDENT COLOR GRAPHICS

Unlike monochrome displays, with color bitmaps, the relation between pixels and memory bits is not one to one. The precise way that color is mapped to memory is typically very much a function of the display adaptor and its capabilities. In other words, it is hardware or device-dependent. From Windows Version 3.0 and on, however, all functions for handling color bitmaps do so in a way that is generic, and independent of the hardware used to display the color. The new formats for icons and cursors also use a format that is device-independent. This is because both icons and cursors are created with sets of device-independent color bitmaps. We will learn more about this when we discuss the SDKPaint tool.

■ THE HELP-BUILDING SYSTEM

The Help-building system is one of the major new additions to Windows. There are two main parts to the SDK Help-building system, the Help engine and the Help compiler. The Help engine itself comes with the retail version of Windows 3.0 and later that all end users will possess. It is this Help engine that Windows uses to process the compiled Help file into a functioning Help session. There are a few different steps involved in creating the final Help file for your program. First of all, you create the text that will appear in the Help system, using any text editor that can produce an ASCII text file. Next control characters are entered in the text file to direct the Help compiler.

■ THE RESOURCE COMPILER

This is the tool you use for compiling Windows resources like menus, cursors, icons, and dialog boxes for a particular application. The Resource Compiler accepts resource scripts with the .RC extension that provides the name and description of all the resources an application will use. It then compiles this into an .RES file, combines this with the .EXE file for the application, and marks the latter with a Windows version stamp. Before using the Resource Compiler you create all the files required for the icons, cursors, fonts, bitmaps, and dialogs your application will need. Then you create a resource script file that describes them.

For resources like fonts, cursors, and dialogs that are specified in their own files, the resource script only needs to contain their name and the name of their file. But for menus, the script needs to contain their entire description, for it is here that they are defined. Once it is complete, you compile it with the Resource Compiler, RC.EXE. There are a number of ways this program can be called up. In a later chapter we will have occasion to use the Resource Compiler and I will give various examples of the alternative ways of using it.

The Debugging Version of Windows

The debugging version of Windows checks on the validity of window handles that are passed to Windows functions. Another advantage is that in the debugging mode symbol information contained in the core dynamic link libraries that make up Windows can be accessed and displayed while Windows is running in the debugging mode, which makes errors easier to diagnose when using a debugger like Codeview for Windows. The debugging version of Windows is also necessary for getting the best use of the HeapWalker program.

Installing the Debugging Version

The debugging version of Windows consists of alternate versions of the core DDLs of the Windows system: KRNL286.EXE, KRNL386.EXE, GDI.EXE, and USER.EXE that are shipped with the MS-Windows SDK and are normally installed in the WIN-

DEV\DEBUG directory. To run Windows in the debugging mode these files and their corresponding symbol files must be copied into the WINDOWS\SYSTEM directory. Before doing this, you will probably want to either rename the nondebugging versions of the DLLs or copy them into another directory for safekeeping.

■ RESOURCE EDITORS AND TOOLS

All Windows programs have to be written so as to guarantee the environment control of shared resources. Memory is one of these shared resources. The system display is also a shared resource. To avoid confusion, I will distinguish between a computer resource and a Windows resource. Windows resources refer to the actual components of programs that are visible on the screen. In the following sections I will give an overview of the various tools provided in the SDK to assist the programmer in creating Windows resources.

■ THE DIALOG EDITOR

This tool provides programmers with a short-cut for creating dialogs. Instead of defining dialog statements in resource scripts, the Dialog Editor (Figure 4.1) allows controls to be designed and tested interactively onscreen. It outputs its specification in a .DLG file

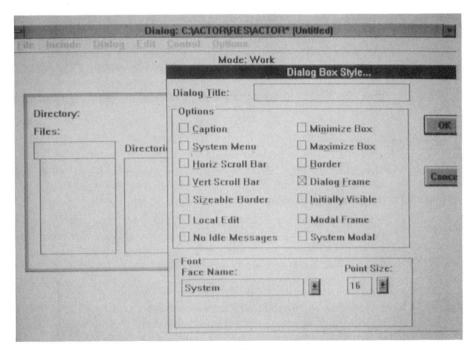

Figure 4.1 The SDK Dialog Editor.

and an .RES file, which is used by the Resource Compiler. The Dialog Editor also produces header files with #define statements to identify controls in dialog boxes. In its latest incarnation the Dialog Editor allows you to build and maintain a catalogue of custom controls for dialogs like an inventory of spare parts.

The Dialog Editor has an alternate user interface called the Toolbox, which works on the same principle as a paint program to give you the identical capabilities you get using menus with this program. The basic operations that can be performed on controls include moving, resizing, copying, deleting, editing text, and modifying a control's identifier or style. You can also move as a group and define a group's "input focus sequence." By default, controls get input focus in the order that they are created, regardless of how they may be repositioned.

∎ SDKPAINT

SDK, a program new with Version 3.0, is a very versatile graphics utility that can create or modify three different types of objects: bitmaps, icons, and cursors. The three types of files corresponding to them, .BMP, .ICO, and .CUR can be included in a resource script so that the appropriate resource (.RES) file can be compiled. Bitmap files are of either color or monochrome device-independent bitmaps. Each bitmap is a unique graphic image. Icons and cursors, on the other hand, represent a family of images, each designed for display on a different type of Windows object.

Opening 2.X bitmap files results in them being automatically converted to the 3.0 format as they load into the SDKPaint editor (Figure 4.2). Because icon and cursor files contain multiple images, you first open the file, and then load the specific image you are interested in. There is a separate menu for loading images. Once a cursor or icon file is open, you can also create new images to be added to it. A number of drawing tools are provided at the bottom of the SDKPaint window for this purpose.

∎ THE FONT EDITOR

FontEdit goes about providing help in creating new fonts by allowing you to edit existing ones to produce what you want. It works only for raster or screen fonts, not for printer fonts. The edit window presents you with an enlarged grid containing any font that has been loaded into the editor. You edit the font by turning individual pixels on or off. Because the only way to create a new font is to modify an existing one, the SDK provides a "seed" font set that can be used for this purpose. When you load this font set, you first see the capital letter 'A' in two different views, one the normal size, and the other blown up into a "fat bits" view where the pixels are represented as small rectangles.

It is possible to move through the whole font set, containing the entire alphabet in both upper- and lowercase for the same typeface. Besides turning pixels on or off one by one, the Font Editor also provides editing operations by row or column of pixels as well. Also powerful are the operations for providing various pattern fills onto the pixel

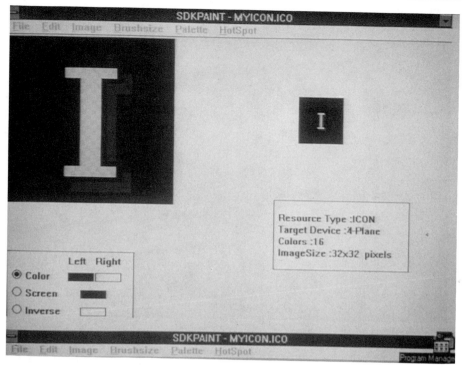

Figure 4.2 The SDKPaint Editor shown in ICM editing mode.

grid. Various commands are also available for varying the entire width of fonts. Changing the height is only possible through the general commands that are used for selecting the overall size of fonts.

■ ZOOMIN

The Windows SDK program that is every bit of fun to use as it is useful is the one called Zoomin (Figure 4.3). What does Zoomin do? You guessed it. It zooms in. That is to say, Zoomin is a special window whose frame shows a rectangle of the screen that will zoom in and out as you work the scroll bar. If you click the mouse on the inside of the window and drag it, while keeping the button depressed, you can move a frame line that represents the zoom rectangle about the screen and the area inside the window will mirror whatever you capture by this frame as you move it. When the frame happens to contain part of the Zoomin window border, then you get a version of the infinitely reflecting mirrors puzzle.

■ PROFILER

There are three parts to the Profiler: 1) a sampling utility, 2) a reporting utility, and 3) a set of functions that can be called from an application. The sampling utility stores information while a program is running about the time spent between adjacent labels

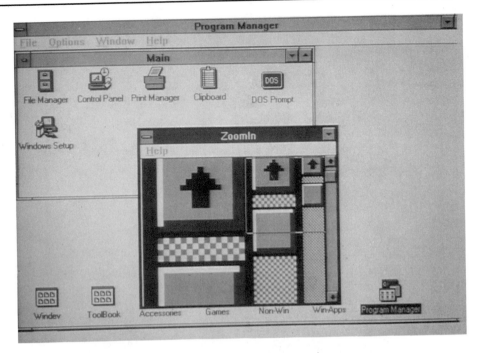

Figure 4.3 The SDK Zoomin utility.

and the memory addresses of code locations. Two different sampling utility programs are provided, depending on whether your application is running in real mode or protected mode. For real mode applications, you run PROF.COM in the normal Windows environment. For protected mode applications you run this program after installing the VPROD.386 driver. The sampler writes the information it gathers into two separate files, one that contains samplings of the instruction pointer register, and another that contains information about the movement of code segments. After the sampling utility has done its information gathering, the SHOWHITS.EXE program uses it to display a report of the results.

You tell Profiler where to start and where to stop sampling code by inserting the ProfStart and ProfStop functions in your code at the appropriate points. ProfStop should not be confused with the ProfFinish function, which is necessary to make the Profiler flush its results to disk without exiting Windows. Once this occurs, then the ShowHits program can be run to develop a report.

■ SPY

The Spy program (Figure 4.4) is a handy device for debugging or just aiding your understanding of how the Windows message system works. An extremely easy program to use, it's best used for monitoring the messages that go to a particular window. To

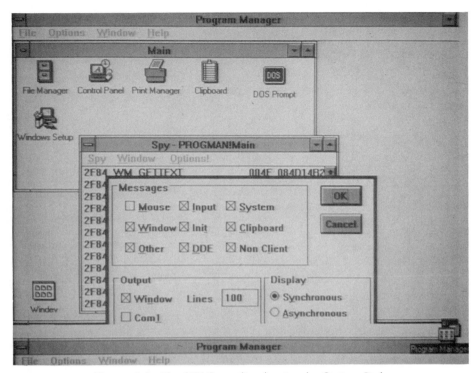

Figure 4.4 The SDK Spy utility showing the Options Dialog.

use it you simply call up the Spy program as you would any Windows application, choose the Set Window command from the Window menu, and click the mouse on the window you want to spy on. From that point on, messages will come streaming in, displayed in the Spy window. Even just moving the mouse around in the chosen window will produce lots of WM_SETCURSOR and WM_MOUSEMOVE messages. The Options menu provides a filter with check boxes that allow you select the types of messages you are interested in viewing. You can select the type of events to spy on as well as whether you will see input or output messages to the selected window or both.

■ HEAPWALKER

This tool (Figure 4.5) is an important one, because it allows you to monitor the global heap, the system memory available for use by Windows. It works whether you are running Windows in real mode or protected mode. If you are running in protected mode, then HeapWalker walks in an area of memory that lives above DOS, any TSR (terminate and stay resident) programs, and drivers that are loaded. HeapWalker can take a number of kinds of walk. A walk is a survey of certain kinds of memory contents that produces a list in the HeapWalker window. For example, there is a walk through the LRU (least recently used) list. This is actually a walk through all discardable memory

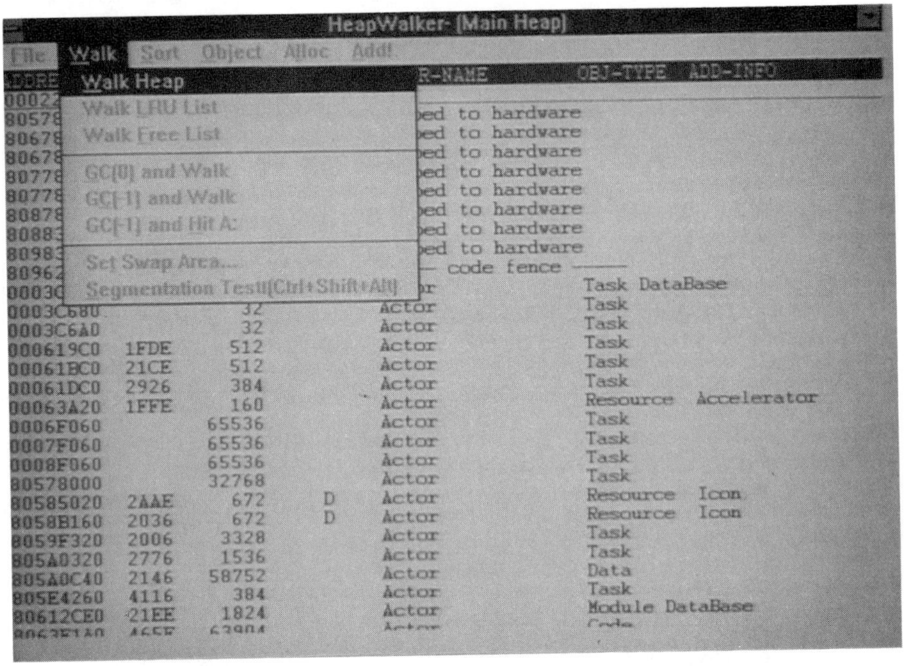

Figure 4.5 The SDK HeapWalker utility showing the Walk menu options.

that has been sorted into a list in the order of least used first. You can select any number of items in such a walk list and choose the Add command from the menu bar, and a dialog will open with a total of bytes for the items selected.

■ SWAP

Swap is a tool used for detecting procedure calls that occur across segment boundaries. This is an aid to improving the performance of programs, because to produce programs that execute as rapidly as possible such calls have to be kept to a minimum. Use of the Swap program requires that the SwapRecording function is embedded in an application. Also needed are .SYM files that are produced when the /map option of the linker is specified. Swap also requires the SKKERNAL.EXE program, which, in the current release of Windows, runs only in the real mode. In the default mode, Swap takes quite a long time to process all the module and symbol names. Usually it will be a good idea to use the -M option to specify those modules that you wish Swap to process.

■ SHAKER

This is a simple program (Figure 4.6) that semirandomly allocates memory from the global heap to force relocation of code and data segments of your program to ensure that no problems result when this happens. For the most part, Shaker runs autono-

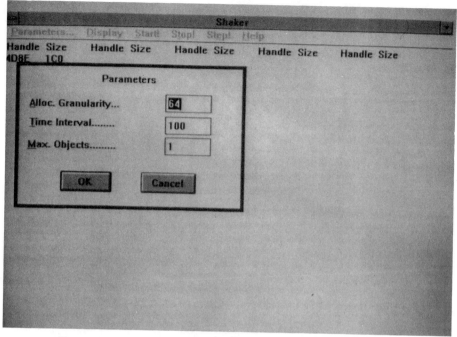

Figure 4.6 The SDK Shaker utility showing the Parameters dialog.

mously, and then you can determine if problems have arisen with your application after it is run. Shaker allows various parameters to be set before its allocation sequence is started, including Granularity, Time Interval, and Max Objects. Granularity sets the minimum size of the memory objects to be allocated. Time Interval sets the time interval measured in system time clicks. Max Objects sets the maximum number of memory objects that will be allocated. The best way to get an understanding of how Shaker works is to run to program. It is quite simple and straightforward to use.

▪ CODEVIEW FOR WINDOWS

As mentioned above, Codeview for Windows is a symbolic debugger of Windows intended for use with a second monitor and runs only in protected mode. There is also the memory requirement of two megabytes of extended memory. The intended setup is for Codeview to be displayed on a second monitor while your program executes on the first. This version of Codeview is quite similar to the DOS version of the program, but there are additional functions designed specifically for the debugging of Windows applications. For example, Codeview for Windows has the ability to track an application's segments and data by readjusting its symbol table appropriately when Windows moves the program's position in memory. The debugger also displays the Windows messages involved when memory is moved or allocated. The five new commands specifically geared toward Windows programming are listed below:

wdl

wdg

wdm

wwm

wbm

■ THE SYMDEB REAL MODE DEBUGGER

The Symbolic Debug Utility, or Symdeb for short, is the tool used for debugging executable programs that run in real mode. Like Codeview for Windows, Symdeb requires an additional monitor, but in this case, a serial terminal is still an option. The Mapsym program works with Symdeb by converting the contents of symbol map (.MAP) files into the .SYM files that the latter program uses.

■ MAINTAINING COMPATIBILITY WITH VERSIONS 2.0 AND 3.0

Some very special rules must be adhered to if a program is to ensure for itself the maximum number of users by virtue of its compatibility with all versions of Windows since version 2.0. One reason for this is the new memory architecture that has been implemented. Besides guidelines on memory management there are two other types of guidelines, those regarding interrupt flags and proportional system fonts.

Any 2.0 Windows application run under Version 3.0 automatically gets proportional system fonts on its menus. To get them on dialogs, controls, and user areas too, instead of the former fixed pitch fonts, the applications have to be marked appropriately. One by-product of the proportional system fonts is that any algorithm based on the assumption that all characters are the same width will not work properly. For aligning things like accelerator key codes on menus, the TAB key rather than space characters should be used. The restriction on interrupt flags refers only to assembly language programs that use the STI and CLI instructions. Since this book does not deal with assembly language, we will not be concerned with this type of restriction.

■ THE STRUCTURE OF WINDOWS PROGRAMS

Typically, an application's WinMain function does four things:

1. It registers the windows classes to be used in an application and performs all other initializations.

2. It creates the main window and other windows the application needs.

3. It begins the message loop that handles messages from its application queue.

4. It waits for the WM_QUIT message, telling it to terminate itself.

Windows passes the WinMain function of each Windows application four parameters, one to receive the instance handle (hInstance), one to receive the previous instance of the application (hPrevInstance), one that receives a long pointer to a null-terminated command line (lpCmdLine), and one that can be passed on to the Show Window function, which displays the application's main window (nCmdShow).

Callback functions are those application functions that are intended to be called by Windows messages.

■ WINDOWS USER INTERFACE STYLE

For various reasons, Microsoft has compiled some guidelines on what is considered good style in utilizing the Windows development tools for building applications.

Here are the two "commandments" as they have been passed down to us:

1. Thou shalt not put menu bars on dialog boxes.

2. Thou shalt embellish modal dialog boxes with framed borders.

■ WRITING RESOURCE SCRIPTS

The MS-Windows Resource Script language provides a method of defining resources that can be compiled and added to the executable file of application programs. This resource script language supports eight different types of statements: 1) single line, 2) user-defined resources, 3) data, 4) string tables, 5) accelerators, 6) menus, 7) dialogs, and 8) directives. Single line statements typically define resources such as icons, fonts, and bitmaps that are contained in separate files by associating an identifier name with the corresponding file name. The format for these single line statements allows for an option that can specify the resource as FIXED, MOVEABLE, or DISCARDABLE. They can also be either preloaded or loaded on call. Raw and user-defined data formats can also be defined. String tables of numbered ASCII strings can be specified, which are retrieved by supplying the corresponding number as an argument to the MS-Windows LoadString function.

Menu labels are followed either by an ID number or a constant name with a predefined integer value.

Table 4.10 shows a list of resource script keywords.

■ CONCLUSIONS

The SDK is an impressive compilation of development tools, which has become obvious during the overview discussion; it is also of formidable complexity. Since there are so many Windows development tools now available from third party developers promoted

Table 4.10 Resource Script Keywords.

RCDATA	RTEXT
STRINGTABLE	CTEXT
ACCELERATORS	CHECKBOX
MENU	PUSHBUTTON
MENUITEM	LISTBOX
POPUP	GROUPBOX
DIALOG	DEFPUSHBUTTON
STYLE	RADIOBUTTON
CAPTION	EDITTEXT
MENU	COMBOBOX
CLASS	ICON
FONT	SCROLLBAR
LTEXT	CONTROL

as aids to make one's life easier, it is certainly worthwhile giving them serious consideration. At this point, if one chooses to just use the SDK and nothing further, then it would appear that one should have a very good reason for doing so. Although there are a couple of products that even allow one to write Windows programs without owning the SDK at all, for serious developers, the tools like Spy, HeapWalker, and Codeview for Windows make the use of the SDK very attractive indeed, regardless of what programming language one chooses.

The MS-Windows architecture has some of the advantages of an object-oriented system. The construction of the actual software systems that can be built under Windows looks very much like one. Things happen by means of messages exchanged between independent modules that operate like autonomously functioning parts whose control does not need to be hand-coded from scratch each time they are used. There are classes of objects that are standard templates, which can be used to stamp out working program parts. However, the similarities virtually stop there. Some of the things about OOP most advantageous to programmers are not present. When it comes to the actual coding, the standard C language-based programming exhibits very little of the object-oriented character found in the Windows architecture itself. One feels, for example, that there is a large amount of code that has to be written to properly take advantage of the Windows resources, even if much of it is standard. It is precisely the fact of this standardization that gives such a sense of the code's redundancy.

From the point of view of OOP, there is therefore a certain incompleteness about the Windows SDK when used with plain C. However, although there is no question that there are difficulties with using other languages than the C recommended by Microsoft, it is also true that, at least in principle, any language can be used. In practice, that language has to be able to produce a very specific kind of code and work with all the memory model conventions associated with Windows, but these are issues concerning the implementation of a language rather than the language itself. For these reasons, you should begin to see some of the strong advantages in using one of the object-oriented languages that have been especially ported for use in the Windows environment. Regardless of which programming language you choose, there is clearly a great deal to learn about how things are done in a system like Windows. The central point of this book is that one of the most natural and appropriate approaches to programming in the Windows environment is the use of OOP technology.

Because there is so much code to write for even relatively simple Windows programs, the practice has naturally arisen of formulating generic application codes that already have most of the bases covered and are ready to receive the application specific code that is unique to the program. The Microsoft Windows SDK comes with a sample generic program that consists of a total of file modules.

■ WINDOWS EDITING CONTROL MESSAGES

EM_CANUNDO

EM_EMPTYUNDOBUFFER

EM_FMTLINES

■ NEW WINDOWS 3.0 FUNCTIONS

AdjustWindowRectEx	Computes the rectangle size of an extended style window.
AllocCStoDSAlias	Returns a data segment selector for writing into the supplied code segment.
AllocDStoCSAlias	Returns a code segment selector for writing into the supplied data segment.
AllocSelector	Returns a new copy of a supplied selector.
AnimatePalette	Replaces entries in a specified logical palette.
AnsiLowerBuff	Converts a string in a buffer to lowercase characters.
AnsiToOemBuff	Translates a specified string from an ANSI character set into an OEM-defined character set.
AnsiUpperBuff	Converts a string in a buffer to uppercase characters.
AppendMenu	Adds a new item to the end of a menu.
ArrangeIconicWindows	Arranges child windows that are minimized as icons.

BeginDeterWindowPos	Allocates memory for a multiple window structure and returns its handle.
ChangeSelector	Generates a temporary code selector for a given data selector or vice versa.
CreateCursor	Creates a cursor of specified height, width, and bit pattern.
CreateDialogIndirectParam	Creates a modeless dialog and allows dialog function to initialize its controls.
CreateDialogParam	Creates a modeless dialog and allows dialog function to initialize its controls.
CreateDLBitmap	Creates a device-specific bitmap from a device-independent one.
CreateDLBPatternBrush	Creates a logical brush from a specific device-independent bitmap.
CreateIcon	Creates an icon of specified height, width, colors, and bit pattern.
CreatePalette	Creates a logical color palette.
CreatePolyPolygonRgn	Creates a region defined by a set of closed polygons.
CreatePopupMenu	Creates an empty popup menu and returns its handle.
CreateRoundRectRegn	Creates a rounded-corner rectangular region.
CreateWindowEx	Creates an overlapped popup or child window with an extended style.
DebugBreak	Forces a break to the debugger.
DefDlgProc	Provides default processing for messages that a dialog with a private window class does not handle.
DeferWindowPos	Updates a multiple window-position data structure.
DefFrameProc	Provides default processing for messages that a window function for an MDI frame window does not handle.
DefineHandleTable	Creates a private handle table in an application's default data segment.
DefMDIChildProc	Provides default processing for messages that a window function for an MDI child window does not handle.

DeleteMenu	Deletes a popup item from a specified menu and releases its allocated memory.
DestroyCursor	Destroys a cursor created by the CreateCursor function and releases its allocated memory.
DestroyIcon	Destroys an icon created by the CreateIcon function and releases its allocated memory.
DeviceCapabilities	Returns the capabilities of a printer device driver.
DialogBoxindirectParam	Creates a modal dialog and allows dialog function to initialize its controls.
DialogBoxParam	Creates a modal dialog and allows dialog function to initialize its controls.
DlgDirListComboBox	Fills the list box of a combo box with a list of all files matching a given path and extension.
DlgDirSelectComboBox	Retrieves the current selection from a combo box list box.
DOS3Call	Permits Windows programs to issue DOS 21H interrupt calls.
DrawFocusRect	Draws rectangles used to indicate control focus.
EndDeferWindowPos	Updates position and size of windows in a screen refresh.
ExitWindows	Initiates the standard Windows shutdown sequence.
ExtDeviceMode	Retrieves or modifies data for a given device driver.
ExtFloodFill	Fills an area of the display with the current brush.
FatalAppExit	Displays a fatal error message and exits Windows.
FreeModule	Decreases the reference count of the loaded module by one.
FreeSelector	Sets free selectors that have already been allocated.
GetClassInfo	Retrieves the specification of a Windows class.
GetCodeInfo	Retrieves pointer to a 16-bit array that stores code segment information.
GetCurrentPDB	Returns paragraph address of the current DOS Program Database.

GetDesktopWindow	Returns window handle of Windows desktop window.
GetDialogBaseUnits	Returns dialog base units used to create dialog boxes.
GetDIBits	Retrieves bits of a specified bitmap and copies them into the specified buffer.
GetDlCntrlID	Returns the ID of the specified child window.
GetDOSEnvironment	Returns a far pointer to the environment string of the currently running task.
GetDriveType	Determines if a drive is removable, fixed, or remote.
GetFreeSpace	Returns the number of bytes available in the global heap.
GetKBCodePage	Determines which OEM/ANSI tables are loaded by Windows.
GetKeyboardType	Returns the system keyboard type.
GetKeyNameText	Retrieves the string that holds the name of a key.
GetLastActivePopup	Determines which popup of a specified window was active most recently.
GetMenuCheckMarkDimensions	Returns the dimensions of default checkmark bitmap.
GetNearestPaletteIndex	Returns matching index of a color value of a logical palette.
GetPaletteEntries	Retrieves a specified range of palette entries in a logical palette.
GetPriorityClipboardFormat	Returns first clipboard format for data in the clipboard.
GetPrivateProfileInt	Returns the value of an integer key from the specified file.
GetPrivateProfileString	Copies a character string from a specified file into a specified buffer.
GetRgnBox	Retrieves the coordinates of the bounding rectangle of a specified region.
GetSystemDirectory	Obtains the path name of the Windows system subdirectory.
GetSystemPaletteEntries	Retrieves a specified range of entries from the system palette.
GetSystemPaletteUse	Determines if an application has access to the full system palette.

GetTabbedTextExtent	Computes the width and height of a specified line of text.
GetWindowsDirectory	Obtains the path name of the Windows directory.
GetWinFlags	Returns 32-bit value with flags specifying the Windows memory configuration.
GlobalDosAlloc	Allocates global memory accessible by DOS running in real mode.
GlobalDosFree	Sets free memory previously allocated by GlobalDosAlloc.
GlobalFix	Prevents specified global memory block from moving in linear memory.
GlobalPageLock	Increments the page lock count associated with specified global selector.
GlobalPageUnlock	Decrements the page lock count associated with specified global selector.
GlobalUnfix	Unlocks the specified global memory block.
InsertMenu	Inserts a new menu item at the specified position.
IsCharAlpha	Tests if a character is an alphabetic character.
IsCharAlphaNumeric	Tests if a character is an alphanumeric character.
IsCharLower	Tests if a character is lowercase.
IsCharUpper	Tests if a character is uppercase.
lstrcmp	Compares two strings lexicographically.
lstrcmpi	Compares two strings lexicographically.
MapVirtualKey	Accepts a virtual key code and returns corresponding scan code.
ModifyMenu	Changes an existing menu item at the specified position.
MulDiv	Multiples two word length numbers and divides them by a third number.
NetBIOSCall	Allows Windows applications to make BIOS 5CH interrupt calls.
OemKeyScan	Maps OEM ASCII codes into OEM key scan codes.
OutputDebugString	Sends a debugging message to debugger or auxiliary device.
PALETTEINDEX	A macro that returns the palette entry index.

PALETTERGB	A macro that returns RGB intensity values.
PolyPolygon	Creates a series of closed polygons.
ProfClear	Discards all samples while the Profiler is running.
ProfFinish	Stops sampling and flushes output buffer to disk while the Profiler is running.
ProfFlush	Unless limits are exceeded, flushes output buffer to disk while the Profiler is running.
ProfInsChk	Determines if Profiler is installed.
ProfSampRate	Sets the code sampling rate for the Profiler.
ProfSetup	Sets parameters for Profiler running in the 386 Enhanced Mode.
ProfStart	Starts sampling while the Profiler is running.
ProfStop	Stops sampling while the Profiler is running.
RealizePalette	Maps entries in logical palette to the system palette.
RectInRegion	Tests if any part of specified rectangle is within specified region.
RemoveMenu	Deletes a menu item with its popup from a specified menu.
ResizePalette	Changes the size of the specified logical palette.
SelectPalette	Selects the specified logical palette.
SetDlBits	Sets the bits of a bitmap to the specified values.
SetDlBitsToDevice	Sets bits from DIB to device.
SetHandleCount	Changes the number of file handles.
SetMenuItemBitmaps	Associates the specified bitmaps with a menu item.
SetPaletteEntries	Sets RGB color values and flags for specified range.
SetSystemPaletteUse	Allows the application to use the full system palette.
StretchDLBits	Moves a DIB from a source to a destination rectangle.
SwapRecording	Toggles analysis on or off while running the Swap program.
SwitchStackBack	Returns the stack of the current task to its data segment.

SwitchStackTo	Changes the stack of the current task to the specified segment.
TabbedTextOut	Writes a string to the specified columns.
ToAscii	Translates specified key code to ANSI characters.
TrackPopupMenu	Displays a floating popup menu at the specified location and tracks selected items.
TranslateMDISysAccel	Processes keyboard accelerators for MDI commands.
UnregisterClass	Removes specified Windows class from class table.
UpdateColors	Updates the client area of specified device context.
ValidateCodeSegments	Outputs debugging information to a terminal.
WinExec	Executes application with command line parameter.
WritePrivateProfileString	Copies the specified character string into a specified initializiation file.
wsprintf	Formats and stores a series of character and values in a buffer.
wvsprintf	Formats and stores a series of character and values in a buffer.

■ NEW WINDOWS 3.0 MESSAGES

CB_ADDSTRING	Add a string to a combo box.
CB_DELETESTRING	Delete a string from a combo box.
CB_DIR	Add a list of files to the combo box from the current directory.
CB_FINDSTRING	Find the first matching string in a combo box list.
CB_GETCOUNT	Return the number of items in a combo box.
CB_GETCURSEL	Return the index of a selected item.
CB_GETEDITSEL	Return the start and end of selected text in edit control of a combo box.
CB_GETITEMDATA	Return the 32-bit value associated with an item in a combo box.
CB_GETLBTEXT	Copy a string from a combo box into a buffer.
CB_GETLBTTEXTLEN	Return the length of a string in a combo box.

CB_INSERTSTRING	Insert a string in a combo box.
CB_LIMITTEXT	Limit the length of text that a user may enter.
CB_RESETCONTENT	Clear all strings from a combo box.
CB_SELECTSTRING	Alter and display the current selection based on prefix characters.
CB_SETCURSEL	Select a string and scroll it into view.
CB_SETEDITSEL	Select all characters between start and end marked.
CB_SETITEMDATA	Assigns a 32-bit value to an item in an owner-draw combo box.
CB_SHOWDROPDOWN	Show or hide dropdown list in combo box.

Combo Box Notification Messages

CBN_DBLCLK	User has double clicked on a combo box string.
CBN_DROPDOWN	Tell child window that the list of its combo box will be dropped down.
CBN_EDITCHANGE	The user has altered text in the combo box's edit control.
CBN_EDITUPDATE	The edit control will display modified text.
CBN_ERRSPACE	The system is out of memory.
CBN_KILLFOCUS	The combo box has lost input focus.
CBN_SELCHANGE	The selection has been changed.
CBN_SETFOCUS	The combo box has received the input focus.

Edit Control Messages

EM_EMPTYUNDOBUFFER	Disables the ability to undo the last edit.
EM_SETPASSWORDCHAR	Changes the password character.
EM_SETTABSTOPS	Sets tab stop positions in multiline edit controls.
EN_MAXTEXT	Announces that the number of characters allowed by an edit control has been exceeded.

List Box Messages

LB_FINDSTRING	Find the first matching string in a list box.
LB_GETHORIZONTALEXTENT	Return the width by which a list can be horizontally scrolled.
LB_GETITEMDATA	Return 32-bit value associated with an item in a list box.

LB_GETITEMRECT	Return the coordinates of the bounding rectangle of a list box item.
LB_GETSELCOUNT	Return the number of selected items in a list box.
LB_GETSELITEMS	Return the indices of the selected items.
LB_GETOPINEX	Return the index of the first visible item in a list box.
LB_SETCOLUMNWIDTH	Set the width in pixels of the columns in multicolumn list boxes.
LB_SETHORIZONTALEXTENT	Set the width by which a list can be horizontally scrolled.
LB_SETITEMDATA	Assign a 32-bit value to an item in an owner-draw list box.
LB_SETTABSTOPS	Set the tab stops in a list box.
LB_SETOPENINDEX	Set the index of the first visible item in a list box.
LBN_KILLFOCUS	Sent when a list box loses input focus.
LBN_SETFOCUS	Sent when a list box receives input focus.
WM_CHARTOITEM	Sent by a list box to its child window on receiving WM_CHAR message.
WM_COMPACTING	Sent to all top-level windows when Windows detects that more than 12.5% of processing time is being spent on compacting memory.
WM_COMPAREITEM	Determine the relative position of a new item in sorted owner-draw combo boxes and list boxes.
WM_DELETEITEM	Inform the window that owns an owner-draw list box or combo box that an item has been deleted.
WM_DRAWITEM	Inform an owner-draw button, menu, or list box that some displayable property has changed.
WM_GETFONT	Retrieve a font from a control that the latter is using to draw text.using.
WM_ICONERASEBKGD	Sent to a minimized window when the icon's background must be filled before it is painted.
WM_MDIACTIVATE	Sent to an MDI client window to tell it to activate a different child window.

WM_MDICASCADE	Cascade the child windows of an MDI frame window.
WM_MDICREATE	Tell an MDI frame window to spawn a new child window.
WM_MDIDESTROY	Tell an MDI client window to close a child window.
WM_MDIGETACTIVE	Return the current active MDI child window.
WM_MDIICONARRANGE	Tells MDI client to arrange its child windows.
WM_MDIMAXIMIZE	Tells MDI client to maximize child window.
WM_MDINEXT	Activates the next MDI child window.
WM_MDIRESTORE	Restores a maximized or minimized MZDI child to normal size.
WM_MDISETMENU	Replaces the menu of an MDI frame window.
WM_MDITITLE	Tiles the child windows of an MDI client.
WM_MEASUREITEM	Tells owner-draw control to fill in MEASUREITEM data structure.
WM_PAINTICON	Tells minimized window to repaint.
WM_PALETTECHANGED	Tells all windows that the window with input focus has changed its palette.
WM_PARENTNOTIFY	Notifies the parent of a window about important changes in its status.
WM_QUERYDRAGICON	Tells a minimized window without a class icon that it is about to be dragged.
WM_QUERYNEWPALETTE	Tells a window it is about to receive input focus.
WM_SETFONT	Specifies the font to be used by a dialog box.
WM_SPOOLERSTATUS	Sent by Print Manager whenever a print task is added or deleted from the queue.

■ NEW WINDOWS 3.0 STRUCTURES

BITMAPCOREHEADER	Holds dimension and color data of DI bitmap.
BITMAPCOREINFO	Full definition of dimension and color data of DI bitmap.
BITMAPFILEHEADER	Holds type, size, and layout data of Windows 3.0 DI bitmap.
BITMAPINFO	Full definition of dimension and color data of Windows 3.0 DI bitmap.

BITMAPINFOHEADER	Holds dimension and color data of Windows 3.0 DI bitmap.
CLIENTCREATESTRUCT	Holds data about menu and first child of MDI client window.
COMPAREITEMSTRUCT	Holds data for two items in owner-draw combo box or list box.
DELETEITEMSTRUCT	Holds data for deleted item of owner-draw combo box or list box.
DEVMODE	Holds device initialization and environment data for printer drivers.
DRAWITEMSTRUCT	Holds data needed to draw owner-draw control.
LOGPALETTE	Defines logical color palettes.
MDICREATESTRUCT	Holds class, title, owner, location, and size data of an MDI child window.
MEASUREITEMSTRUCT	Holds the dimensions of an owner-draw control.
PALETTEENTRY	Specifies the color and usage of entries in logical color palettes.
RGBQUAD	Holds RGB color intensity data quad structure.
RGBTRIPLE	Holds RGB color intensity data triple structure.

5

INTRODUCTION TO THE ACTOR PROGRAMMING SYSTEM

■ THE ACTOR LANGUAGE VERSION 3.0

To gain an introduction to object-oriented programming (OOP) for Windows, a very good place to begin is the Actor language from the Whitewater Group. Actor not only runs under MS-Windows, but was the first OOP tool specifically designed for writing applications that run in the Windows environment. Using Actor is one of the easiest ways to learn OOP under Windows, and you do not have to own the Windows SDK to do so. In this chapter, first I'll describe the Actor programming environment. Then I'll introduce you to the Actor syntax. Finally, I'll get into Windows programming under Actor and the various tools that are provided to assist you in the process.

■ THE ACTOR PROGRAMMING ENVIRONMENT

The Actor programming environment consists of the Actor display screen, a workspace window, and whatever other optional facilities are in use at the time. Particularly important among these are the: Browser, Inspectors, Debugger, and File Editors.

Actor uses the Windows facilities to implement objects that allow an interactive, windowing environment for development very much like the one used in Smalltalk. As with many MS-Windows programs, you virtually need a mouse to use Actor. The main items used on the Actor desktop are the workspace windows, browsers, and inspectors modeled on those used in Smalltalk. When the system first comes up, it shows a workspace window (Figure 5.1) with two rows of command options along the top bar of the workspace window. The commands include File, Edit, Doit!, Browse!, Inspect!, Show Room!, and Templates.

The editing area of a Workspace window behaves just like an interpreter. If you type in an expression and then ENTER, Actor attempts to compile and execute it. If there

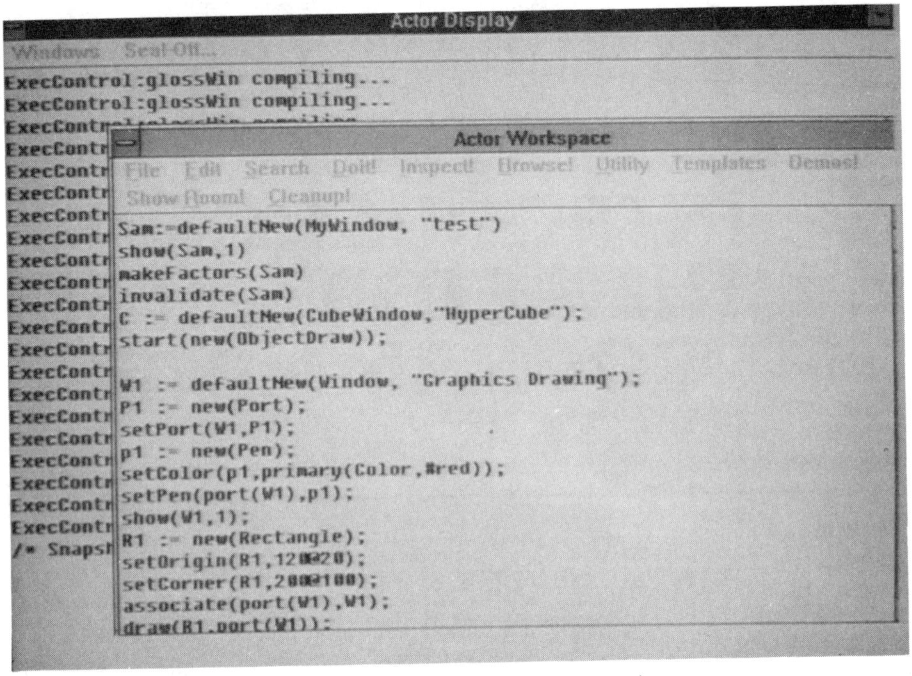

Figure 5.1 An Actor Workspace window.

is Actor code already in an editing window, then highlighting a portion of the code and clicking on Doit! will result in that portion of code being compiled and executed. The Browse! and Inspect! options result in a brand new instance of these tools opening like a popup window on the Actor desktop.

■ ACTOR'S BROWSER

A Browser (Figure 5.2) provides a similar function to that of an Inspector, but instead of opening an interactive window on a single object, it does this for the entire system of classes currently loaded. Its scrollable list box contains a list of all the classes currently in the Actor class hierarchy. The right-hand list box contains the methods for the current class. By first selecting a class, and then a method in that class, you may access the code in the bottom window and edit it. An Options selection on the Browser menu bar allows you to choose whether the classes are listed in hierarchical or alphabetical order. An even easier way to find a class is to use the GoTo Class selection under the Options menu. Also under this menu are selections for defining class variables and class initialization routines. I'll save the topic of class variables for a later section.

A separate menu of the Browser is devoted to search and replace operations in the text pane. As a convenience, various templates can be selected from Templates option on

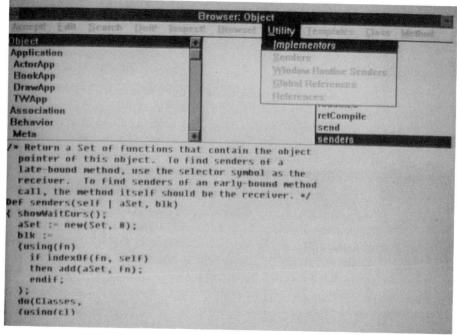

Figure 5.2 The Actor class Browser window.

the Browser menu bar that are inserted into the editing pane to help speed up the coding process and limit the chances for typing and syntax errors.

The Browser's Utility menu contains some powerful facilities:

Implementors, Senders, Window Routine Senders, Global References, and References.

The **Implementors** option searches the entire development environment for all the classes that implement a method of a given name. **Senders** does a similar thing, but it builds a list of all the methods that use the selected method in sending a message. The **Window Routine Senders** option is a particularly handy one. With this, you can find all the methods in the development environment that call a particular Windows function. **Global References** builds a list of all the methods that reference a selected global variable. Finally, **References** returns a list of all the early bound references to a method. Early binding is a special syntax in Actor that can be used to write more efficient code when you are sure of what the exact type of an argument will be.

For any given class, the Browser shows only those methods that are newly implemented for the class. The inherited methods are not listed in the method pane. However, inherited variables *are* listed in the variable pane. The Browser is one of the must tools for OOP. Once you have used one, you will never wish to do OOP without one again.

Unlike some browsers that can be used with key commands as well as a mouse, the Actor Browser is designed for use with the mouse exclusively.

■ INSPECTORS

An Inspector is a popup window that can be used to view the contents of all objects, instances as well as classes, one at a time. Using them is very easy. If you want to inspect an instance, first highlight the name of the instance in a workspace and then select Inspect! from an Actor window in the development environment. If the object is an instance of one of the Collection classes, in the upper right pane you will find a list of index numbers corresponding to the objects in the collection. Clicking on any of these will select the object and its name will be displayed in the main window.

Inspectors are used for focusing in on a particular object. You use them to examine the contents of objects in detail as well as making modifications to them. The upper left pane of an inspector window contains a list box that displays all the instance variables of an object. Clicking the mouse on any of the items in the scrollable list of variables results in its value being displayed in the bottom pane of the inspector, its edit window. Both class objects and their instances can be accessed using an Inspector.

■ ACTOR CLASSES

Actor comes with a surprisingly large class library of ready-made code that can be used for building applications fairly quickly once you bridge the learning curve of using the system and knowing what's there. Here is a partial list of the classes used for data structures and the graphics facilities subsumed under them.

```
Object
  Collection
    Indexed Collection
      Array
        Function
        Ordered-Collection
          Sorted-Collection
          Text-Collection
      Byte-Collection
        String
          Symbol
      Struct
        DosStruct
        Graphics-Object
          WinPolygon
          Rect
            WinEllipse
            RndRect
```

                        Proc
                    Interval
                        CharInterval
                KeyedCollection
                    Dictionary
                        Method-Dictionary
                            Identity-Dictionary

The System class is a unique construct in Actor because it is the only class with methods
that can be used to send messages without a receiver.

■ MS-WINDOWS CLASSES

One of the most attractive things about the Actor system is that it provides built-in
classes for making the use of the MS-Windows user interface easier. Three main classes
are concerned with this: Window, Control, and Dialog. First let's look at the branch
of the hierarchy that contains all of the Windows classes. Here is the outline of this
branch:

Object
    Windows-Object
        Control
                Button
            Edit
            ListBox
                    ClassList
                    MethodList
                    VarList
            ScrollBar
        Dialog
            ClVarDialog
            ClassDialog
                DebugDialog
            DialogDesign
            DirtyCLD
            FileDialog
            InputDialog
                ReplaceDialog
            PrintDialog
            SealDialog
        Window
            AboutWindow
            TextWindow
                EditWindow
                    WorkEdit

```
                    BrowEdit
                      DBBrowEdit
                      DebugEdit
                    FileWindow
                      PrintFileWindow
                      Workspace
              ToolWindow
              Browser
              DebugWindow
              Inspector
```

To make things easier, I will break this down into three main branches: the Window branch, the Control branch, and the Dialog branch. Though relatively large, the Window class is just a formal or abstract class. This means it implements the methods that will be used by the subclasses, which implement the specialized windows that actually get instantiated and used. In particular, Window implements the routines that communicate with MS-Windows.

To understand how Actor works, it is important to keep in mind that there is a difference between Windows messages and Actor messages. Windows doesn't understand any of the messages at the Actor level, so it ignores them. Actor doesn't understand most of the Windows messages either because it doesn't need to respond to them. However, it is possible to make Actor respond to any Windows messages one wishes in any way desired. All that's necessary to do this is to define a method of a class in Actor with the same name as a Windows message, and in the definition of the method specify how the Actor object that receives the message is to respond.

Whenever a window object is created in Actor the message Call CreateWindow is sent to Windows with no fewer than eleven parameters. When a window object is created in this way, Windows sends the handle or name of the window created and this handle must be stored by Actor. At the level of OOP in Actor, it is the **create** method of the Window class and its descendants that results in the MS-Windows message CreateWindow being sent. When an Actor window is closed, the window object actually still exists unless it is somehow explicitly removed from the system. The handle of a window's menu is stored in the hMenu instance variable. The **loadMenu** method takes care of loading menu resources and assigning a value to hMenu.

The TextWindow class is one of the simplest descendants of Windows that allows you to actually do real things. This class allows you to create tiled windows that can print text. It does this with the **printString** and **printChar** methods, which call the Textout GDI (Graphics Display Interface) function in MS-Windows. Often you will want text windows that can do more that just show text, that can allow you to go in and edit that text. The subclass of TextWindow called EditWindow provides the code that supports this editing ability. The WorkEdit class takes this one step further by allowing you to create windows that not only can edit, but also enter Actor language statements to be evaluated. The three subclasses of WorkEdit provide the types of windows that are like those most often used: browsers, file browsers, and general purpose workspace windows. The main difference, though, is that, like their ancestor TextWindow, these are tiled windows. The windows most often used in Actor come from another branch of the tree that is implemented with the class PopupWindow.

The windows that you get by instantiating PopupWindow are the familiar layered windows that stack up on top of one another. However, unlike the tiled windows, they do not permit you to zoom or contract them down to an icon. As is dictated by MS-Windows, popup windows require a "parent" text window. When this parent window is contracted into an icon, then the popup windows associated with it temporarily become invisible.

■ CONTROLS

As in MS-Windows, in Actor a control is a special type of window that is used for routine input and output in a user interface. Examples of controls include things like buttons, list boxes, and scroll bars. The branch of the class tree concerned with controls looks like this:

```
Object
   Control
      Button
      Edit
      ListBox
          ClassList
         MethodList
          VarList
      Scrollbar
```

Like Window, the Control class in Actor is just a formal one; its subclasses are the ones that are actually instantiated in applications. Controls are handled in Actor in an almost identical way to Windows. New instances are created by sending the **new** message, and they are displayed by sending the **show** message.

The ListBox class is a subclass of Control that creates a small popup window that is associated with a parent window and displays a list of items. Usually the list box is used to present items that a user can select with the mouse. The Scrollbar class is not used for all the scroll bars on all the windows as you might have assumed. The style definition for windows typically handles this automatically. This class is used when scroll bars are needed in some other location than the standard one that windows typically get automatically. So with this class, you can create a set of horizontal and vertical scroll bars that are on a separate part of the screen from the parent window they control. Similarly, the Button class is for creating buttons in ways other than the routine ones. Buttons come with built-in dialog boxes, but there are other things you might want to do with them. You might want to put them in regular windows, for example.

This brings us to the Dialog class and its subclasses:

```
Object
  Dialog
       ClVarDialog
     ClassDialog
       DebugDialog
     DialogDesign
       DirtyCLD
       FileDialog
     InputDialog
       ReplaceDialog
     PrintDialog
     SealDialog
```

Dialog boxes resemble popup windows in that they stack on top of other windows and they need a parent window with which they are associated. Like Window and Control, Dialog is basically an abstract class that implements code intended for use by its descendants. The FileDialog class in Actor is used to create the dialog boxes that routinely appear in MS-Windows when you load a file by using a pull-down menu. The ClassDialog class is for dialog objects used when a class is being edited or created with a browser.

■ DYNAMIC MENUS AND DIALOGS

Another advantage of Actor is that it offers an alternative way of creating menus and dialogs besides that of compiling static resources. While static menus and dialogs are more efficient, dynamic resources, because they are created dynamically, can be more easily customized. To create dynamic menus, you use the Menu class, which initially is not present in the class hierarchy, but can be easily loaded with the statement:

```
load("classes\menu.cls"); <CR>
```

Alternatively, if you want to save typing, you can go to the File menu of the Actor Display window and choose Load, and then select menu.cls from the classes directory.

■ CALLBACKS

There are often occasions when you want to have some operation iterate over all objects of a certain kind, all windows of a certain type, all instances of a certain class, and so on. To do this in Actor, the address of the function over which you wish to iterate has to be sent to Windows so that it can call back to it on each iteration through Windows objects. To simplify this process the Callback class has been provided that supports all types of constructions in which a callback function is involved. Table 5.1 lists the Windows enumeration functions that can be utilized this way.

To use the Callback class in Actor, you first write:

Table 5.1 Windows Enumeration Functions.

EnumChildWindows	EnumObjects
Enum ClipboardFormats	EnumProps
EnumFonts	EnumTaskWindows
EnumMetaFile	EnumWindows

```
Def enumWindows(self | cb, set)
{ set := new(Set, 4);
  cb := create(Callback, #(0, 1), {using(hnd, lVal) add(set, hnd); 1});
  Call EnumWindows(lock(cb), 1L);
  free(cb);
  ^set;
```

∎ LIST STRUCTURES

For intelligent applications, and many other types of application as well, processing linked lists is essential. How does one go about doing that in Actor? One way might be to work with the Ordered Collection class and add subclasses to it with the necessary methods defined for list processing. However, listing a demo originally provided with a previous release of Actor offers another approach. The new class ListNode is defined as a subclass of the Collection class. The methods **append, do, isAtom, printOn,** and **rPrintOn** are defined for this new class. New methods are also defined for Object; the root class, including **isAtom, rPrintOn,** and **cons.** If you inspect the code for **cons** you will see that there is a routine for sending the message **new** to the ListNode class and creating a new instance of it. Obviously, this is only the rudimentary beginning of what a functional list processing class would encompass.

The structures used by the Ordered Collection class differ significantly from dynamically modifiable linked lists. In the terminology of OOP, ordered collections are fixed collections that are nevertheless 'growable'. This means that when you create an OrderedCollection, you must create one with a maximum number of elements. If the elements already stored in the collection have not yet reached the maximum, it is easy to add new elements to the beginning or end of the list. When the maximum is reached, and you need more, you must send the **grow** message to the collection. What really happens when you do this is that a new array of the needed size is created and the elements of the old array are copied into it.

∎ PROGRAMMING IN ACTOR

As we saw earlier, the Actor language is something of a hybrid tongue. It behaves very much like Smalltalk, but its syntax has a strong resemblance to C. It is, in some programmers' views, this one included, a very welcome accomplishment to have re-created an environment like Smalltalk without the peculiar Smalltalk syntax. The C programmers will surely like the Actor syntax, but I think most will agree that this syntax makes OOP quite readable. What are the basic features of this syntax? I was hoping you would ask, because that's the thing that I'll be discussing next.

■ ACTOR SYNTAX BASIC

In Actor, the beginning is the act, so to speak. That is, the name of the method or procedure, the "verb" in the program code, is the thing that comes first in an Actor message. First the action term, then a parenthesis, and then a list of terms within it. That's the general format for all statements in Actor. The very next item after the parenthesis opens is always the name of the object to which the message is being sent. So, in the hypothetical message:

verify(program77, rapidMode);

the message **verify** is being sent to an object called program77. The 'rapidMode' term is an argument that further qualifies the verify message. The last thing in an Actor message statement, the 'terminator' if you like, is always a semicolon, just as in C. There is also a resemblance to C in the use of brackets ({}) to set off code blocks.

One important thing to keep in view is that Actor is case sensitive. For some, that may take getting used to at first. What this means is that Actor will not recognize a term unless the exact sequence of upper- and lower-case characters is exactly correct. One small error and Actor will complain that it doesn't know what you're referring to.

As with languages like C and Pascal, Actor encloses arguments to a method in parentheses immediately following the method's name or selector. And like Pascal and Smalltalk, variable assignments are made using the colon-equal (:=) symbol. Also as in Smalltalk, the way you create new instances is usually by sending the "new" message to a class and assigning this new instance a name. So, for example, we could create an instance of the Turtle class by saying:

Barney := new(Turtle);

In general, sending messages in Actor is like passing arguments, treated as an argument. So now that we have created the turtle messages that he can recognize, like any authorized Turtle, Barney knows that the message 'r' means turn right, 'l' turn left, 'f' move forward, and 'b' move backward. He also knows that '**down**' means to put his tail to the ground for drawing purposes, and '**up**' means to pick it back up again. So if we wanted Barney to perform a turtle walk in the shape of a square, the messages we would send him would be:

down(Barney);
f(Barney, 10);

```
r(Barney, 90);
f(Barney, 10);
l(Barney, 90);
b(Barney, 10);
r(Barney, 90);
f(Barney, 10);
up(Barney);
```

In Actor, the keyword Def is used to define methods. So, if we want to teach, not only Barney, but all authorized Turtles, the new message walkSquare, we would define the method:

```
Def walkSquare(self, size)
{   down(self);
    f(self,size);
    r(self, 90);
    f(self, size);
    l(self, 90);
    b(self, size);
    r(self, 90);
    f(self, size);
    up(self);
};
```

Henceforth, to get Barney or any of his relatives to perform the above maneuver, all we would have to do is to say:

```
walkSquare(Barney, 10);
```

You may have noticed that this turtle walk is only one orientation for the general type of maneuver. There is another species of turtle, admittedly rather rare, that instinctively will do its square-walking counterclockwise. Fortunately, object-oriented systems like Actor provide a way of mirroring this little idiosyncrasy of natural history. What we can do to handle this additional detail is to define a new class of turtle called CounterTurtle and provide a **walkSquare** method for turtles of this species that do the counterclockwise variant of the standard turtle square walk. And by coincidence, this will also provide us with the opportunity of illustrating how to define new classes in Actor.

The way new classes are usually created in Actor is from within the Browser, so I'll start with how to do it that way. First, you select the class Turtle from the class list in the upper left window. Then, you go to the Options pull-down menu and select 'Make Descendant'. A popup window opens that serves as a template for creating the new class. Now, enter CounterTurtle as the name of the class. Then, click on the Accept button, and the system will create this new class and its name will be added to the class list and become part of the Actor class hierarchy.

The other way to create new classes, which is what the Browser is actually doing behind the scenes, is to write the code for it directly. The 'inherit' statement is used for this. So we could write:

```
inherit(Turtle, #CounterTurtle)
```

All versions of Actor from version 2.0 and on have supported class variables. A class variable is a variable that is defined for a class and can have a value even when there are no instances of the class. In fact, the class variable belongs to the class and, in general, is completely independent of instances. One possible use of a class variable would be to store a list of all instances of the class. Another important use of them is for storing any information that is to be stored by instances of the class.

■ A LITTLE MUSIC?

If you'd like to hear a little Bach, evaluating these messages starts the performance:

```
A := defaultNew(AboutWindow, "New");
bach(A);
```

■ CODE BLOCKS

The use of blocks in Actor is an adaptation of the block structure used in Smalltalk. A block is a piece of code that has not been assigned a name. It is a way that code itself can become a little more modular. Every block is itself an object, which is an instance of the class BlockContext. The only method in this class that you really need to use is the eval method. What does eval do? You guessed it. It evaluates blocks. Whenever any block is sent the eval message, it executes itself. Blocks provide a way of allowing algorithms to be specialized rather easily. Whenever there are whole groups of algorithms that all work essentially the same way, you can take the code that differentiates each of them and define it as a block. That way the only change that needs to be made is switching blocks.

Actor does not have a 'for' statement.

■ FILE FORMATS

There are two different types of files in which Actor source code may be stored. There are .ACT files and there are .CLS files. The latter are reserved for Actor class definitions and have a more structured format. The .ACT files are used mainly for storing Actor statements and programs based on existing classes. Actor resembles Smalltalk in its use of image files for storing the exact state of the development environment so that when Actor is restarted it will be in the exact state when the last image was saved. Saving the image involves taking a "snapshot," which can be done at any time during an Actor session.

■ ACTOR WORKOUTS

As a special convenience to readers unfamiliar with Actor, I have devised a series of speedy workouts that take you rapidly through the most important aspects of the language in interactive sessions. Those who are familiar with C and Smalltalk will soon find themselves on familiar ground.

First of all, there are a couple of things you might like to know about the way the interactive environment in Actor works. You can type the name of any Actor object followed by a semicolon, and Actor will echo back a general description of the object. For something more detailed, an Inspector should be used. So, for example:

```
ThePort;
<a WorkSpace>

OutPorts;
Set(<a WorkWindow> )
```

■ NUMBER CLASS SESSION

As with most object-oriented languages, doing arithmetic is a matter of sending messages to objects of the Number class, telling them what operations to perform on themselves. Actor uses an infix approach for doing arithmetic, as the following examples illustrate:

```
2 + 2;
4

4 * 5;
20

7 * (4 + (3 * 2));
70

sqrt(144);
12

exp(2);
7.389056099

4**3;
64.
```

```
random(666);
47
Def average(self,other | ans)
{
ans := (self + other)/2;
^ans
}
```

The following definition of the method square for the Number class is incorrect. Why?

```
Def square(self)
{ self * self;
}
```

Here is the correct definition of square:

```
Def square(self | ans)
{
ans := self * self;
^ans
}
```

The square method can now be used to define other new methods like sumsquare:

```
Def sumsquare(self, other | ans)
{
ans := square(self) + square(other);
^ans
}

sumsquare(3,4);
25
```

■ STRINGS

```
Bs := fillWith("b",22);
"bbbbbbbbbbbbbbbbbbbbbb"

insert(Bs, "x",10);
"bbbbbbbbbbxbbbbbbbbbbbb"
```

hash(Bs);
3004

■ CONTROL STRUCTURES

Actor provides a full range of control structures expected of a modern programming language such as: conditionals, iterative loops, enumeration, case structures, and recursion. The templates provided on the Templates menu provide ready assistance if you've forgotten the right syntax for one of the control structures. Most programmers are thoroughly familiar with the iterative loop control structure. The following section will explain the use of them in Actor.

■ LOOPS

```
i := 0;
loop  while i < 10
print(i);
i := i + 1;
endLoop;

As := fillWith("a",22);
"aaaaaaaaaaaaaaaaaaaaaa"

i := 0;
loop  while i < 10
As := insert(As,"x",i);
i := i + 1;
endLoop;
^As;
"xxxxxxxxxxaaaaaaaaaaaaaaaaaaaaaa"

delete(As,0,10);
"aaaaaaaaaaaa"

i := 0;
loop  while i < 22
As := insert(As," ",i);
i := i + 1;
endLoop;
^As;
"                      aaaaaaaaaaaaaaaaaaaaaa"
```

```
leadingBlanks(As);
22

leftJustify(As);
"aaaaaaaaaaaaaaaaaaaaaaa"

print(As);
"                    aaaaaaaaaaaaaaaaaaaaaaa"

delete(As,0,10);
"aaaaaaaaaaaaa"

i := 1;
loop while i < 45
As := insert(As,"x",i);
i := i + 2;
endLoop;
^As;
"axaxaxaxaxaxaxaxaxaxaxaxaxaxaxaxaxaxaxaxaxax"

i := 2;
loop while i < 67
As := insert(As,"e",i);
i := i + 3;
endLoop;
^As;
"axeaxeaxeaxeaxeaxeaxeaxeaxeaxeaxeaxeaxeaxeaxeaxeaxe
axeaxeaxeaxe"

i := 3;
loop while i < 89
As := insert(As," ",i);
i := i + 4;
endLoop;
^As;
"axe axe axe axe axe axe axe axe axe axe axe axe axe
axe axe axe axe axe axe axe axe axe "

words(As);
OrderedCollection("axe" "axe" "axe" "axe" "axe" "axe"
"axe" "axe" "axe" "axe" "axe" "axe" "axe" "axe" "axe"
"axe" "axe" "axe" "axe" "axe" "axe" "axe" )
```

▪ COLLECTIONS

In most object-oriented systems, the Collection or Container classes provide the core of a system of prefabricated data structures, ready to take off the shelf and use. Actor is no exception to this. The following is the branch of the Actor class hierarchy that is concerned with Collection objects:

```
Object
  Collection
    Bag
    IndexedCollection
      Array
        Function
          OrderedCollection
            CircularQueue
            TextCollection
            SortedCollection
              SortedSet
      ByteCollection
        String
          Symbol
        Struct
      Interval
        CharInterval
    KeyedCollection
      Dictionary
        Frame
        FrameList
        Slot
```

The Collection class itself is an abstract or formal class. You can't do anything with its instances. It serves as the basis for a large range of descendant collection classes. When you create a member of one of the Collection classes with a **new** message, you must specify an argument that tells the system the maximum number of items there will be in the collection. However, the **size** method will return the number of items that have been actually added to the collection, not the maximum size specified in the **new** message.

▪ ARRAYS

Working with arrays in Actor means working with instances of the Array class. There are two main constructions used to create arrays:

```
A4  := new(Array,4);

AR4 := #(1,2,3,4);
```

Here's how a 2-D array is constructed:

```
AA := #(#(1,0),#(1,1),#(0,1),#(0,0));
```

Now build a 3-D array:

```
AAA := #(#(#(1,1,1),#(1,1,0),#(1,0,0)),#(#(0,1,1),#(0,1,0),#(0,0,0)),#(#(1,0,1),#(0,0,1),
#(0,0,0)));
```

An Actor array can be composed of a mixture of different data types:

```
Mix := #("String", 77, #(a,b,c));
```

```
AA2 := copyFrom(AA,0,3);
```

You can also assemble arrays of arrays by first creating the arrays and then using the put message to stuff one array into another as evaluating the following code illustrates:

```
A1 := #(1,2,3,4);
A2 := #(5,6,7,8);
A3 := #(9,10,11,12);
A4 := #(13,14,15,16);
AAAA := new(Array,4);
put(AAAA,A1,0);
put(AAAA,A2,1);
put(AAAA,A3,2);
put(AAAA,A4,3);
```

To check that the array really has all the things you put into it, you can use the print message to display the array's content. Here is the message sent and what is returned:

```
print(AAAA);
Array(Array(1 2 3 4 ) Array(5 6 7 8 ) Array(9 10 11 12) Array(13 14 15 16 ) )
```

■ OTHER COLLECTIONS

The descendants of Array add properties that address issues simple arrays are not meant to tackle. OrderedCollection objects have two instance variables, firstElement and lastElement. SortedCollection objects inherit these two, and also have a third variable, compareBlock. The value of the compareBlock variable determines how the elements of a SortedCollection object will be sorted. Here's a simple interactive session with a SortedCollection:

```
S := new(SortedCollection,7);
add(S, "f");
```

```
add(S,"d");
add(S, "y");
add(S, "a");

print(S);
SortedCollection("a" "d" "f" "y" )

add(S, "k");
add(S, "c");
add(S, "x");

print(S);
SortedCollection("a" "c" "d" "f" "k" "x" "y" )

size(S);
7

add(S, "q");
size(S);
8

"a" in S;
1

"r" in S;
nil

findItemIndex(S,"x");
Array(1 6 )

remove(S,"x");
"x"

size(S);
7
```

One thing to notice is that the **setCompareBlock** message allows you to re-sort a SortedCollection with a new criterion for the comparison of its elements. I've jumped ahead a little to emphasize some of the power that's readily available with these classes. Now let's backtrack and take a look at where SortedCollections inherit some of their power.

■ ORDERED COLLECTIONS

The SortedCollection class that I just introduced in the section above is a direct subclass of OrderedCollection. These are not abstract classes. You can use them to make working objects. Let's look at an example of some things that can be built with the

OrderedCollection class. The following are two variants on the same theme. First, an object is initialized. Then, members are added to it. Finally, an enumeration loop is used it iterate through the members and output them each to the screen. You might also like to use an Inspector to view these and other collection objects that you create.

```
OC := new(OrderedCollection,9);
add(OC,"One");
add(OC,"Two");
add(OC,"Three");
do(OC, { using(i) printLine(i)});

Assassins := new(OrderedCollection, 3);
add(Assassins, "Ruby");
add(Assassins, "Ray");
add(Assassins, "Bremer");
do(Assassins,{using(a) printLine(a)});
```

■ DICTIONARIES

Here is a simple example of how you can use Dictionary objects:

```
Capitals := new(Dictionary,10);
add(Capitals,"USA","Washington");
add(Capitals,"USSR","Moscow");
add(Capitals,"Italy","Rome");
add(Capitals,"France","Paris");
add(Capitals,"Germany","Berlin");
add(Capitals,"Japan","Tokyo");
add(Capitals,"China","Peking");
add(Capitals,"Sweden","Stockholm");
add(Capitals,"England","London");
add(Capitals,"Greece","Athens");

at(Capitals,"USA");
"Washington"
```

MethodDictionaries hold key/value pairs whose lookups are based on equivalence, as opposed to equality. This is more efficient in terms of both time and space than Dictionary, but less general. Since the keys are looked up on the basis of equivalence rather than equality, this restricts the keys of MethodDictionaries to be objects for which equivalence is meaningful, such as Char, Int, and Symbol.

■ TEXT COLLECTIONS

Instances of the TextCollection class are Ordered Collections of strings. The following is an example that illustrates how you can use TextCollection objects to assemble and disassemble various words and sentences from collections of word strings. Obviously, the possibilities are by no means exhausted by this example.

```
Tc := new(TextCollection, 12);
add(Tc, "What");
add(Tc, "goes");
add(Tc, "on");
add(Tc, "in");
add(Tc, "your");
add(Tc, "heart");

makeString(Tc);
"What goes on in your heart"

add(Tc, "mind");
makeString(copyFrom(Tc,0,6));
"What goes on in your heart"
```

▪ QUEUES

There is also the CircularQueue class distributed with Actor. CircularQueue objects can be used for just about any of the purposes normally associated with circular queue data structures. The following example demonstrates how a CircularQueue object can be used to represent the repeating calendar cycle of weeks:

```
WeekDays := new(CircularQueue,7);
add(WeekDays,"Monday");
add(WeekDays,"Tuesday");
add(WeekDays,"Wednesday");
add(WeekDays,"Thursday");
add(WeekDays, "Friday");
add(WeekDays,"Saturday");
add(WeekDays,"Sunday");
do(WeekDays, { using(i) printLine(i)});
```

The last message is an enumeration loop that iterates through all the entries of the CircularQueue and prints them on the screen. Here is an interactive session that uses the WeekDays CircularQueue to demonstrate some of the functions and properties of CircularQueue objects:

```
size(WeekDays);
7

next(WeekDays);
"Monday"
next(WeekDays);
"Tuesday"
```

next(WeekDays);
"Wednesday"
next(WeekDays);
"Thursday"
next(WeekDays);
"Friday"
next(WeekDays);
"Saturday"
next(WeekDays);
"Sunday"

WeekDays[0];
"Monday"
WeekDays[6];
"Sunday"

■ CLASS VARIABLES

In the Actor system, class variables are used very infrequently. The few classes that utilize them are: ErrorHandler; File and its descendants, ActorAnalyzer, System, VarList; Dialog and its descendants, AboutWindow, ClockWindow; and ToolWindow and its descendants. What are class variables usually used for? First of all, for things whose value will never change for any instance. Second, for things whose value may change over time, but will change simultaneously for all instances. As you can see from this, class variables are not usually things that ought to be easy for the user or programmer to change inadvertently or whimsically. For this reason, the convention used in Actor is that their name string begins with a leading dollar sign, as in the $Dialogs class variable of the Dialog class.

A particularly interesting class variable is $Clocks, in the ClockWindow class. This variable stores the set of instances of the class. In a later chapter we will examine the mechanism that is used in ClockWindow.

■ CALLING DYNAMIC LINK LIBRARIES

To access Windows DLLs, the Library class is available in Actor, which also utilizes the Proc class in making the facilities of the DLLs available. A Proc is an object that defines a dynamically linked library procedure. Procs are descendants of the Struct class. To use Library to access DLLs, you have to create a separate instance of the class for each library file you need to access. The instances of Library associate a name with the DLL files and define separate dictionaries of procedures. Library's setName method is used to set the name instance variable.

So, for example, to initialize a Library instance to use with PBRUSH.DLL, a module that is shipped with Windows, you would do something very much like the following, but probably with a different drive and pathname:

```
pblib := new(Library);
setName(pblib, "e:\windows\pbrush.dll");
```

Once this has been done, then instances of Proc must be created for each function in the DLL that you wish to use. This is accomplished with the **add** message, which enters a procedure name and args descriptor in the Library object, as well as creating a new instance of Proc. Library also has its own **load** message that is used to load the DLL file modules. Actually calling DLL procedures involves sending **pcall** messages to the appropriate Proc instances. Before exiting Actor or an application built with Actor, it is also necessary to explicitly close the DLL module using the **free** message. The limitation of using DLLs is that some time must taken to load and free these modules each time they are used, but it is not an excessive price to pay for the versatility that is gained.

■ REPRESENTING KNOWLEDGE

Actor includes a set of classes that define a Frame Representation Language (FRL) that is very useful for representing knowledge. This capability is provided in the Frame, FrameList, and Slot classes. Frame, FrameList, and Slot are all descendants of the Dictionary class. What is provided is a structure for representing organized knowledge in terms of frames, slots, and facets. Instances of the FrameList class provide a dictionary of all the frames that will be used by a given application. FrameLists are dictionaries of Frames, Frames are dictionaries of Slots, and Slots are dictionaries of facets. Facets are not represented by a separate class in Actor, but can be any class or object.

The first thing to do to create an FRL knowledge base is to create a new instance of the FrameList class. In the example I will be discussing, I will be using FRL to keep track of case histories. So the statement used to create the FrameList instance will be:

```
History := new(FrameList, 12);

set(History, #event, #date, #location, #principal,);
set(History, #event, #time,#value,nil);
setValue(History,#event,#value,#ElectionofChairman);
^Z
setValue(History,#ElectionofChairman,#date,date(new(Date),11,7,1992));
```

In this last statement, the value of the #date slot is provided by creating an instance of Actor's Date class that supplies its own format for storing dates and routines for manipulating them.

```
getValue(History,#ElectionofChairman,#date);
11-7-1992

setValue(History,#ElectionofChairman,#location,"San Francisco");
```

```
setValue(History,#ElectionofChairman,#time,time(new(Time),13,00,0));
13:00:00

setValue(History,#event,#value,#SigningofContract);
setValue(History,#SigningofContract,#date,date(new(Date),1,1,1993));

dayOfWeek(getValue(History,#ElectionofChairman,#date));
"Tuesday"

dayOfWeek(getValue(History,#SigningofContract,#date));
"Wednesday"

asLongString(getValue(History,#SigningofContract,#date));
"January 1, 1993"

asDayString(getValue(History,#SigningofContract,#date));
"Friday, January 1, 1993"
```

■ DEBUGGING

Routine errors in code evaluated by Actor typically result in a dialog box opening that contains a stack history up to the point of the error. The dialog box will usually also contain a message that diagnoses the type of error. If you wish, when a dialog box is open due to an error, you can click on the "debug" button and cause a Debug Window to open. This is a versatile debugging tool that combines some of the features of a Browser and some of those of an Inspector, as well as the ability to change any of the values associated with a method. With this tool you can also resume processing on the fly immediately after an error has been fixed.

■ THE PROFILER

You can begin profiling an application at any time in Actor by evaluating the message:

```
profile(System);
```

At that point Actor will begin collecting information on how many times every method is executed. The same message, profile(System), is also used to tell Actor to stop collecting profiling information. When it is sent for the second time, the collected data is automatically written to a file called PROFILE.DAT.

■ EXECUTING EXTERNAL PROGRAMS

External programs can be executed using the **exec** method of the String class, for example:

```
exec("D:\excel\excel.exe");
```

The **exec** method accepts command line arguments, so that commands like this also work:

exec("D:\excel\excel d:\excel\library\goalseek.xlm");

The result of an **exec** method is that control is transferred to the application that is loaded and executed. The user must then manually exit the external application to return to the home Actor application.

In Actor, the Behavior class provides the root class for metaclasses just as Object provides the root class for ordinary classes.

■ SEALING OFF APPLICATIONS

Because Actor is incrementally compiled, and Actor programs need the presence of the environment to run, instead of linking compiled code with run-time libraries, another method is provided for preparing deliverable applications. In the Actor approach, this is called sealing the application off. To make this process easier, a menu called Seal-off is provided on the Actor display window. Choosing this menu with the mouse opens a dialog window, which has a template for entering the information needed for the sealing-off process. You need to supply the name of the application's class, the name of the image it will use, and the settings for its static and dynamic memory.

■ THE APPLICATION CLASS

In the previous paragraph I mentioned that the seal-off facility required the name of the application's class. This needs further explanation, because not just any class will allow the facility to work properly. Typically, an application will include several classes. But to produce a sealed-off application, one of them must be a subclass of the special class called Application. Let's look at some of the features of this class. The Application class has two instance variables, 'mainWindow' and 'commandLine'. The values of these instance variables tell the seal-off facility the name of the application's main window and a command line argument that will be passed to the class's **init** method. This and other methods of the class are not concerned with things the application does, but with the process of sealing it off and functioning in the run-time environment.

Calling Windows Functions

An example of a Windows function call is provided in the **createMenu** method of the Windows class:

```
Def createMenu(self)
{ if setMenu(self, Call CreateMenu())
then Call DrawMenuBar(getHWnd(self))
else ^nil
```

```
    endif;
  }
```

An even simpler example is the frequently used show method of the WindowObject class:

```
Def show(self, val)
{ Call ShowWindow(getHWnd(self), val);
  update(self);
}
```

Another instructive use of Windows function calls is in the appendItem method of the Menu class:

```
Def appendItem(self, menuItem, hM | pC hPopup)
{ if pC := popupColl(menuItem)
  then hPopup := Call CreateMenu();
  do(pC,
  {using(mi) appendItem(self, mi, hPopup);
  });
  Call AppendMenu(hM, MF_POPUP, hPopup,
    asciiz(text(menuItem)));
  else addToMenu(menuItem, hM);
    setAction(self, id(menuItem), actionSym(menuItem));
  endif;
}
```

First, the menu item called hPopup is created by calling the CreateMenu function. Then, the AppendMenu function is called using hPopup as an argument. A menu item with the temporary variable name hPopup is created and appended to the menu that sends the message. The easiest call messages are those that take no arguments, because then there's no problem of determining the proper format for those arguments.

```
    Call GetCurrentTime();

    Def loadList(self | str)
    { str := asciiz(fileSpec);
      if (Call DlgDirListComboBox(hWnd, str, FILE_LB, 0, 0x0000L) = 0)
      then ^nil
      endif;
      Call DlgDirList(hWnd, str, FILE_DIRLB, FILE_DIR, 0xC010L);
      fileSpec := removeNulls(str);
      setItemText(self, FILE_LB, fileSpec);
      pathSpec := getItemText(self, FILE_DIR);
    }
```

```
Def draw(self| nFrame, hdc, lpBuf)
{ nFrame := 0;
lpBuf := lpImage + 4L;
loop
 checkMessage();
while alive(self) cand nFrame < frameCount
begin
 nFrame := nFrame + 1;
 hdc := getContext(self);
 Call SetMapMode(hdc, MM_ANISOTROPIC);
 Call SetWindowOrg(hdc, 0, 0);
 Call SetWindowExt(hdc, 640, 200);
 Call SetViewportOrg(hdc, 0, 0);
 Call SetViewportExt(hdc, x(vpExt), y(vpExt));
 Call SelectObject(hdc, hBrush);
 Call SelectObject(hdc, hPen);
 Call PatBlt(hdc, x, y, 640, 200, PATCOPY);
 Call Polyline(hdc, lpBuf + 8L, ptCount);
 Call ReleaseDC(hWnd, hdc);
 x := wordAt(lpBuf);
 y := wordAt(lpBuf + 2L);
 lpBuf := lpBuf + asLong(frameSize);
endLoop;
}
```

■ ADDING PRIMITIVES TO ACTOR

A Primitive is a built-in method that is efficient because it runs machine code directly rather than first being compiled from Actor code. Actor allows new primitives to be added to it by using either assembly language or C. The CStruct class allows nested structures to be defined, just as in the C language.

The Whitewater Group also offers the Support Packages:

> The Actor Extensions
>
> The Resource Toolkit
>
> Object Graphics
>
> The Wintrieve Database Toolkit
>
> Actor vs Smalltalk

There are so many similarities between Smalltalk and Actor that one may well ask why so much effort was expended to create a new language when implementations of Smalltalk already exist. There are two main reasons. First, Actor was designed to be compatible with the commercial environment of PCs; hence, its built-in compatibility with Microsoft Windows. Second, the syntax of Actor has been designed to be more familiar to programmers who program in C and Pascal. In short, Actor is intended to provide a system incorporating all that was good about Smalltalk, but repackaged for the specific needs of today's programmers working on PCs. Last but not least, of course, is the fact that Actor runs under MS-Windows. Smalltalk typically has its own user interface and windowing system.

One thing in the Actor language I continue to miss, though, is a facility for multiple inheritance. With systems intended for real-world applications, multiple inheritance will increasingly become a standard feature. The reason is simple. In the real world, it is an important fact that many things fulfill multiple roles and multiple functions. Multiple inheritance provides a ready way of handling this in an explicit way. Vendors of object-oriented tools who fail to include multiple inheritance typically give the reasons either that they do not want to make the system too complex for users or that none of their customers have requested it. I do not find either of these answers particularly convincing. I have had no great difficulty in using multiple inheritance in systems that have it and have difficulty conceiving of a serious object-oriented application where it will not be missed. In response to this, it might be said that you can still create classes of the same definition in a system without multiple inheritance the hard way by simply defining them to be exactly what you want. My feeling about this is that, while true in theory, it tends to be something that will never be done in practice. Personally, in the five years or so that I have worked with OOP systems, I have only done this once or twice unless the system provided for multiple inheritance, in which case it is often a routine practice. The reason is the same one that makes interactive systems like Actor significant, and not just a mere convenience. The more you make basic things easy to do, the more you tend to launch out into the more difficult areas creatively, trying things that otherwise you might not have tried. If you are a user of an OOP tool that lacks this feature, I strongly recommend that you pester the vendor to put it at the top of the list for new features. I feel almost certain that you will not regret the results of having exercised your prerogative as a customer.

■ MANAGING TIME

The importance of the handling of time is an area that is particularly apparent in an environment like Windows. It is also one where the advantages of the object-oriented approach are very clear and conspicuous. In many of the system level operations, the object-oriented model does not apply especially well. As the System class in Actor illustrates, there are many system functions that are not well expressed by the model of sending messages to objects. For that reason, all the methods of System are class methods, and there are no instances of the class. On the other hand, the encoding of temporal records as objects that encapsulate all the facilities needed for handling them actually provides a classic example of the advantages of object-oriented systems.

The Windows API provides Timers as a limited resource. Several of the Windows desk accessories make use of the Timers, including the Clock, Calendar, Terminal, and Control Panel. These facilities can always be accessed making direct calls of Windows functions. Calling the GetCurrentTime() function that does not require any arguments returns the Windows time, which is the number of milliseconds that have elapsed since the system was booted.

GetTickCount()

The Windows SetTimer function creates system timer events. Windows uses the WM_TIMER message to respond to calls by an application of the SetTimer function. The argument format for SetTimer is:

SetTimer(hWnd, nIDEvent, wElapse, lpTimerFunc)

The hWnd argument is an optional one for associating the timer with a particular window, by supplying its handle. If the hWnd argument is not NULL, then nIDEvent is used to provide an event ID for the timer. The wElapse argument is used to specify the time interval between timer updates. The lpTimerFunc argument is used to supply Windows with the name of a callback function to which it is to send WM_TIMER messages. The SetTimer function returns a value indicating whether Windows has succeeded in creating a timer resource. If zero is returned, the resource was not created.

When a system timer is no longer needed, the KillTimer function can be used to terminate it. The format for KillTimer is:

KillTimer(hWnd, nIDEvent)

When the hWnd parameter used to call SetTimer is Null, the nIDEvent argument used for calling KillTimer is the value returned by the SetTimer call.

■ WORKING WITH DATES AND TIMES

The Time and Date classes provide a variety of services in the handling of data formats that are used in processing temporal records.

A new Date object can be created manually in the following way:

day1 := date(new(Date),7,27,90);
7-27-90

The Date class contains the code for being able to determine what day of the week it was for any date in the past, present, or future. To make use of this, it is simply a matter of sending a dayOfWeek message to any date object, like this:

> *dayOfWeek(day1);*
> *"Wednesday"*

Alternatively, the dayOfWeekNumber message can be sent to return a number instead of a string to represent the day of the week. Here the number 3 is returned instead of "Wednesday."

> *dayOfWeekNumber(day1);*
> *3*

In an analogous manner to the way the Date class takes care of the calculations necessary for providing correct date formats, Time provides facilities for handling the data format used to record the time of day or night.

Manual creation of Time objects can be accomplished by sending a message like this:

> *T1 := time(new(Time), 12,30,0);*
> *12:30:00*

The normal time format can also be converted to a time array format using the as-TimeArray message:

> *asTimeArray(T1);*
> *Array(12 30 0 nil)*

As the relevant branch of the class hierarchy indicates, Time and Date are both peer classes that descend from the Long class.

Object
  Magnitude
    Number
    Long
      Date
      Time

The internal represention for dates is a long number that corresponds to the number of days since the establishment of the Gregorian calendar.

It is of interest to compare the implementation of the Time and Date classes because they are so similar, even though the needs of the two are in some ways quite different. The biggest difference, of course, is that the Time class has to be able to deal with time changes down to the second, whereas the Date class only has to be concerned with changes by the day. The two classes are so close in design and implementation that a number of their methods are precisely identical. The methods that are exactly the same in both classes are the asLong, set, printOn, and sysPrintOn object methods and the new class method. Even the current class methods are so close that they only differ by a single data value. An alternate design that takes advantage of this close correspondence of the classes would be to create a formal class called TemporalObject, which incorporates all of the methods that are identical for both of the classes. Date and Time would then be descendants of TemporalObject and add only the methods that need to be specialized. The current class method could also be implemented in the formal class, allowing the differing value to be incorporated as a class variable. This is not of great practical interest in this particular case, though, because it would still take additional different methods to initialize the class variables.

The Temporal Object Class

```
inherit(Long, #TemporalObject, nil, 1, nil)!!

now(class(TemporalObject))!!

/* Create a new Date object and initialize. */
Def new(self)
{ ^init(new(self:Behavior));
}!!

now(TemporalObject)!!

/* Put a date onto the specified Stream. */
Def sysPrintOn(self, aStrm)
{ printOn(asString(self), aStrm)
}!!

/* Sets the (indexed) value of self with the passed value. */
Def set(self, value | temp)
{ temp := new(Struct, 4);
  putLong(temp, value, 0);
  setClass(temp, class(self));
  swapProperties(self, temp);
  swap(self, temp);
}!!

/* Puts a date onto the specified Stream. */
Def printOn(self, aStrm)
{ printOn(asString(self), aStrm)
}!!

/* Returns self as a long number for arithmetic purposes. */
Def asLong(self | temp)
{ ^setClass(temp := copy(self), Long)
}!!
```

The Timer Class

```
inherit(TemporalObject, #Timer, nil, 1, nil)!!

now(class(Timer))!!

/* Return current time. */
Def current(self | ds)
{ ds := new(Struct, 18);
  putMSB(ds, 0x2c, 4);
  call(ds);
  ^time(new(self),
   atMSB(ds, 8), /* Hour */
   atLSB(ds, 8), /* Minute */
   atMSB(ds, 10) /* Second */);
}!!

now(Timer)!!

/* Normalize the time by setting the time to be
 within a single 24 hour period. */
Def normalize(self)
{ set(self, asLong(self) mod 86400)
}!!

/* Set the time object from the passed parameters. */
Def time(self, hr, min, sec)
{ set(self, (hr*3600)+(min*60)+sec)
}!!

/* Initialize time to 0:00:00. */
Def init(self)
{ set(self, 0L);
}!!

/* Return an array with 4 elements - hour, minute, second,
 overflow. Overflow indicates a time past a 24 hour clock.
 Overflowed times should be normalized. */
Def asTimeArray(self | hour, min, sec, over, time)
{ if (time := (asLong(self) mod 86400)) < self /* more than 24 Hour */
 then over := asLong(self) / 86400;
 endif;
 hour := time / 3600;
 min := time - (hour * 3600);
 sec := min mod 60;
```

```
min := min / 60;
 ^tuple(asInt(hour), asInt(min), asInt(sec), over)
}!!
```

```
/* Converts self to a time object. */
Def asTime(self)
{ ^self
}!!
```

```
/* Convert Timer object to a String. */
Def asString(self | ta)
{ ta := asTimeArray(self);
 ^asString(ta[0]) + ":" +
 asPaddedString(ta[1], 2) + ":" +
 asPaddedString(ta[2], 2)
}!!
```

The Dating Class

```
inherit(TemporalObject, #Dating, nil, 1, nil)!!
```

```
now(class(Dating))!!
```

```
/* Returns the current date. */
Def current(self | ds)
{ ds := new(Struct, 18);
 putMSB(ds, 0x2a, 4);
 call(ds);
 ^date(new(self),
  atMSB(ds, 10), /* Month */
  atLSB(ds, 10), /* Day */
  wordAt(ds, 8)  /* Year */);
}!!
```

```
now(Dating)!!
```

```
/* Given a date, returns the previous date while preserving the original date. */
Def previous(self)
{ ^asDate(self - 1)
}!!
```

```
/* Given a date, returns the next date while preserving the original date. */
Def next(self)
{ ^asDate(self + 1)
```

```
}!!

/* The limit of a date object is 2. */
Def limit(self)
{ ^2
}!!

/* Initializes all new dates to 1/1/1980. */
Def init(self)
{ ^date(self, 1, 1, 1980);
}!!

/* Returns the day of week number (0=Sunday...7=Saturday). */
Def dayOfWeekNumber(self)
{ ^asInt((asLong(self)+4L) mod 7)
}!!

/* Returns the day of the week. */
Def dayOfWeek(self)
{ ^#("Sunday" "Monday" "Tuesday" "Wednesday" "Thursday"
   "Friday" "Saturday")[dayOfWeekNumber(self)]
}!!

/* Returns a new Dating object with the passed month, day and year.
 Calculated as month months plus day days from the first day of
 the year i.e. date(new(Date), 11, 31, 1990) returns 12-01-1990.
 This is based on algorithm 199, from collected algorithms from the ACM */

Def date(self, month, day, year | century)
{ if month > 2
 then month := month - 3;
 else month := month + 9;
  year := year - 1;
 endif;
 century := year / 100;
 year := year - (century * 100);
 ^set(self, ((asLong(century) * 146097L) / 4L)
   + ((asLong(year) * 1461L) / 4L)
   + (((asLong(month) * 153L) + 2L) / 5L)
   + (asLong(day) - 578041L));
}!!

/* Returns a date in the abbreviated string format. */
Def asString(self | da)
{ da := asDateArray(self);
```

```
^asString(da[0]) + "-" +
asString(da[1]) + "-" +
asString(da[2])
}!!
```

```
/* Return date in long string format. */
Def asLongString(self| da)
{ da := asDateArray(self);
 ^#("January" "February" "March" "April" "May" "June" "July"
 "August" "September" "October" "November" "December")[da[0]-1] +
 " " + asString(da[1]) + ", " + asString(da[2])
}!!
```

```
/* Return date in 'day of the week' format. */
Def asDayString(self)
{ ^dayOfWeek(self) + ", " + asLongString(self)
}!!
```

```
/* Returns an array with three elements - month, day, year.
 [algorithm 199, from collected algorithms from the ACM] */
Def asDateArray(self| gregorian, month, day, year)
{ gregorian := asLong(self) + 578041L;
 year := ((gregorian * 4) - 1) / 146097L;
 gregorian := ((gregorian * 4) - 1) - (year * 146097L);
 day := (gregorian / 4);
 gregorian := ((day * 4) + 3) / 1461;
 day := ((day * 4) + 3) - (gregorian * 1461);
 day := (day + 4) / 4;
 month := ((day * 5) - 3) / 153;
 day := ((day * 5) - 3) - (month * 153);
 day := (day + 5) / 5;
 year := (year * 100) + gregorian;
 if month < 10
 then month := month + 3;
 else month := month - 9;
  year := year + 1;
 endif;
 ^tuple(asInt(month), asInt(day), asInt(year))
}!!
```

```
/* Converts the supplied number to a date. */
Def asDate(self)
{ ^self
}!!
```

```
day1 := date(new(Dating),8,15,90);
8-15-90

T1 := time(new(Timer),12,30,0);
12:30:00
```

■ WHAT TIME IS IT?

In the following few sections you will see various examples that demonstrate how easy it is to handle time management with an object-oriented system like Actor, and how appropriate the object-oriented approach is for this sort of thing.

First of all, there is a simple digital clock that you can bring into your development environment by making sure the ClockWindow class is loaded, and evaluating the messages:

```
CW := defaultNew(ClockWindow, "Current Time");
show(CW,1);
```

This sample ClockWindow class shows how easy it is to implement a digital clock under Windows in Actor. As descendants of the TextWindow class, ClockWindow objects provide a character oriented display of the current time. One of the special features of ClockWindow is the ability to synchronize several different instances of the class by timing the update intervals on a regular basis. ClockWindow utilizes class variables to accomplish this. The $Interval and $Clocks class variables provide all the information for the simple updating procedure. The $Interval variable stores the interval of time between time updates of ClockWindow objects.The $Clocks variable stores the names of all of ClockWindow's current instances.

■ DIGITAL CLOCKS

The ClockWindow class has some interesting features beyond just telling you the correct time of day. The class initialization for ClockWindow contains the lines:

```
$Interval := 5;
$Clocks := new(Set, 4);
```

This states that ClockWindows will be updated every five seconds and that the $Clocks class variable will be initialized as an empty instance of the Set class with a size able to contain four objects.

Every five seconds is not really prompt enough for many purposes, particularly if there are several clocks (Figure 5.3).

```
CW1 := new(ClockWindow,nil,nil, "First Clock", &(50,50,175,125));
show(CW1,1);
```

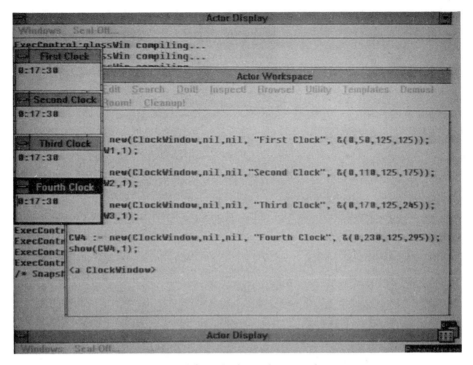

Figure 5.3 The four clocks in close synchronization.

```
CW2 := new(ClockWindow,nil,nil,"Second Clock", &(50,110,175,175));
show(CW2,1);

CW3 := new(ClockWindow,nil,nil, "Third Clock", &(50,170,175,245));
show(CW3,1);

CW4 := new(ClockWindow,nil,nil, "Fourth Clock", &(50,230,175,295));
show(CW4,1);
```

If it bothers you that all the clocks do not always have the same reading, then evaluate the message:

```
setInterval(ClockWindow,0);
```

Here's how the init method of ClockWindow is written:

```
Def init(self)
{ init(self:ancestor);
  add($Clocks, self);
  tick(self);
```

```
    setTimer(self, $Interval);
}

Def close(self)
{ killTimer(self);
  remove($Clocks, self);
  close(self:ancestor);
}
```

As you can see, this method sets the values of both the class variables of the ClockWindow class. A simple extension to the ClockWindow can be made by adding an override to the new class method that allows a time zone to be specified, which allows a number of clocks in different time zones to be simultaneously synchronized. The new class method can be written:

```
Def new(self, parent, menu, windowName, rect, timeZone | aClock)
{ aClock := new(self:WindowClass, parent, menu, windowName, rect);
  aClock[timeZone] := ((timeZone mod 24) + 24) mod 24;
  ^aClock;
}
```

The SetTimer Windows function implements Timers in the Windows environment as a limited global resource.

The Windows functions for accessing System Time and Date are among the easiest to use because they don't require any arguments.

```
Call GetCurrentTime();
Call GetTickCount();
```

■ TIME MANAGEMENT CLASS DESCRIPTIONS

ClockWindow

Source file: CLOCKWIN.CLS

Inherits from: TextWindow

Class Variables:

$Interval

$Clocks

Class methods:

setInterval Sets clock interval (number of seconds). The clock interval specifies how often each clock window object should update its display. When the clock interval changes, each clock instance is informed so that it can modify its timer interval.

sizeRect	Returns a sizing rectangle. Changes the window sizing rect so that it is simply a quarter of the size of the default sizing rect.

Object methods:

close	Turns off the timer, then closes the window.
drawTime	Draws time in the TextWindow just by overwriting the previously drawn string.
init	
killTimer	Kills the timer.
setTimer	Starts the timer. Will cause a WM_TIMER message every n seconds as specified by the argument. Expected resolution in milliseconds, so adjust appropriately.
tic	Processes a timer tick. Gets the current time and display.
timeStr	Returns current time string. Calls DOS Get Time function. Interrupt 21H Function 2CH
update	Updates timer interval. Resets receiver's timer to tick every n number of seconds specified by the $Interval class variable.

StopWatch

Source file:	STOPWATC.CLS
Inherits from:	Object

Instance Variables:

startTime	Time at start of block execution.
stopTime	Time at end of block execution.

Object methods:

lap	Returns the time between the start time and now.
start	Starts the StopWatch and records the start time.
stop	Stops the StopWatch and returns the total time elapsed.

Clock

Note: This is from a public domain application written by Jim Cauthorn. The class description is provided here for study purposes.

Source file:	CLOCK.CLS
Inherits from:	Window

Instance Variables:

brForeground	Foreground brush.
penBackground	Background pen.
penForeground	Foreground pen.

bIconic	Non-nil if the app is iconic.
aspectD	
aspectN	
clockRect	
clockRadius	
clockCenter	
VertRes	
HorzRes	
MapSize	The scaling factor.
TimerID	Timer-ID number.
oTime	Last time read.
nTime	Newest time read.
timeZone	# of hours to add to time.
IconDrawMode	Drawing clock icon directly to screen, or to bitmap first, then screen?
daylight	Non-nil if daylight hours, nil if nighttime.
Object methods:	
clockPaint	The main handler for painting and repainting the Clock.
clockSize	Resizes between iconic and windowed operation of the clock.
clockTimer	Handles timer messages sent to the clock command.
compClockDim	Computes the clock's dimensions.
create	Decide whether to create a POPUP or TILED window.
createTools	Constructs the pens and brushes used to draw the clock.
deleteTools	Deletes the pens and brushes.
drawFace	Draws the clock face as a circle of ticks and dots.
drawFatHand	Draws the hour and minute hands when in a window.
drawHand	Draws the second hand, or the minute and hour hands when iconic.
drawHandsIcon	Paints the minute and hour hands in the icon.
drawHandsWnd	Paints the minute and hour hands in the window.
killTimer	Kills the system timer.
paint	Repaints the screen.
setTimer	Sets the system timer.
show	Displays the clock according to value of val. The order of events is important. The clock must have its window 'shown' before it can have the error box attached to it. Tools must be created before 'show' is executed.

■ ADDITIONAL SAMPLE CODE

I have included some additional sample programs in Listings 1 through 4, three of which are familiar benchmark type programs, the prime number, Fibonacci, and Hanoi, and the last of which includes some extensions for list processing. Since these algorithms have been implemented so many times in so many of the popular programming languages they can be of help to experienced programmers who are interested in seeing rather quickly how Actor is used to do things they are used to doing with their favorite language. As you gain familiarity with Actor, you will probably find that it supports just about all constructions you are familiar with and some others as well.

Listing 1. Eratosthenes' Sieve Benchmark.

```
inherit(Object, #Sieve, nil, nil, nil);

now(Sieve);

/* Returns the number of prime numbers between 0 and cnt,
inclusive. */
Def sieve(self, cnt | flags, count, c)
{     c := cnt + 1;
    flags := new(Array, c);
    fill(flags, true);
    count := 1;
    do( over(2, c),
        { using(i | triple)
            if flags[i]
            then triple := i*3;
                        if triple < cnt
                    then  do( overBy(triple-1, c, i+i-1),
                        { using(j) flags[j] := nil });
                    endif;
                    count := count + 1;
            endif;
        });
    ^count;

}

Actor[#Sam] := new(Sieve)
/* To run type: sieve(Sam, 100) */
```

Listing 2. Fibonacci Program.

```
now(Int)

/* Recursive way of finding the nth Fibonacci term.
```

*This way of finding the Fibonacci terms is intentionally very inefficient because each message "spawns" two recursive messages. */*

```
Def fib(self)
{ if self < 3
  then ^1
  endif;  ^fib(self - 1) + fib(self - 2);
}
```

/* Iterative way of finding the nth Fibonacci term. */

```
Def fib2(self | term, term1Before, term2Before)
{ if self < 3
  then ^1
  else term := 2; term1Before := 1; term2Before := 1;
  do(new(Interval, 3, self + 1, 1),
    {using(i) term := term1Before + term2Before;
    term2Before := term1Before;
    term1Before := term;
    });
    ^term
  endif;
}
```

Listing 3. Tower of Hanoi.

/* ref. Byte August, 86 p. 146   cbd 8.13.86 */

inherit(Object, #TowerOfHanoi, nil, nil, nil);

now(TowerOfHanoi);

```
Def moveTower(self, height, from, to, use)
{ if height > 0
  then
  moveTower(self, height - 1, from, use, to);
  moveTower(self, height - 1, use, to, from);
  endif;
}
```

```
Def moveTower2(self, height, from, to, use)
{ if height > 0
  then
  moveTower(self:TowerOfHanoi, height - 1, from, use, to);
```

```
moveTower(self:TowerOfHanoi, height - 1, use, to, from);
endif;
}


Actor[#Hanoi] := new(TowerOfHanoi);

/* Example solves runs the Tower of Hanoi problem */
moveTower(Hanoi, 3, 1, 3, 2);
```

Listing 4. List Handling Support in Actor.

```
/*
C.B.Duff 7.13.86
(c) Copyright, 1986
*/
now(NilClass);
/* append nil to a node */
Def append(self, aNode)
{ ^aNode }

Def cons(self, aNode)
{ ^aNode }

Def rPrintOn(self, aStrm)
{ printOn('[', aStrm);
}

inherit(Collection, #ListNode, #(left right), nil,nil);

now(ListNode);

Def append(self, aNode)
{ ^cons( left, append(right, aNode));
}

Def do(self, aBlock)
{ if isAtom(left)
  then eval(aBlock, left);
  else do(left, aBlock);
  endif;
  if right
  then do(right, aBlock);
  endif;
}
```

```
Def isAtom(self)
{ ^nil }

Def printOn(self, aStrm)
{ printOn('[', aStrm);
  printOn(left, aStrm);
  rPrintOn(right, aStrm);
}

Def rPrintOn(self, aStrm)
{ printOn(' ', aStrm); printOn(left, aStrm);
  rPrintOn(right, aStrm);
  printOn(']', aStrm);
}

now(Object);

Def isAtom(self)
{ }!!

Def rPrintOn(self, aStrm)
{ printOn('.', aStrm);
  printOn(' ', aStrm);
  printOn(self, aStrm);
  printOn(']', aStrm);
}

Def cons(self, aNode | newNode)
{ if isAtom(aNode)
  then newNode := new(ListNode);
  else newNode := copy(aNode);
  endif;
  newNode.left := self;
  newNode.right := aNode;
  ^newNode;
}
```

6

OBJECT-ORIENTED USER INTERFACES FOR WINDOWS

Central to all MS-Windows development is the use of the available facilities for building an application's user interface. As a matter of fact, the user interface issues are so conspicuous in most Windows programming approaches that a determined effort has to be made to keep them distinct from the internal problem solving aspects of applications. Fortunately, this is something at which object-oriented systems excel, for the very good reason that it is exactly the sort of modularity for which they are specifically intended. We will be continuing to use the Actor programming language, which I introduced in the previous chapter. The emphasis, however, will be on issues that apply to all object-oriented systems in the Windows environment.

■ CREATING WINDOWS

The process of creating a window in Actor may seem a little complex at first, because there are some important things to remember, but you should get the hang of it rather quickly. The class methods 'new' and 'defaultNew' are very often used for this purpose. The 'defaultNew' method is a version of 'new' that supplies its own default arguments and is consequently quicker and easier to use. The class method 'new' makes a call to the object method 'create', which in turn makes a call on the CreateWindow function at the MS-Windows level.

A rudimentary window can be created and opened by sending the messages:

W := defaultNew(Window, "Basic Window");
show(W,1);

This creates and displays a basic empty window that is not yet equipped to really do anything important. It is generally the subclasses of Windows that are often used to do specific things. Another general purpose method for creating windows of practically any type is the **newStyle** method. The price you pay for this generality is that **newStyle** requires quite a large assortment of arguments to be specified. There's seven of them in fact. The first specifies the name of the class of the type of window you are creating. Next comes the name of the parent window if it is a child window you wish to create. In a large number of cases, the windows that are created are child windows of one sort or another. The **newChild** method is usually used for this purpose.

Below is the branch of the Actor class hierarchy that shows the various specialized window classes:

```
Object
    WindowsObject
        Window
        TextWindow
            EditWindow
            WorkEdit
                BrowEdit
                FileWindow
                WorkSpace
        ToolWindow
            Browser
            Inspector
```

The WindowsObject class is the formal root class that lays the foundation for creating any of the main objects used in constructing windows, such as controls, dialogs, and windows themselves. It is at the level of the Window class that menu support is first provided. Its default style is the popup window style, and its default pointer is the generic mouse pointer. Although Windows is a formal class for the most part, its instances can be used to display graphics.

```
FW := newMain(FileWindow, "editmenu", "Editor", nil);
show(FW, 1);
```

Whenever a window object is created in Actor the message Call CreateWindow is sent to Windows with no fewer than eleven tparameters. When a window object is created in this way, Windows sends the handle or name of the window created and this handle must be stored by Actor. At the level of object-oriented programming (OOP) in Actor, it is the **create** method of the Window class and its descendants that results in the MS-Windows function CreateWindow being called. The handle of a window's menu is stored in the hMenu instance variable. The **loadMenu** method takes care of loading static menu resources and assigning a value to hMenu.

The **defaultNew** method really amounts to calling the new method with some special default arguments, as its simple definition shows:

```
Def defaultNew(self, name)
{ ^new(self, mainWindow(TheApp:late), nil, name, nil);
}
```

Similarly, the **new** method is simply defined in terms of the **newStyle** method:

```
Def new(self, par, menuName, wName, rect)
{ ^newStyle(self, par, menuName, wName, rect, nil, nil)
}
```

In the **newStyle** method, which does some of the real work, the major calls are to the **create** and **init** methods. Here is how **newStyle** is defined:

```
Def newStyle(self, par, menuName, wName, rect, id, style | theWnd)
{ theWnd := new(self:Behavior);
  if menuName
  then loadMenu(theWnd, menuName);
  else setHMenu(theWnd, setContID(theWnd, id));
  endif;
  setPaintStruct(theWnd, new(Struct, 32));
  create(theWnd, par, wName cor "", rect cor sizeRect(self),
  style cor style(self));
  setLocRect(theWnd);
   ^init(theWnd);
}
```

As we move forward to the real workhorse methods, we see where the calls are made to the basic Windows level functions like CreateWindow. For example, in the definition of the **create** method that follows, the CreateWindow function is called two different ways, depending on whether an actual value is supplied for the rect argument. When it is nil, a default size is supplied:

```
Def create(self, par, wName, rect, style | wndCls, parHWnd)
{ parHWnd :=
  if parent := par
  then handle(par)
  else 0
  endif;
  wndCls := wndClass(class(self));
  if Call GetClassInfo(HInstance, asciiz(wndCls),
   new(Struct, 26)) = 0
  then register(class(self));
  endif;
  caption := wName;
  wStyle := style;
```

```
    setCurWindow(System, self);
    hWnd :=
    if rect
    then Call CreateWindow(asciiz(wndCls), asciiz(caption), style,
     left(rect), top(rect), width(rect), height(rect),
     parHWnd, hMenu cor 0, HInstance, 0L);
    else Call CreateWindow(asciiz(wndCls), asciiz(caption), style,
     0x80 * 0x100, 0, 0x80 * 0x100, 0,
     parHWnd, hMenu cor 0, HInstance, 0L);
    endif;
    if hWnd = 0
    then alert(System, self, #windCreateError);
    endif;
    add(Windows, self);
    if not(parent)
    then add(OpenWindows, self);
    endif;
    }
```

The **newMain** message is an important one because it is used to create and return a
new window usable as an application's main window. It is defined simply:

```
Def newMain(self, menu, caption, rect)
{ ^newStyle(self, nil, menu, caption, rect, nil, WS_OVERLAPPEDWINDOW)
}
```

The menu argument requires a string corresponding to the name of the menu defined
in a resource script, or nil if there is no such menu. The caption argument is another
string, this one expecting the window's title, or nil. Finally, the rect argument expects
a rectangle structure specifying the coordinates on the screen for the window, or nil,
for the default.

■ TEXT WINDOWS

The TextWindow class is one of the simplest descendants of Window that you can get
to do some really useful things. This class allows you to create tiled windows that can
print text. It does this with the **printString** and **printChar** methods, which call the
Textout GDI (Graphics Display Interface) function in MS-Windows. Often you will
want text windows that can do more that just show text, that can allow you to go in
and edit that text. The subclass of TextWindow called EditWindow provides the code
that supports this editing ability. The WorkEdit class takes this one step further by
allowing you to create windows that not only allow editing, but also permit Actor
language statements to be evaluated. The three subclasses of WorkEdit provide the
types of windows that are like those most often used: browsers, file browsers, and general

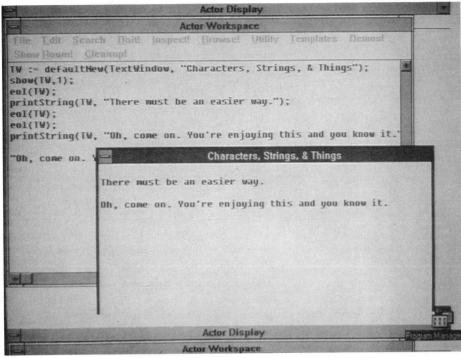

Figure 6.1 Outputting strings in a window.

purpose workspace windows. The main difference, though, is that, like their ancestor TextWindow, these are tiled windows. The windows most often used in Actor come from another branch of the tree, which is implemented with the class PopupWindow.

A TextWindow object can be created and opened by evaluating the messages:

```
TW := defaultNew(TextWindow, "Characters, Strings, & Things");
show(TW,1);
```

The window this creates does not allow you to type text directly. But you can send text to it (Figure 6.1). For example, these messages tell the window to display various text strings:

```
eol(TW);
printString(TW, "There must be an easier way.");
eol(TW);
eol(TW);
printString(TW, "Oh, come on. You're enjoying this and you know it.");
```

Another good thing about Text Windows is that they keep track of the insertion point for text, which they store in the xPos and yPos instance variables. This insertion point can be changed using the **moveCaret** message. For example:

```
setXPos(TW,50);
moveCaret(TW);
```

TextWindow objects also have the property of being able to redisplay text after it has been temporarily obscured by another window. TextWindow has a setXPos method that allows the xPos variable to be set. Although there is no setYPos method in TextWindow, it is very easy to define one as follows:

```
Def setYPos(self, yp)
{     ^yPos := yp;
}
```

The windows that you get by instantiating a popup style window are the familiar layered windows that stack up on top of one another. However, unlike the tiled windows, they do not permit you to zoom or contract them down to an icon. As is dictated by MS-Windows, popup windows have to have a "parent" text window. When this parent window is contracted into an icon, then the popup windows associated with it temporarily become invisible. Popup style windows are generally instances of classes Control, Dialog, or their descendants. I will devote several sections to Windows objects of this type at a later point.

■ EDITWINDOWS

An example of a full-fledged editing window can be seen if these messages are evaluated in a workspace:

```
E := new(EditWindow,ThePort, "editmenu", "Basic Editor", nil);
show(E,1);
```

Thus, the editor created has two command menus on its main bar, one with basic text editing operations, and the other for searching and replacing text. This provides you with a rudimentary editor, but one that lacks file I/O and other amenities for a satisfactory stand-alone program. What would it take to turn the basic editor object into something more streamlined and useful? To answer this, you first have to know more about how EditWindow (Figure 6.2) objects work. Two other file classes that are useful are FileWindow (see Table 6.1) and FileEditor.

The menu management methods used by EditWindow are actually inherited from the Window and WindowObject classes. In the Window class, the createMenu, drawMenu, loadMenu, setHMenu, and setMenu object methods are defined for handling menus as static resources. The new, newMain, and newStyle class methods take menu parameters or names as arguments. The hMenu and menu instance variables are also inherited from the Window class. The menu instance variable is for use with dynamic menus.

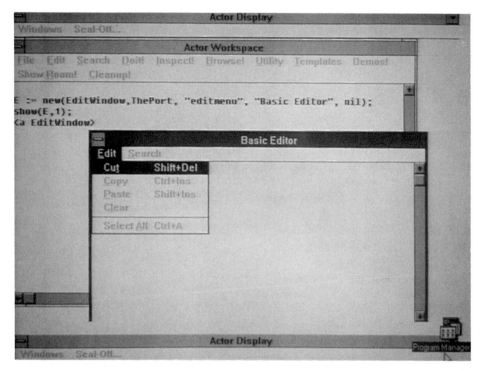

Figure 6.2 An editor window based on the EditWindow class.

Unlike the EditWindow objects, WorkSpaces do have menu options for file operations. To create a new fully functional Workspace using the precompiled menu resources in Actor.EXE Evaluate:

```
WS := new(Classes[#WorkSpace], mainWindow,
loadString(320), loadString(321), nil);
show(WS, 1);
```

The **loadstring** messages are used to activate strings that have been defined as static resources and compiled as part of the ACTOR.EXE file.

The EditWindow **getClipText** message returns a text string from the Clipboard.

```
Def getClipText(self | hStr, aStr)
{ if Call OpenClipboard(hWnd) <> 0
  then hStr := Call GetClipboardData(CF_TEXT);
  aStr := getText(hStr);
  Call CloseClipboard();
  ^removeNulls(aStr);
  endif;
```

```
        Call CloseClipboard();
        ^nil
    }
```

■ FILEEDITOR

Another important class for creating editor windows is FileEditor. As the name suggests, this class provides an editing window with a menu for performing various file operations. The **open** message is implemented as a class method so that only one message is needed for both creating and opening a FileEditor object, as, for example:

```
        FE := open(FileEditor,"New");
```

■ CLASS DESCRIPTIONS

FileEditor

Source file:	FILEEDIT.CLS
Inherits from:	EditWindow
Instance Variables:	
fileDlg	File loader dialog.
file	Name of the file being edited.
inputDelimiter	The input file delimiter.
outputDelimiter	The output file delimiter.
Class methods:	
open	Opens a new file editor on the specified file.
style	Returns the default window style.
wndClass	Returns the name of the MS-Windows window class for the objects of this class.
wndIcon	Returns the name of this class's MS-Windows window class either for registration or new window creation.

Table 6.1 FileWindow Instance Variables.

fileDlg	File loader dialog
file	Name of file being edited
inputDelimiter	input file delimiter
outputDelimiter	output file delimiter

Object methods:

charIn	Handles auto-indent.
checkDirty	Asks the user if they want to lose edits. Returns true (self) if they do. Error box text defined as resource strings.
command	Handles menu events.
create	Creates a Filewindow using all defaults. Attaches a default FileDialog to it.
init	Initializes the delimiter variables.
maxFileSize	Returns the maximum file size available to read.
openFile	Opens a new file and replaces worktext with its contents.
openSaveAs	Asks the user for a file name and tries to open it. Returns a DOS file name or nil.
readText	Replaces the selection range with the contents of a file. fName is a string naming the DOS file to be read, for example, "new.doc."
recreate	Recreates self according to the data in instance variables.
save	Saves the text to the current file.
setFileDlg	Sets and returns the file dialog.
shouldClose	Makes sure the user really wants to close the window.
showTitle	Displays the current title of the file being edited or "Untitled" if no name has been specified.
writeText	Writes contents of workText to a file. fName is a string containing the name of the DOS file, for example, "new.doc."

ActorApp

Source file:	ACTORAPP.CLS
Inherits from:	Application.

Instance Variables:

workspace	The Actor workspace window display for compatibility only.
imageName	Name for the next snapshot file.
dynamic	Dynamic for next snapshot.
static	Static for next snapshot.

Class methods:

Object methods:

abort	Clears the mainWindow and redraws the current window if necessary. This method returns true (self) to indicate that the sender may continue the abort process.

■ THE ACTORAPP CLASS

One of the most informative ways to see how a user interface is built in Actor is to make a careful study of the ActorApp class, because this is the class that provides most of the user interface that is used in the Actor development environment. A single instance of ActorApp is stored in a variable name called TheApp and is sent an **init** message at startup. Any completed application to be sealed up should have an object stored in TheApp that can respond to **init**, **abort**, and **shouldClose** messages.

The ActorApp **init** method starts up Actor with a tiled display window, which has to be created first. After that, it creates a workspace window, if possible, and then recreates any other windows that respond to the **recreate** message. The ActorApp **init** method is always executed at startup to initialize the complete Actor development environment.

```
Def init(self, str)
{ init(self:ancestor, str);
 DeadWindows := new(Set, 4);
 if mainWindow
 then recreate(mainWindow);
  forceOnScreen(mainWindow);
 else startMainWindow(self);
  add(OutPorts:late, mainWindow);
 endif;
 addAbout(mainWindow);
 removeUsing(OpenWindows, mainWindow, {});
 if workspace
 then recreate(workspace);
 else
  if Classes[#WorkSpace]
  then startWorkSpace(self);
  endif;
 endif;
 removeUsing(OpenWindows, workspace, {});
 do(OpenWindows:late, {using(window) recreate(window);});
 if size(DeadWindows:late) > 0
 then do(DeadWindows:late,
  {using(window)
   remove(OpenWindows:late, window);
 });
  beep();
  printLine(loadString(382));
  beep();
 endif;
 initDirty(self);
 if workspace
 then forceOnScreen(workspace);
```

```
changeLog(workspace,
 "/* Started image: " + imageInfo(self) + " */");
setFocus(workspace);
Call PostMessage(handle(workspace), messageID(#WM_SYSCOMMAND),
IDSABOUT, 0);
endif;
initMemory();
^messageLoop(self);
}
```

The **startMainWindow** message initializes a window for the first time. Once such a window is created, the method could theoretically be removed from the system, the point being that it only has to be used once.

```
Def startMainWindow(self)
{ display := mainWindow := newMain(WorkWindow, nil, loadString(160), nil);
setBuffer(mainWindow, new(String, 120));
fill(buffer(mainWindow), ' ');
home(mainWindow);
show(mainWindow, CmdShow);
}
```

The ActorApp **startWorkSpace** message starts just the workspace for the first time. Once a workspace object belongs to OpenWindows, like startMain, this method can theoretically be removed from the system.

```
Def startWorkSpace(self)
{ workspace := new(Classes[#WorkSpace], mainWindow,
 loadString(320), loadString(321), nil);
show(workspace, 1);
}
```

The ActorApp **reset** message sets up the entire Actor Application again. In doing so, it clears both the mainWindow and the workspace window.

```
Def reset(self)
{ mainWindow cand cls(initWorkText(resetLocRect(mainWindow)));
 workspace cand cls(initWorkText(resetLocRect(workspace)));
}
```

■ BUTTONS, DIALOGS, AND OTHER CONTROLS

The branch of the Actor class hierarchy that applies to controls has the following structure:

Object
  DlgItem

WindowsObject
Control
  Button
  Edit
  ScrollBar
  ListBox
    ComboBox
Dialog
  DialogDesign
  FileDialog
  InputDialog

■ CREATING BUTTONS

A Button class is supplied with Actor that descends from the Control class, which in turn descends from WindowsObject. Buttons are really small child windows with special control and display properties (Figures 6.3, 6.4, and 6.5). An example of the various types of buttons can be seen by evaluating this code in a workspace window:

```
WB := new(Window,ThePort, nil, "Window For Buttons", &(275,60,500,200));
show(WB,1);
```

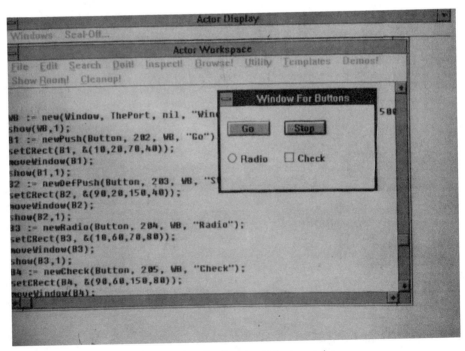

Figure 6.3 The four basic button styles.

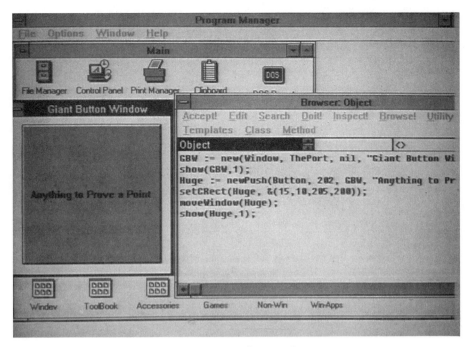

Figure 6.4 A window size button.

```
B1 := newPush(Button, 202, WB, "Go");
setCRect(B1, &(10,20,70,40));
moveWindow(B1);
show(B1,1);
B2 := newDefPush(Button, 203, WB, "Stop");
setCRect(B2, &(90,20,150,40));
moveWindow(B2);
show(B2,1);
B3 := newRadio(Button, 204, WB, "Radio");
setCRect(B3, &(10,60,70,80));
moveWindow(B3);
show(B3,1);
B4 := newCheck(Button, 205, WB, "Check");
setCRect(B4, &(90,60,150,80));
moveWindow(B4);
show(B4,1);
```

If you have any doubts or hesitations about the available freedom in selecting button sizes, this example should dispel them:

```
GBW := new(Window, ThePort, nil, "Giant Button Window", &(275, 60, 500, 300));
show(GBW,1);
```

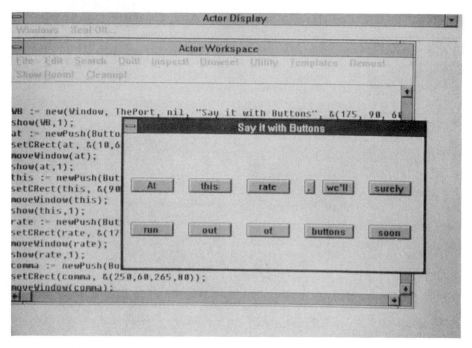

Figure 6.5 The text area of Buttons opens various opportunities for effective user interface design (UID).

```
Huge := newPush(Button, 202, GBW, "Anything to Prove a Point");
setCRect(Huge, &(15,10,205,200));
moveWindow(Huge);
show(Huge,1);
```

Windows supports up to 255 buttons on a window or dialog. Here's an example of a window with a lot of buttons on it:

```
WB := new(Window, ThePort, nil, "Say it with Buttons", &(175, 90, 600, 300));
show(WB,1);
at := newPush(Button, 202, WB, "At");
setCRect(at, &(10,60,70,80));
moveWindow(at);
show(at,1);
this := newPush(Button, 203, WB, "this");
setCRect(this, &(90,60,150,80));
moveWindow(this);
show(this,1);
rate := newPush(Button, 204, WB, "rate");
setCRect(rate, &(170,60,230,80));
```

```
moveWindow(rate);
show(rate, 1);
comma := newPush(Button, 205, WB, ",");
setCRect(comma, &(250,60,265,80));
moveWindow(comma);
show(comma, 1);
well := newPush(Button, 205, WB, "we'll");
setCRect(well, &(275,60,320,80));
moveWindow(well);
show(well, 1);
surely := newPush(Button, 205, WB, "surely");
setCRect(surely, &(340,60,400,80));
moveWindow(surely);
show(surely, 1);
run := newPush(Button, 202, WB, "run");
setCRect(run, &(10,120,70,140));
moveWindow(run);
show(run, 1);
out := newPush(Button, 203, WB, "out");
setCRect(out, &(90,120,150,140));
moveWindow(out);
show(out, 1);
of := newPush(Button, 204, WB, "of");
setCRect(of, &(170,120,230,140));
moveWindow(of);
show(of, 1);
buttons := newPush(Button, 205, WB, "buttons");
setCRect(buttons, &(250,120,320,140));
moveWindow(buttons);
show(buttons, 1);
soon := newPush(Button, 205, WB, "soon");
setCRect(soon, &(340,120,400,140));
moveWindow(soon);
show(soon, 1);
```

■ CREATING FILE DIALOGS

File dialogs are different from the usual type because a large variety of conveniences have been built into them. Typically, they automatically handle the supplying of a file extension and compiling and displaying of a list of files in a list box window that can be scrolled and selected. It is also customary to provide a second list box that allows selection of alternative directories and disk drives. The following messages are sufficient for creating a basic File Dialog:

```
F := new(FileDialog, "*.*");
runModal(F, FILE_BOX, ThePort);
```

As you can see, this type of File Dialog is set up for loading files from a list box.

■ WORKSPACES

An excellent way to see how complete user interfaces are built with Actor is to study the WorkSpace class, whose instances are used for the workspace windows that you've already had some experience in using.

Workspaces are designed to be the first child window of the main window. Other child windows of the main window use the WorkSpace class method sizeRect.

Here is how the loadFile method of the WorkSpace Class is defined:

```
Def loadFile(self)
{ if not(fileDlg)
  then fileDlg := new(FileDialog, "*.*");
  endif;
  if runModal(fileDlg, FILE_BOX, self) == IDOK
  then load(loadFile(fileDlg));
  endif;
  repaint(self);
  setFocus(self);
}
```

The strategy of this routine is that of using the same file dialog each time, since it stores the string for the most recent path specification.

WorkSpace has the same thirty-nine instance variables as its ancestor EditWindow.

WorkSpace uses the instance variable fileDlg to store the windows file dialog object.

■ THE TEXTFILE CLASS

This is a subclass of the File class that is equipped for reading and writing text buffers. To initialize a new TextFile, you must usually do something like this:

```
TF := new(TextFile);
setName(TF, "newfile.txt");
create(TF);
open(TF, 1);
```

Remember that TextFile objects are not windows. To actually view a TextFile object you need to use a window of a class that is equipped for loading displaying text files like FileEdit. TextFile objects are equipped with a 512K buffer and are able to recognize delimiting characters. This allows TextFile objects to keep track of when they've come to the end of a legitimate line of text. TextFile objects all have an instance variable called delimiter that stores the delimiter character that is being used. The readLine method uses this to determine what constitutes a complete line of text.

■ CREATING DYNAMIC MENUS

As mentioned earlier, dynamic menus are those that can be created without the need for preparing precompiled resource files. The two main classes involved are Menu and MenuItem. There are two types of items that can appear on a menu, those that perform actions and those that pop up another list of menu choices. Dynamic menus are stored in the 'menu' instance variable that is implemented in the Window class.

The MenuWindow class approaches the problem of creating an application with cascading menus by creating a class that is devoted to just that one application. This is not the ideal way of doing things of course. You will want to be able to use these special types of menu in a variety of different circumstances. So the thing to do is to break the problem down into some general purpose functions that do the job, and either place them in their own subclass, or paste them into the Window class itself. The approach taken here will be to create a new class that holds them. This way, the documentation for the Window class will remain accurate, and all that is new will be contained in the documentation for the new class.

Let's consider a simple dynamic File menu that can activate a File Dialog. There are two main steps to building such a menu. First you create the command line popup for the menu, and then you would create the action event to activate your File Dialog. To do this, you might create a new class called FileMenuWindow that is a subclass of Window. First you would need to define a new **command** method for the new class. This method simply interprets menu commands that are action events and then performs the actions associated with them. The code can be very simple if the way you approach it is to just use a **perform** message to pass on the control to a message to be specified elswhere:

```
Def command(self, wp, lp | msg)
{ if msg := action(menu, wp)
  then ^perform(self, wp, msg)
  endif;
}
```

This is the basis for allowing events generated by users interacting with menus to be transmitted to the objects that can perform the operations specified. Besides a **command** method, an **init** method is also necessary for building dynamic menus. Here is a generic **init** method for dynamic menus that can be used as a template to be edited for the application you have in mind:

```
Def init(self | pMenu)
{ menu := create(new(Menu), self);
```

```
addItem(menu, appPopup(self));
pMenu := newPopup(MenuItem, "&Menu1");
 addItem(pMenu, new(MenuItem, "&Option1" + asString(Tab) + "Ctrl+W",
COMMAND1, #message1));
 addItem(pMenu, new(MenuItem, "&Option2" + asString(Tab) + "Ctrl+S",
COMMAND2, #message2));
 addItem(menu, pMenu);
pMenu := newPopup(MenuItem, "&Menu2");
 addItem(pMenu, new(MenuItem, "&Option1", COMMAND1, #message1));
 addItem(pMenu, new(MenuItem, "Option2", COMMAND2, #message2));
 addItem(menu, pMenu);
 addItem(menu, new(MenuItem, "&Help!", HELP, #help));
 do(over(COMMAND1, COMMAND2 + 1),
{using(item) grayMenuItem(menu, item);
 });
 drawMenu(self);
 }
```

Naturally the number of menus and submenus provided in the template is arbitrary and the lines can be deleted or copied to provide what is needed for a given purpose.

■ CREATING DYNAMIC DIALOGS

You can create dynamic dialogs similar to the way dynamic menus are built. The two main classes involved are DlgItem and DialogDesign (Figure 6.6). If these two classes are not presently in your system you should load them now. Dynamic dialogs are not only useful for interactive development, when you are not ready yet to compile static dialog resources. To create a simple dynamic dialog, evaluate these messages in a workspace window:

```
D := new(DialogDesign);
setText(D,"Hard Dialog");
addItem(D, newButton(DlgItem, "Shut", IDOK, 40@40, 32@16,0));
addItem(D, newStatic(DlgItem, "Make Your Move", 100, 25@20,60@16,0));
setSize(D, 0@0,110@70);
runModal(D,nil,ThePort);
```

Now let's try to get a good overview of what's actually going on with dynamic dialogs. The main instance variable of the DailogDesign class is itemColl, which is a collection that contains all the child controls used in a dialog. The prompter class method of the DailogDesign class is used to create dynamic dialogs that allow users to enter text in fields interactively. Controls are added to a dialog using addItem messages, much the way items are added to menus. The addItem message is usually used with various initialization methods of the DlgItem class. All of these methods have the same basic format and take six arguments:

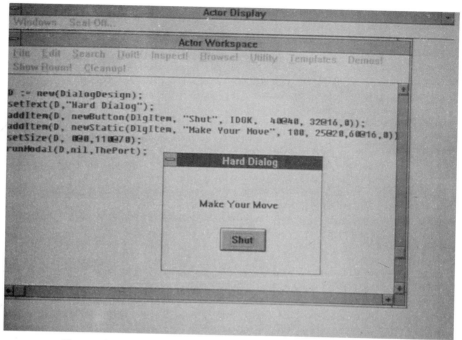

Figure 6.6 A dynamic dialog based on the Dialog Design class.

1. the target of the message

2. the caption text for the dialog to display

3. the ID number integer

4. the control's coordinates on the dialog

5. the control's size

6. the type of control

A simple way of creating a very similar dialog to the previous example can be accomplished by using the ErrorBox class (Figure 6.7). Load this class if you do not already have it loaded and evaluate:

E := new(ErrorBox,ThePort, "Make Your Move","HardDialog",MB_ICONHAND);

■ MODELESS DIALOGS

A modeless dialog is one that the user is not forced to respond to before performing other tasks. The dialog can be allowed to stand until later. All that's needed to make a dialog act modelessly is to use the runModeless message in place of runModal. To run the "Hard Dialog" modelessly evaluate:

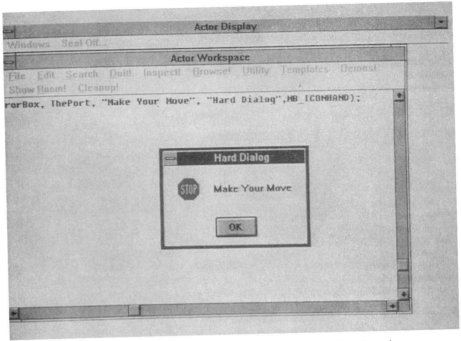

Figure 6.7 A dynamic dialog with icon based on the ErrorBox class.

```
D := new(DialogDesign);
setText(D, "Hard Dialog");
addItem(D, newButton(DlgItem, "Shut", IDOK, 4040, 3216,0));
addItem(D, newStatic(DlgItem, "Make Your Move", 100, 2520,6016,0));
setSize(D, 00,11070);
runModeless(D,nil,ThePort);
```

Modeless dialogs are important for parts of an application where you want to give the user an opportunity to take over the initiative and perform another task rather than being forced to respond one way. They can also be important in preventing the user from being "moded in" where a situation arises in which there is no possible response and the computer has to be rebooted.

■ CUSTOM DYNAMIC DIALOGS

There are endless uses for dialogs and therefore no end to the types of dialog that may be appropriate for a given purpose. For example, one common use of prompter dialogs and other controls is to allow the user to supply arguments for messages. One good way of accomplishing this is to write a special command method that will specify what is to be done with the user's input after it is received.

■ CREATING LIST BOXES

List boxes are an important type of control in the Windows environment that have an endless variety of uses that can offer significant productive benefits when incorporated into well-thought-out designs. In Actor the ListBox (Figure 6.8) class is a descendant of Control that serves both as a template for initializing working objects as well as a class whose properties are inherited by more elaborate controls, such as combo boxes. A simple list box can be created and displayed with the messages:

```
WW := new(Window, ThePort, nil, "Window For List Box", &(275, 60,500,200));
show(WW,1);
L := new(ListBox, 200, WW);
setCRect(L, &(100,0,200,80));
moveWindow(L);
addString(L, "Alpha");
show(L,1);
addString(L, "Beta");
addString(L, "Gamma");
```

■ CREATING COMBO BOXES

A special ComboBox (Figure 6.9) class is devoted to creating combo boxes in Actor. It is a subclass of ListBox, as is only right, since combo boxes really are a special type of List Box. A combo box is a special Dialog that can include various different lists

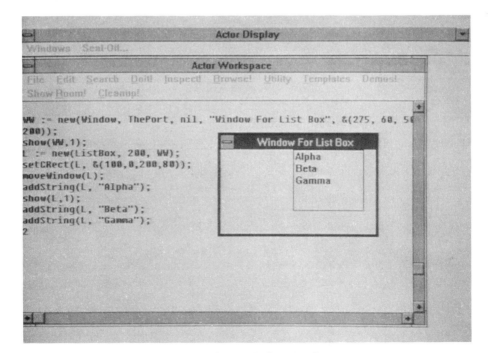

Figure 6.8 A Windows List Box.

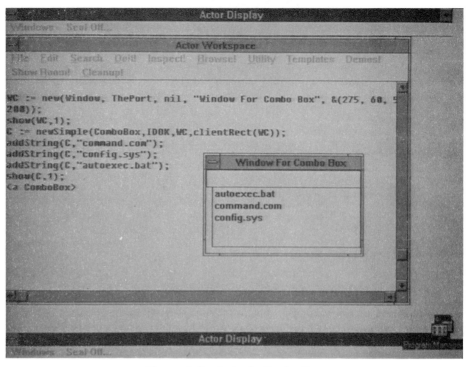

Figure 6.9 A simple Combo Box.

and options to choose from. There are three different kinds: simple, dropdown, and dropdown-list (Figure 6.10). These messages can be evaluated to create a simple combo box:

```
WC := new(Window,ThePort,nil, "Window For Combo Box",&(275,60,500,200));
show(WC,1);
C := newSimple(ComboBox,IDOK,WC,clientRect(WC));
addString(C,"command.com");
addString(C,"config.sys");
addString(C,"autoexec.bat");
show(C,1);
WC := new(Window, ThePort, nil, "Window For Combo Box", &(275, 60, 500, 200));
show(WC,1);
C := newDropDownList(ComboBox,IDOK,WC,clientRect(WC));
addString(C,"happiness");
addString(C,"freedom");
addString(C,"prosperity");
show(C,1);
```

Click on the arrow to see the dropdown sorted list of text items. Although this example appears to work well enough, there is a problem with combo boxes created in this way,

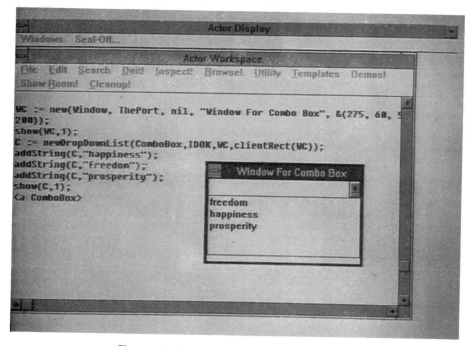

Figure 6.10 A dropdown Combo Box open.

which you will notice if you move the window across the screen. Although the window moves, the combo box stays put. In applications where the user is unable to move the window, no problem really arises. To deal with the matter in applications where the user is allowed to move the list box window, a simple mechanism must be introduced that automatically moves the list box the correct way whenever the window that owns it moves.

▪ CREATING MAIN WINDOW MENU BARS

A technique that has long been used in software engineering is to prototype one part of a working program while using stubs or dummy functions to provide hooks for what can be added later. This is a technique that is particularly suitable for designing the main bar of a Windows user interface. In the next two sections I will provide two examples of this, where all the menus and menu items are created, but the action items are just stubs that don't do anything other than open a dialog to indicate where the real messages will go later. Here is an example of the main init message for a hypothetical application for displaying business graphics (Figure 6.11):

```
Def init(self | pMenu)
{ menu := create(new(Menu), self);
```

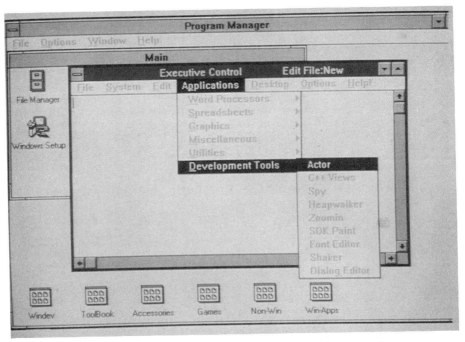

Figure 6.11 The Executive Control menu bar (first version).

```
pMenu := newPopup(MenuItem, "&File");
addItem(pMenu, new(MenuItem, "&Load" + asString(Tab) + "Ctrl+W",
100, #load));
addItem(pMenu, new(MenuItem, "&Save" + asString(Tab) + "Ctrl+S",
101, #save));
addItem(menu, pMenu);
pMenu := newPopup(MenuItem,  "&Charts");
addItem(pMenu, new(MenuItem, "Vertical", 102, #drawChart));
addItem(pMenu, new(MenuItem, "Horizontal", 103, #drawChart));
addItem(pMenu, new(MenuItem, "Pie Chart", 104, #drawChart));
addItem(menu, pMenu);
addItem(menu, chartsPopup(self));
addItem(menu, new(MenuItem, "&Help!", HELP, #help));
drawMenu(self);
}

Def chartsPopup(self | popup)
{ popup := newPopup(MenuItem, "&Options");
addItem(popup, stylePopup(self));
addItem(popup, new(MenuItem, "Brushes", 206, #brushes));
addItem(popup, new(MenuItem, "Colors", 207, #palette));
```

```
      ^popup
   }

Def stylePopup(self | popup)
{ popup := newPopup(MenuItem, "&Styles");
  addItem(popup, new(MenuItem, "Dashed", 208, #style));
  addItem(popup, new(MenuItem, "Dotted", 209, #style));
  addItem(popup, new(MenuItem, "Spray", 210, #style));
   ^popup
}

Def command(self, wp, lp | msg)
{ if msg := action(menu, wp)
  then ^perform(self, wp, msg)
  endif;
}
```

The Stub Methods for this example simply use simple error box dialogs to produce some action when a menu item is selected and inform the user of what is supposed to happen when the program is completed. These methods are written as follows:

```
Def brushes(self, wp)
{
errorBox(getString(menu, wp),"Brushes dialog goes here");
}

Def drawChart(self, wp)
{
errorBox(getString(menu, wp),"Chart will go here");
}

Def help(self, wp)
{
errorBox(getString(menu, wp),"Help dialog goes here");
}

Def load(self, wp)
{
errorBox(getString(menu, wp),"Load routine goes here");
}

Def palette(self, wp)
{
errorBox(getString(menu, wp), "Palette dialog goes here");
}
```

```
Def save(self, wp)
{
errorBox(getString(menu, wp),"Save routine goes here");
}

Def style(self, wp)
{
errorBox(getString(menu, wp), "Style dialog goes here");
}
```

When you've entered these methods in the ChartWindow class, evaluate these messages in a workspace:

```
W := defaultNew(ChartWindow, "Chart Sampler");
show(W,1);
```

■ SIMPLE EXECUTIVE CONTROLLER

The next example (Listing 1) is similar to the previous one, but provides the initial prototype for a more elaborate application that will go through various alterations until it becomes the completed example of Chapter 9. Here, we are just interested in designing the main menu bar, and as with the previous example, stubs are used for the action items that are yet to be implemented.

In this case just a listing for the class file is provided because this class does not really present any new material. The techniques used have already been covered, and now they are being applied to prototype an application that will be quite useful.

Listing 1. User Interface version ExecWindow class (stub menus).

```
/***********************/!!
/*                     */!!
/* The ExecWindow class */!!
/*   (User Interface Only) */!!
/*                     */!!
/***********************/!!

inherit(Window, #ExecWindow, #(actions fileDlg), 2, nil)!!

now(class(ExecWindow))!!

now(ExecWindow)!!
```

```
/* Method for hierarchical menu for graphics program items */

Def graphPopup(self | popup)
{ popup := newPopup(MenuItem, "&Graphics");
  addItem(popup, new(MenuItem, "Zing", 208, #type));
  addItem(popup, new(MenuItem, "Windows CAD", 209, #type));
  addItem(popup, new(MenuItem, "Designer", 210, #type));
  addItem(popup, new(MenuItem, "Object Draw", 211, #type));
  ^popup
} !!

/* Method for hierarchical menu for utility program items */

Def utilityPopup(self | popup)
{ popup := newPopup(MenuItem, "&Utilities";
  addItem(popup, new(MenuItem, "Norton", 217, #type));
  addItem(popup, new(MenuItem, "Xtree Gold", 218, #type));
  addItem(popup, new(MenuItem, "Archive", 219, #type));
  addItem(popup, new(MenuItem, "Other", 220, #type));
  ^popup
} !!

/* Method for hierarchical menu for word proc. program items */

Def wpPopup(self | popup)
{ popup := newPopup(MenuItem, "&Word Processors");
  addItem(popup, new(MenuItem, "Word for Windows", 208, #type));
  addItem(popup, new(MenuItem, "Ami", 209, #type));
  ^popup
} !!

/* stub method for unfinished menu commands */

Def stub(self, wp)
{
errorBox(getString(menu, wp), "Hurry up and replace this with the real thing!");
}
!!

/* stub method for unfinished menu commands */

Def type(self, wp)
{
errorBox(getString(menu, wp), "For now, imagine this executing the Program");
}
```

```
!!

/* Method for hierarchical menu for spreadsheet program items */

Def ssPopup(self | popup)
{ popup := newPopup(MenuItem, "&Spreadsheets");
 addItem(popup, new(MenuItem, "Excel", 208, #type));
 addItem(popup, new(MenuItem, "Zing", 209, #type));
 addItem(popup, new(MenuItem, "Quattro Pro", 210, #type));
 ^popup
} !!

/* Method for hierarchical menu for miscellaneous program items */

Def miscPopup(self | popup)
{ popup := newPopup(MenuItem, "&Miscellaneous");
 addItem(popup, new(MenuItem, "Toolbook", 208, #type));
 addItem(popup, new(MenuItem, "Project", 209, #type));
 addItem(popup, new(MenuItem, "Almanac", 210, #type));
 ^popup
} !!

/* Method for file loading */
Def fileLoad(self, wp | newfileName)

{ if not(fileDlg)
 then fileDlg := new(FileDialog, "*.*");
 endif;
 if runModal(fileDlg, FILE_BOX, self) == IDOK
 then load(loadFile(fileDlg));
 endif;
 repaint(self);
 setFocus(self);
}

!!

/* Method for hierarchical menu for developer program items */
Def develPopup(self | popup)
{ popup := newPopup(MenuItem, "&Development Tools");
 addItem(popup, new(MenuItem, "Actor", 212, #type));
 addItem(popup, new(MenuItem, "C++ Views", 213, #type));
 addItem(popup, new(MenuItem, "Spy", 214, #type));
 addItem(popup, new(MenuItem, "Heapwalker", 215, #type));
 addItem(popup, new(MenuItem, "Zoomin", 216, #type));
```

```
  ^popup
} !!


/* Method for hierarchical menu for application program items */

Def appsPopup(self | popup)
{ popup := newPopup(MenuItem, "A&pplications");
 addItem(popup, wpPopup(self));
 addItem(popup, ssPopup(self));
 addItem(popup, graphPopup(self));
 addItem(popup, miscPopup(self));
 addItem(popup, utilityPopup(self));
 addItem(popup, develPopup(self));
  ^popup
}!!


/* stub method for unfinished menu commands */
Def save(self, wp)
{
errorBox(getString(menu, wp), "Save routine goes here");
}
!!


Def help(self, wp)
{
errorBox(getString(menu, wp), "Help dialog goes here");
}
!!


/* Initializes a new window with a dynamic hierarchical  menu. */

Def init(self | pMenu)
{ menu := create(new(Menu), self);
 pMenu := newPopup(MenuItem, "&File");
 addItem(pMenu, new(MenuItem, "&Load" + asString(Tab) + "Ctrl+W",
100, #fileLoad));
 addItem(pMenu, new(MenuItem, "&Save" + asString(Tab) + "Ctrl+S",
101, #save));
 addItem(menu, pMenu);
 pMenu := newPopup(MenuItem, "&Accessories");
 addItem(pMenu, new(MenuItem, "Calculator", 102, #stub));
  ^Z
 addItem(pMenu, new(MenuItem, "Clock", 103, #stub));
 addItem(pMenu, new(MenuItem, "Notepad", 104, #stub));
 addItem(pMenu, new(MenuItem, "Control Panel", 105, #stub));
```

```
addItem(pMenu, new(MenuItem, "Cardfile", 106, #stub));
addItem(pMenu, new(MenuItem, "Calendar", 107, #stub));
addItem(pMenu, new(MenuItem, "Write", 108, #stub));
addItem(pMenu, new(MenuItem, "Paintbrush", 109, #stub));
addItem(pMenu, new(MenuItem, "Recorder", 110, #stub));
addItem(menu, pMenu);
addItem(menu, appsPopup(self));
addItem(menu, new(MenuItem, "&Help!", 99, #help));
drawMenu(self);
}
!!


/* Responds to the menu events.
 The wp argument gives the selected menu ID.
 Gets a message symbol from the menu object. */


Def command(self, wp, lp | msg)
{ if msg := action(menu, wp)
  then ^perform(self, wp, msg)
  endif;

}!!
```

■ SAMPLE RESOURCE FILE SELECTIONS

This section (Listing 2) just contains a reference of selected sections from a sample resource script file used in setting up the Actor environment. It is particularly useful when studied in conjunction with the ActorApp class.

Listing 2. Resource Script Syntax Sample.

```
#include "style.h"
#include "actor.h"
#include "track.h"
#include "demos.h"


work          ICON    work.ico
Browser       ICON    browser.ico
FileWindow    ICON    filewind.ico
Inspector     ICON    inspect.ico
cube        DATA    cube.dat
700         BITMAP  actlogo.bmp
701         BITMAP  act30.bmp
702         BITMAP  acttext1.bmp
```

```
703          BITMAP acttext2.bmp
704          BITMAP acttext3.bmp
705          BITMAP acttext4.bmp
706          BITMAP acteye.bmp

Actor ACCELERATORS
BEGIN
VK_INSERT, EDIT_PASTE, VIRTKEY
VK_DELETE, EDIT_CUT, VIRTKEY
VK_SUBTRACT, EDIT_CUT, VIRTKEY
VK_ADD, EDIT_COPY, VIRTKEY

VK_LEFT, VK_LEFT, VIRTKEY
VK_UP, VK_UP, VIRTKEY
VK_RIGHT, VK_RIGHT, VIRTKEY
VK_DOWN, VK_DOWN, VIRTKEY

"^a", EDIT_SELALL
"^g", BR_CGOTO
"^r", BR_REFORM
"^z", BR_ZOOM

VK_TAB, EDIT_TAB, VIRTKEY
VK_PRIOR, EDIT_PRIOR, VIRTKEY
VK_NEXT, EDIT_NEXT, VIRTKEY
VK_HOME, EDIT_HOME, VIRTKEY
VK_END, EDIT_END, VIRTKEY
VK_F1,  VK_F1,  VIRTKEY
VK_F2,  VK_F2,  VIRTKEY
VK_F3,  VK_F3,  VIRTKEY
VK_F4,  VK_F4,  VIRTKEY
VK_F5,  VK_F5,  VIRTKEY
VK_F6,  VK_F6,  VIRTKEY
VK_F7,  VK_F7,  VIRTKEY
VK_F8,  VK_F8,  VIRTKEY
VK_F9,  VK_F9,  VIRTKEY
VK_F11, VK_F11, VIRTKEY
VK_F12, VK_F12, VIRTKEY


VK_DELETE, EDIT_CUT, VIRTKEY, SHIFT
VK_INSERT, EDIT_COPY, VIRTKEY, CONTROL
VK_INSERT, EDIT_PASTE, VIRTKEY, SHIFT
END
```

```
ABOUT_BOX DIALOG DISCARDABLE 59, 79, 151, 128
STYLE WS_POPUP | WS_DLGFRAME
BEGIN
 CTEXT "Actor\256 3.0" -1, 1, 12, 147, 10
 CTEXT "Copyright \251 1986-1990" -1, 1, 28, 147, 10
 CTEXT "The Whitewater Group, Inc." -1, 1, 39, 147, 10
 CTEXT "All rights reserved." -1, 1, 50, 147, 10
 ICON "work" 5, 24, 98, 13, 17
 ICON "browser" 6, 114, 98, 13, 17
 CTEXT "Portions Copyright \251 1987-1990", -1, 1, 68, 147, 10
 CTEXT "Microsoft Corporation", -1, 1, 79, 147, 10
 DEFPUSHBUTTON "&OK" IDOK, 57, 99, 32, 14, WS_GROUP
END


INPUT_BOX DIALOG DISCARDABLE 77, 94, 165, 71
STYLE WS_BORDER | WS_CAPTION | WS_DLGFRAME | WS_POPUP
BEGIN
 EDITTEXT FILE_EDIT, 10, 32, 138, 12, WS_BORDER | WS_CHILD |
WS_TABSTOP | ES_AUTOHSCROLL
 LTEXT "", INPUT_MSG, 11, 5, 143, 18, WS_CHILD
 DEFPUSHBUTTON "&OK" IDOK, 32, 50, 32, 14, WS_CHILD
 PUSHBUTTON "&Cancel" IDCANCEL, 99, 50, 32, 14, WS_CHILD
END


REPLACE_BOX DIALOG DISCARDABLE 77, 94, 165, 85
STYLE WS_BORDER | WS_CAPTION | WS_DLGFRAME | WS_POPUP
BEGIN
 CONTROL "", FILE_EDIT, "EDIT", WS_CHILD | WS_VISIBLE |
WS_BORDER | WS_TABSTOP | 0x80L, 10, 16, 138, 12
 CONTROL "", RPLC_EDIT, "EDIT", WS_CHILD | WS_VISIBLE |
WS_BORDER | WS_TABSTOP | 0x80L, 10, 46, 138, 12
 CONTROL "", INPUT_MSG, "STATIC", WS_CHILD | WS_VISIBLE |
WS_GROUP, 11, 5, 143, 9
 CONTROL "Replace with:", 501, "STATIC", WS_CHILD | WS_VISIBLE |
WS_GROUP, 11, 34, 143, 9
 CONTROL "&OK", IDOK, "BUTTON", WS_CHILD | WS_VISIBLE |
WS_TABSTOP | 0x1L, 10, 64, 32, 14
 CONTROL "&Replace All", RPLC_ALL, "BUTTON", WS_CHILD |
WS_VISIBLE | WS_TABSTOP, 48, 64, 64, 14
 CONTROL "&Cancel", IDCANCEL, "BUTTON", WS_CHILD |
WS_VISIBLE | WS_TABSTOP, 117, 64, 32, 14
END


ERR_BOX DIALOG DISCARDABLE 48, 32, 210, 85
```

```
STYLE WS_POPUP | WS_CAPTION
CAPTION "Error Dialog"
BEGIN
 DEFPUSHBUTTON "&OK", IDOK, 172, 8, 28, 14, WS_GROUP
 PUSHBUTTON "&Debug", IDYES, 172, 28, 28, 14, WS_GROUP
 LISTBOX ERR_LB, 4, 8, 160, 70
END


DW_BOX DIALOG DISCARDABLE 27, 27, 201, 105
STYLE WS_DLGFRAME | WS_POPUP
BEGIN
 LTEXT "The text in the Browser edit window has been" 2, 10, 11, 180, 10
 LTEXT "changed.  Accept or Cut to Clipboard?" 3, 10, 24, 150, 10
 PUSHBUTTON "&Accept", DW_ACC, 10, 47, 75, 14, WS_CHILD
 PUSHBUTTON "Cut to C&lipboard", DW_CTC, 10, 74, 75, 14, WS_CHILD
 DEFPUSHBUTTON "A&bandon", DW_ABA, 110, 47, 75, 14, WS_CHILD
 PUSHBUTTON "&Cancel", IDCANCEL, 110, 74, 75, 14, WS_CHILD
END


FILE_BOX DIALOG DISCARDABLE 27, 23, 170, 116
STYLE WS_DLGFRAME | WS_POPUP | DS_ABSALIGN
BEGIN
 CONTROL "" FILE_LB, "ComboBox", CBS_SIMPLE | CBS_SORT |
WS_VSCROLL | WS_TABSTOP | WS_CHILD, 4, 30, 55, 80
 CONTROL "Files:" 3, "static", SS_LEFT | WS_CHILD, 4, 19, 31, 10
 CONTROL "" FILE_DIRLB, "ListBox", LBS_STANDARD | WS_TABSTOP
| WS_CHILD, 65, 42, 55, 68
 CONTROL "Directories:" 3, "static", SS_LEFT | WS_CHILD, 65, 31, 38, 10
 DEFPUSHBUTTON "&Open", IDOK, 130, 37, 30, 15, WS_CHILD
 PUSHBUTTON "&Cancel", IDCANCEL, 130, 63, 30, 15, WS_CHILD
 CONTROL "Directory:" 3, "static", SS_LEFT | WS_CHILD, 4, 7, 32, 11
 CONTROL "" FILE_DIR, "static", SS_LEFT | WS_CHILD, 39, 7, 146, 11
END


MBrowMenu MENU
BEGIN
 MENUITEM "&Accept!", BR_ACCEPT
 POPUP "&Edit"
  BEGIN
   MENUITEM "Cu&t\tShift+Del", EDIT_CUT
   MENUITEM "&Copy\tCtrl+Ins", EDIT_COPY
   MENUITEM "&Paste\tShift+Ins", EDIT_PASTE
   MENUITEM "C&lear", EDIT_CLEAR
   MENUITEM SEPARATOR
   MENUITEM "Select &All\tCtrl+A", EDIT_SELALL
```

```
            MENUITEM "&Reformat\tCtrl+R", BR_REFORM
        END
        POPUP "&Search"
        BEGIN
         MENUITEM "&Find...", EDIT_SRCH
         MENUITEM "Find &Next"\tF3",VK_F3
         MENUITEM "&Replace...", EDIT_RPLC
        END
        MENUITEM "&Doit!", INSP_DOIT
        MENUITEM "&Inspect!", INSP_ISEL
        MENUITEM "&Browse!", WORK_BROWSE
        POPUP "&Utility"
        BEGIN
         MENUITEM "&Implementors", WORK_IMP
         MENUITEM "&Senders", WORK_SYMSEND
         MENUITEM "&Window Routine Senders", WORK_WINDSEND
         MENUITEM "&Global Reference", WORK_GLOSEND
         MENUITEM "&References", WORK_SEND
        END
        POPUP "&Templates"
        BEGIN
         MENUITEM "&do", TEMP_DO
         MENUITEM "&if/then", TEMP_IF
         MENUITEM "if/&else", TEMP_IFEL
         MENUITEM "&block", TEMP_BLOCK
         MENUITEM "&select/case", TEMP_CASE
         MENUITEM "&loop", TEMP_LOOP
         MENUITEM SEPARATOR
         MENUITEM "&New method", TEMP_NMETH
        END
      END
```

■ DOS DIRECTORIES

Manipulating DOS directories and pathnames is something that is not as straightforward in Windows as one might expect, because there are no Windows functions for handling this directly. There is the GetSystemDirectory function, but for some reason, there is no corresponding SetSystemDirectory function. The DlgDirListComboBox function is a specialized function that works only in special file dialogs. In the supplied classes of Actor there is also no direct support for modifying paths directly. The **setFileSpec** method of the FileDialog class is for use only with FileDialog objects. However, there are some Public Domain classes started by Mark Solinski and greatly extended by James Howe that address the issue quite adequately. Because they will be used by some later examples, I will supply these Public Domain classes here (see Listings 3–6.)

There are two classes used to handle directory and pathname manipulation, the FileString and Directory classes. There is also some code that updates the Actor SortedCollection class.

In the Directory class, the full path is broken up into two instance variables, diskDrive, which stores the disk drive letter name, and pathName, which stores the rest of the path, not including the drive name.

Directory makes an extensive use of class methods.

```
fullName(current(Directory));
"C:\Actor"

Dir := current(Directory);
<a Directory>

fullName(Dir);
"C:\Actor"

setDiskDrive(Dir,"D");
<a Directory>

setPathName(Dir,"/");
<a Directory>

fullName(Dir);
"D:/"
```

Listing 3. SYSCHNG.ACT.

```
/*
** System changes to support the Directory class.
**
** Modified By:   James W. Howe
** Date:        06/30/1988
*/!!

add(Constants, #DOS_OFFSET, 700);!!

now(DosStruct)!!
/* Take a long pointer and place the value in the correct segment/offset
   registers. */
```

```
Def setPtr(self lPtr, Segment, Offset)
{
 putWord(self, high(lPtr), Segment);
 putWord(self, low(lPtr), Offset);
}!!


now(Struct)!!
/* Given a memory location, fill self with Struct:size data */

Def fillStruct(self, lpMem)
{
 do(overBy(0, size(self), 2),
  {
  using(i) putWord(self, wordAt(lpMem + asLong(i)), i);
  });

 ^ self;
}!!


/*
** System changes made to the SortedCollection class.  These changes
** allow you to set the compare block when you create an instance
** of the class rather than having to do it in a separate step.
** The new method works the same way as it used to.  A new method,
** "sortBlock" takes a sort block parameter in addition to the
** size parameter.
**
** Modified By:    James W. Howe
** Date:        06/30/1988
*/!!


now(SortedCollectionClass)!!
/* Answer a new SortedCollection object using the default sorting
 method.  This method sets the compare block explicitly instead
 of relying on the init method to do it. */

Def new(self, size | aCollection)
{
 aCollection := init(variableNew(self:Behavior, size));
 aCollection.compareBlock := { using(item1,item2) item1 < item2 };
 ^ aCollection;
} !!
now(SortedCollectionClass)!!
/* Answer a new SortedCollection object using the given sorting
 method. */
```

```
Def sortBlock(self, size, sortBlock | aCollection)
{
  aCollection := init(variableNew(self:Behavior, size));
  aCollection.compareBlock := sortBlock;
  ^ aCollection;
} !!
now(SortedCollection)!!
/* Initializes the SortedCollection object.
  Note:  This method no longer sets the default sort block.
      That is accomplished in the new method for the class. */

Def init(self)
{
  firstElement := lastElement := 0;
} !!
```

Listing 4. The FileString Class file: FILESTRI.CLS.

```
/* This class is used to parse information from a string that
  contains a file name.  */!!

inherit(Object, #FileString, #(fileString ), 2, nil)!!

now(FileStringClass)!!

/* Answer a new FileString object using the string given as its name. */
Def new(self, aString)
{
  ^ setName(new(self:Behavior), aString);
} !!

now(FileString)!!

/* Answer the path specification contained in fileString.  This does
  not include the disk drive or the file name.  This method assumes
  that all information after the disk drive is a path definition only. */
Def asPath(self | startPos)
{
  startPos := indexOf(fileString, ':', 0);
  if startPos
    startPos := startPos;
  else
    startPos := -1;
```

```
  endif;

  ^ subString(fileString, startPos + 1, size(fileString) + 1);
} !!

/* Append aString as a file name to fileString.  This is useful if
   the current fileString refers to a directory. */
Def appendFile(self, aString)
{
  if at(fileString, size(fileString) - 1) = '\'
    fileString := fileString + aString;
  else
    fileString := fileString + "\" + aString;
  endif;
} !!

/* Answer the file extension contained in fileString.  This does
   not include the disk drive, the path specification or file
   name. */
Def fileExtension(self| fileSpec, dotPos)
{
  fileSpec := fileSpec(self);
  dotPos := indexOf(fileSpec, '.', 0);
  if not(dotPos)
    ^ "";
  else
    ^ subString(fileSpec, dotPos + 1, size(fileSpec) + 1);
  endif;
} !!

/* Answer the file specification contained in fileString.  This does
   not include the disk drive or the path specification but is the
   full file name including any extension. */
Def fileSpec(self| curSlash, lastSlash, startPos)
{
  startPos := indexOf(fileString, ':', 0);
  if startPos
    startPos := startPos;
  else
    startPos := -1;
  endif;

  lastSlash := startPos;
  loop
  while (curSlash := indexOf(fileString, '\', lastSlash+1))
```

```
      lastSlash := curSlash;
    endLoop;
    ^ subString(fileString, lastSlash+1, size(fileString) + 1);
  } !!


  /* Answer the contents of fileString */
  Def fileString(self)
  {
    ^ fileString;
  } !!


  /* Answer the file name contained in fileString.  This does
     not include the disk drive, the path specification or file
     extension */
  Def fileName(self | fileSpec, dotPos)
  {
    fileSpec := fileSpec(self);
    dotPos := indexOf(fileSpec, '.', 0);
    if not(dotPos)
      ^ fileSpec;
    else
      ^ subString(fileSpec, 0, dotPos);
    endif;
  } !!


  /* Answer the path specification contained in fileString.  This does
     not include the disk drive or the file name. */
  Def pathSpec(self | curSlash, lastSlash, startPos)
  {
    startPos := indexOf(fileString, ':', 0);
    if startPos
      startPos := startPos;
    else
      startPos := -1;
    endif;

    lastSlash := startPos;
    loop
    while (curSlash := indexOf(fileString, '\', lastSlash+1))
      lastSlash := curSlash;
    endLoop;
    ^subString(fileString, startPos, lastSlash+1);
  } !!


  /* Answer a string containing the disk drive letter followed by a
```

```
    colon.  If the fileString has no drive letter, return an empty
    string. */
Def diskDrive(self)
{
 if indexOf(fileString, ':', 0) = 1
   ^ subString(fileString, 0, 2);
 else
   ^ "";
 endif;
} !!


/* Set the fileString variable to aString. */
Def setName(self, aString)
{
 fileString := aString;
} !!
```

Listing 5. The Directory Class file: DIRECTOR.CLS.

```
/********************************************
**
**     A Directory object represents a disk directory with a
** drive letter and a path name specification.  The methods
** used by this object were derived from the DirStuff class
** created by Mark Solinski of The Whitewater Group.
** A Public Domain Class Written by:
** James W. Howe    Date: 06/29/1988
********************************************/!!


inherit(Object, #Directory, #(diskDrive   /* Disk drive letter */
pathName   /* Not including drive */), 2, nil)!!


now(DirectoryClass)!!


/* Answer a new directory object corresponding to the
   specified file name */

Def pathName(self, aString | theDir, aFileString)
{
 aFileString := new(FileString, aString);
 theDir := new(Directory);
 theDir.pathName := asPath(aFileString);
 theDir.diskDrive := diskDrive(aFileString);
 if diskDrive(theDir) = ""
```

```
      theDir.diskDrive := currentDisk(self);
    endif;

     ^ theDir;
 }    !!


/* Answer the full path specification, including disk drive letter, for
  the current directory. */

Def fullName(self)
{
  ^ currentDisk(self) + currentPath(self);
}  !!


/* Change to the specified directory. */

Def makeCurrent(self, aPathName | aDTA, ds, lpPN, result)
{
 aDTA := getDTA(Directory);
 ds := new(DosStruct);
 lpPN := IP(aPathName);



 fill(ds, 0);
 setPtr(ds, lpPN, DOS_DS, DOS_DX);
 setCall(ds, 0x3B);   /* DOS CHDIR Function */
 call(ds);
 result := getError(ds);
 if result <> 0
   errorBox("Dos Error", loadString(DOS_OFFSET+result));
 endif;

 freeHandle(aPathName);
}   !!


/* Remove the specified directory. */

Def remove(self, aPathName | aDTA, ds, lpPN, result)
{
 aDTA := getDTA(Directory);
 ds := new(DosStruct);
 lpPN := IP(aPathName);



 fill(ds, 0);
```

```
setPtr(ds, lpPN, DOS_DS, DOS_DX);
setCall(ds, 0x3A);   /* DOS RMDIR Function */
call(ds);
result := getError(ds);
if result <> 0
  errorBox("Dos Error", loadString(DOS_OFFSET+result));
endif;


freeHandle(aPathName);
}   !!


/* Create the specified directory. */


Def create(self, aPathName | aDTA, ds, lpPN, result)
{
aDTA := getDTA(Directory);
ds := new(DosStruct);
lpPN := lP(aPathName);



fill(ds, 0);
setPtr(ds, lpPN, DOS_DS, DOS_DX);
setCall(ds, 0x39);   /* DOS MKDIR Function */
call(ds);
result := getError(ds);
if result <> 0
  errorBox("Dos Error", loadString(DOS_OFFSET+result));
endif;


freeHandle(aPathName);
}   !!


/* Answer a sorted collection of files for the given path. */


Def filesOf(self, dir, fileStr, mask | ds, lpPN, aDTA, files, result,
                      aPathName, aFileString, anArray, errors)

{
files := sortBlock(SortedCollection, 1,
            {using(elem1, elem2) at(elem1, 0) < at(elem2, 0)});

ds := new(DosStruct);
aDTA := getDTA(self);


fileStr := if fileStr then
          fileStr;
```

```
        else
          "*.*";

        endif;
mask := if mask then
        mask;
      else
        0x0;
      endif;
aFileString := if dir then
           new(FileString, dir);
         else
           new(FileString,
               currentDisk(self) + currentPath(self));
         endif;
aPathName := fileString(appendFile(aFileString, fileStr));
lpPN := lP(aPathName);

fill(ds, 0);
setPtr(ds, lpPN, DOS_DS, DOS_DX);
putWord(ds, mask, DOS_CX);
setCall(ds, 0x4E);
call(ds);
getError(ds);

errors := new(Set, 2);
add(errors, 2);
add(errors, 18);

loop result := wordAt(ds, DOS_AX);
while not(result in errors)
begin
 anArray := new(Array, 2);
 put(anArray,
     removeNulls(setClass(fillStruct(new(Struct, 13), aDTA + 30L),
                     String)), 0);
 put(anArray, (wordAt(aDTA + 21L) bitAnd 0xFF), 1);
 add(files, anArray);

fill(ds, 0);
setPtr(ds, lpPN, DOS_DS, DOS_DX);
putWord(ds, mask, DOS_CX);
setCall(ds, 0x4F);    /* DOS Find Subsequent function */
call(ds);
getError(ds);
```

```
        endLoop;

        freeHandle(aPathName);

        ^ files;
    }       !!

/* Answer a sorted collection of subdirectories for the given path. */

Def subdirectoriesOf(self, dir, fileStr | ds, result, lpPN, aDTA, subdirs,
                    aPathName, aFileString errors)
{
    subdirs := new(SortedCollection, 1);
    ds := new(DosStruct);
    aDTA := getDTA(self);

    fileStr := if fileStr
            fileStr;
        else
            "*.*";
        endif;

    aFileString := if dir then
            new(FileString, dir);
        else
            new(FileString,
                            currentDisk(self) + currentPath(self));
                endif;
    aPathName := fileString(appendFile(aFileString, fileStr));
    lpPN := lP(aPathName);

    fill(ds, 0);
    setPtr(ds, lpPN, DOS_DS, DOS_DX);
    putWord(ds, 0x10, DOS_CX);
    setCall(ds, 0x4E);
    call(ds);
    getError(ds);

    errors := new(Set, 2);
    add(errors, 2);
    add(errors, 18);

    loop result := wordAt(ds, DOS_AX);
    while not(result in errors)
    begin
```

```
    if (wordAt(aDTA + 21L) bitAnd 0xFF) = 16   /* A Directory */
      add(subdirs,
         removeNulls(setClass(fillStruct(new(Struct, 13), aDTA + 30L),
                        String)));
    endif;

    fill(ds, 0);
    setPtr(ds, lpPN, DOS_DS, DOS_DX);
    putWord(ds, 0x10, DOS_CX);
    setCall(ds, 0x4F);   /* DOS Find Subsequent function */
    call(ds);
    getError(ds);
    endLoop;

    freeHandle(aPathName);

    ^ subdirs;
}    !!

/* Answer the default DTA */

Def getDTA(self | ds)
{
  ds := new(DosStruct);
  setCall(ds, 0x2F);
  call(ds);
  getError(ds);

  ^ pack(wordAt(ds, DOS_BX), wordAt(ds, DOS_ES))
} !!

/* Answer a new directory object corresponding to the current directory */
Def current(self | theDir)
{
  theDir := new(Directory);
  theDir.pathName := currentPath(self);
  theDir.diskDrive := currentDisk(self);

  ^ theDir;
}    !!

/* Answer the volume label for the disk containing the current directory. */

Def volumeLabel(self | ds, lpPN, aDTA, result, volumeLabel,
                aPathName, aFileString, errors)
```

```
{
ds := new(DosStruct);
aDTA := getDTA(self);

aFileString := new(FileString, fullName(self));
aPathName := fileString(appendFile(aFileString, "*.*"));
lpPN := lP(aPathName);

fill(ds, 0);
setPtr(ds, lpPN, DOS_DS, DOS_DX);
putWord(ds, 0x8, DOS_CX);
setCall(ds, 0x4E);
call(ds);
getError(ds);

errors := new(Set, 2);
add(errors, 2);
add(errors, 18);

result := wordAt(ds, DOS_AX);
if not(result in errors) then
 volumeLabel := removeNulls(setClass(fillStruct(new(Struct, 13),
                                aDTA + 30L),
                        String));
else
 volumeLabel := nil;
endif;

freeHandle(aPathName);

^ volumeLabel;
}     !!

/* Answer a string corresponding to the current directory path. */

Def currentPath(self | ds, lpDir, aTC, aStr, bStr)
{
ds := new(DosStruct);
fill(ds, 0);
lpDir := lP(aStr := new(String, 128));
setPtr(ds, lpDir, DOS_DS, DOS_SI);
setCall(ds, 0x47);
call(ds);
bStr := "\" + removeNulls(getText(Handles[aStr]));
freeHandle(aStr);
```

```
    getError(ds);

    ^ bStr;
} !!


/* Answer the current disk drive letter. */

Def currentDisk(self | ds)
{
  ds := new(DosStruct);
  setCall(ds, 0x19);
  call(ds);
  getError(ds);
  ^ asString(asChar(atLSB(ds, DOS_AX) + asInt('A'))) + ":"
} !!


now(Directory)!!


/* Answer a sorted collection of files for self. */

Def filesOf(self, fileStr, mask | ds, lpPN, aDTA, files, result, aFileString,
                aPathName, anArray, errors)
{

  files := sortBlock(SortedCollection, 1,
              {using(elem1, elem2) at(elem1, 0) < at(elem2, 0)});
  ds := new(DosStruct);
  aDTA := getDTA(Directory);

  fileStr := if fileStr then
          fileStr;
        else
          "*.*";
        endif;
  mask := if mask then
        mask;
      else
        0x0;
      endif;

  aFileString := new(FileString, fullName(self));
  aPathName := fileString(appendFile(aFileString, fileStr));
  lpPN := lP(aPathName);

  fill(ds, 0);
```

```
setPtr(ds, lpPN, DOS_DS, DOS_DX);
putWord(ds, mask, DOS_CX);
setCall(ds, 0x4E);
call(ds);
getError(ds);

errors := new(Set, 2);
add(errors, 2);
add(errors, 18);

loop result := wordAt(ds, DOS_AX);
while not(result in errors)
begin
 anArray := new(Array, 2);
 put(anArray,
    removeNulls(setClass(fillStruct(new(Struct, 13), aDTA + 30L),
                  String)), 0);
 put(anArray, (wordAt(aDTA + 21L) bitAnd 0xFF), 1);
 add(files, anArray);

 fill(ds, 0);
 setPtr(ds, lpPN, DOS_DS, DOS_DX);
 putWord(ds, mask, DOS_CX);
 setCall(ds, 0x4F);   /* DOS Find Subsequent function */
 call(ds);
 getError(ds);
endLoop;

freeHandle(aPathName);

 ^ files;
}          !!
```

```
/* Answer true if aDirectory represents the same directory as the
  receiver, otherwise answer false. */
Def = (self, aDirectory)
{
 ^ fullName(self) = fullName(aDirectory)
} !!
```

```
/* Answer true if the receiver has at least one subdirectory */

Def hasSubdirectory(self | ds, result, lpPN, aDTA, aFileString,
                 aPathName, errors)
```

```
{
ds := new(DosStruct);
aDTA := getDTA(Directory);

aFileString := new(FileString, fullName(self));
aPathName := fileString(appendFile(aFileString, "*.*"));
lpPN := lP(aPathName);

fill(ds, 0);
setPtr(ds, lpPN, DOS_DS, DOS_DX);
putWord(ds, 0x10, DOS_CX);
setCall(ds, 0x4E);
call(ds);
getError(ds);

errors := new(Set, 2);
add(errors, 2);
add(errors, 18);

result := wordAt(ds, DOS_AX);
if result = 0 then
  result := true;
else
  if not(result in errors) then
    errorBox("DosError", loadString(DOS_OFFSET+result));
  endif;
  result := false;
endif;

freeHandle(aPathName);

^ result;
}      !!

/* Remove the directory specified by self. */

Def remove(self | aPathName, aDTA, ds, lpPN, result)
{
aDTA := getDTA(Directory);
ds := new(DosStruct);
aPathName := fullName(self);
lpPN := lP(aPathName);


fill(ds, 0);
```

```
setPtr(ds, lpPN, DOS_DS, DOS_DX);
setCall(ds, 0x3A);  /* DOS RMDIR Function */
call(ds);
result := getError(ds);
if result <> 0
  errorBox("Dos Error", loadString(DOS_OFFSET+result));
endif;

freeHandle(aPathName);
}   !!


/* Create a directory corresponding to self. */

Def create(self| aPathName, aDTA, ds, lpPN, result)
{
aDTA := getDTA(Directory);
ds := new(DosStruct);
aPathName := fullName(self);
lpPN := lP(aPathName);


fill(ds, 0);
setPtr(ds, lpPN, DOS_DS, DOS_DX);
setCall(ds, 0x39);  /* DOS MKDIR Function */
call(ds);
result := getError(ds);
if result <> 0
  errorBox("Dos Error", loadString(DOS_OFFSET+result));
endif;

freeHandle(aPathName);
}   !!


/* Change directory to self. */

Def makeCurrent(self| aDTA, ds, lpPN, result, aPathName)
{
aDTA := getDTA(Directory);
ds := new(DosStruct);
aPathName := fullName(self);
lpPN := lP(aPathName);


fill(ds, 0);
setPtr(ds, lpPN, DOS_DS, DOS_DX);
```

```
setCall(ds, 0x3B);   /* DOS CHDIR Function */
call(ds);
result := getError(ds);
if result <> 0
  errorBox("Dos Error", loadString(DOS_OFFSET+result));
endif;


freeHandle(aPathName);
} !!


/* Answer a sorted collection of subdirectories for the object. */

Def subdirectories(self, fileStr | ds, result, lpPN, aDTA, subdirs,
                  aFileString, aPathName, errors)
{
subdirs := new(SortedCollection, 1);
ds := new(DosStruct);
aDTA := getDTA(Directory);

if fileStr = nil
  fileStr := "*.*";
endif;

aFileString := new(FileString, fullName(self));
aPathName := fileString(appendFile(aFileString, fileStr));
lpPN := lP(aPathName);

fill(ds, 0);
setPtr(ds, lpPN, DOS_DS, DOS_DX);
putWord(ds, 0x10, DOS_CX);
setCall(ds, 0x4E);
call(ds);
getError(ds);

errors := new(Set, 2);
add(errors, 2);
add(errors, 18);

loop result := wordAt(ds, DOS_AX);
while not(result in errors)
begin
 if (wordAt(aDTA + 21L) bitAnd 0xFF) = 16   /* A Directory */
   add(subdirs,
     removeNulls(setClass(fillStruct(new(Struct, 13), aDTA + 30L),
                 String)));
```

```
            endif;

            fill(ds, 0);
            setPtr(ds, lpPN, DOS_DS, DOS_DX);
            putWord(ds, 0x10, DOS_CX);
            setCall(ds, 0x4F);   /* DOS Find Subsequent function */
            call(ds);
            getError(ds);
        endLoop;

        freeHandle(aPathName);

         ^ subdirs;
        }   !!

/* Set the path name associated with the directory object to aString. */

Def setPathName(self, aString)
{
 pathName := aString;
}   !!

/* Set the disk drive associated with the directory object to aCharacter. */
Def setDiskDrive(self, aCharacter)
{
 diskDrive := asString(aCharacter) + ":";
}   !!

/* Answer the full path specification, including disk drive letter, for
   the directory. */

Def fullName(self)
{
 ^ diskDrive(self) + pathName(self);
}   !!

/* Answer the volume label for the disk containing self. */

Def volumeLabel(self| ds, lpPN, aDTA, result, volumeLabel,
                     aFileString, aPathName, errors)
{
 ds := new(DosStruct);
 aDTA := getDTA(Directory);

 aFileString := new(FileString, fullName(self));
```

```
aPathName := fileString(appendFile(aFileString, "*.*"));
lpPN := IP(aPathName);

fill(ds, 0);
setPtr(ds, lpPN, DOS_DS, DOS_DX);
putWord(ds, 0x8, DOS_CX);
setCall(ds, 0x4E);
call(ds);
getError(ds);

errors := new(Set, 2);
add(errors, 2);
add(errors, 18);

result := wordAt(ds, DOS_AX);
if not(result in errors) then
 volumeLabel := removeNulls(setClass(fillStruct(new(Struct, 13),
                              aDTA + 30L),
                     String));
else
 volumeLabel := nil;
endif;

freeHandle(aPathName);

^ volumeLabel;
}          !!
```

/* Answer the path name associated with the directory object. */

```
Def pathName(self)
{
 ^ pathName;
} !!
```

/* Answer the disk drive associated with the directory object. */

```
Def diskDrive(self)
{
 ^ diskDrive;
} !!
```

Listing 6. DIRECT.RC.

```
; Dos error messages  (Error number + DOS_OFFSET)
DOS_OFFSET+1,  "Invalid function number"
DOS_OFFSET+2,  "File not found"
```

```
DOS_OFFSET+3,  "Path not found"
DOS_OFFSET+4,  "Too many open files"
DOS_OFFSET+5,  "Invalid function number"
DOS_OFFSET+6,  "File not found"
DOS_OFFSET+7,  "Path not found"
DOS_OFFSET+8,  "Too many open files"
DOS_OFFSET+9,  "Invalid function number"
DOS_OFFSET+10, "Invalid environment"
DOS_OFFSET+11, "Invalid format"
DOS_OFFSET+12, "Invalid access code"
DOS_OFFSET+13, "Invalid data"

DOS_OFFSET+15, "Invalid drive specified"
DOS_OFFSET+16, "Attempt to remove current directory"
DOS_OFFSET+17, "Not same device"
DOS_OFFSET+18, "No more files"
DOS_OFFSET+19, "Attempt to write on write-protected diskette"
DOS_OFFSET+20, "Unknown unit"
DOS_OFFSET+21, "Drive not ready"
DOS_OFFSET+22, "Unknown command"
DOS_OFFSET+23, "Data error (CRC)"
DOS_OFFSET+24, "Bad request structure length"
DOS_OFFSET+25, "Seek error"
DOS_OFFSET+26, "Unknown media type"
DOS_OFFSET+27, "Sector not found"
DOS_OFFSET+28, "Printer out of paper"
DOS_OFFSET+29, "Write fault"
DOS_OFFSET+30, "Read fault"
DOS_OFFSET+31, "General failure"
DOS_OFFSET+32, "Sharing violation"
DOS_OFFSET+33, "Lock violation"
DOS_OFFSET+34, "Invalid disk change"
DOS_OFFSET+35, "FCB unavailable"
DOS_OFFSET+36, "Sharing buffer overflow"
DOS_OFFSET+50, "Network request not supported"
DOS_OFFSET+51, "Remote computer not listening"
DOS_OFFSET+52, "Duplicate name on network"
DOS_OFFSET+53, "Network name not found"
DOS_OFFSET+54, "Network busy"
DOS_OFFSET+55, "Network device no longer exists"
DOS_OFFSET+56, "NETBIOS command limit exceeded"
DOS_OFFSET+57, "Network adapter hardware error"
DOS_OFFSET+58, "Incorrect response from network"
DOS_OFFSET+59, "Unexpected network error"
DOS_OFFSET+60, "Incompatible remote adapter"
```

DOS_OFFSET+61, "Print queue full"
DOS_OFFSET+62, "Not enough space for print file"
DOS_OFFSET+63, "Print file was deleted"
DOS_OFFSET+64, "Network name was deleted"
DOS_OFFSET+65, "Access denied"
DOS_OFFSET+66, "Network device type incorrect"
DOS_OFFSET+67, "Network name not found"
DOS_OFFSET+68, "Network name limit exceeded"
DOS_OFFSET+69, "NETBIOS session limit exceeded"
DOS_OFFSET+70, "Temporarily paused"
DOS_OFFSET+71, "Network request not accepted"
DOS_OFFSET+72, "Print or disk redirection is paused"

DOS_OFFSET+80, "File exists"
DOS_OFFSET+82, "Cannot make directory entry"
DOS_OFFSET+83, "Fail on INT 24"
DOS_OFFSET+84, "Too many redirections"
DOS_OFFSET+85, "Duplicate redirection"
DOS_OFFSET+86, "Invalid password"
DOS_OFFSET+87, "Invalid parameter"
DOS_OFFSET+88, "Network data fault"

7

OBJECT-ORIENTED GRAPHICS PROGRAMMING FOR WINDOWS

In this chapter we will explore some of the rudiments of object-oriented Windows graphics programming using some of the built-in features of Actor. Some of the topics covered will include color rectangles, ellipses, polygons, bitmaps, and charts.

It may not come as a tremendous surprise that graphics programming in the Windows environment involves drawing graphics objects in windows. However, some of the consequences of this fact may not be quite as obvious. One of the first hurdles you will have to overcome has to do with coordinates. Any window in an environment like Windows is intended to be movable about the screen. However, you would expect that a graphics object drawn on a window would move with the window and stay put as far as its own borders are concerned when its window is displaced across the screen. This implies that there are two different coordinate systems, one for the screen and one for the window. In most Windows programming systems, this is something that you must deal with as a matter of routine.

■ BUILT-IN GRAPHICS CLASSES

In Actor, there are a total of six basic built-in graphics classes: Point, GraphicsObject, Rect, RndRect, WinPolygon, and WinEllipse. It is not true that all the others are descendants of the class Point, however. As a matter of fact they are descendants of the Struct class. They are built as collections of Point objects, not specializations of them. In a system with multiple inheritance, it would be possible for graphics classes to inherit from more than one inheritance line, so as to automatically acquire both graphics and other types of properties. As a group, all classes of graphics objects respond to their own versions of the **draw** message.

The class hierarchy in Actor as it leads into the built-in graphics classes looks like this:

```
Object
  Collection
    IndexedCollection
      ByteCollection
        Struct
            GraphicsObject
      Rect
            RndRect
    WinEllipse
        WinPolygon
```

In the following sections I will go over the most important of these built-in graphics classes.

■ THE POINT CLASS

Point objects in Actor are two dimensional, with two instance variables, x and y, which represent the coordinate pairs that define a 2-D point. Point objects can be created three different ways: 1) using a **new** message, and then setting the values with the **setX** and **setY** messages, 2) creating a literal point directly, analogous to the way you might create an array, and 3) by using the **point** message. Here is an example of how the three different ways might be used to create the same identical point:

```
Start := new(Point);
setX(Start,30);
setY(Start,40);

Start := 30@40;

Start := point(30,40);
```

■ SCRIBBLE

A sample Scribble demo is provided with Actor using a class also called scribble, which affords a good example of how relatively simple it is to get started doing useful things in graphics. To create a Scribble window, evaluate these messages:

```
Sc := defaultNew(Scribble, "Scribble Away");
show(Sc,1);
```

Generally, the Scribble class is a good introduction to graphics programming with Actor and with object-oriented systems because it establishes freehand drawing with the mouse by implementing just four methods and a single instance variable. We will look at each of these components of the Scribble application in turn.

As with all interactive graphics programs using the mouse in Actor, the mouse control for Scribble is handled by three methods called **beginDrag**, **drag**, and **endDrag**, respectively. These three methods correspond to the Windows messages: WM_LBUTTONDOWN, WM_MOUSEMOVE, and WM_LBUTTONUP. These messages are sent when the left mouse button is pressed down, when the mouse moves while it is held down, and when it is released.

The single instance variable of Scribble is dragDC, which keeps track of the position to which the mouse has been dragged. The **beginDrag** message stores the display context in the dragDC instance variable and sets the location of point at the current mouse position. It is written:

```
Def beginDrag(self, wP, point)
{ dragDC := getContext(self);
  moveTo(point, dragDC);
}
```

The drag method simply draws a line from the position of point to that of dragDC.

```
Def drag(self, wP, point)
{ lineTo(point, dragDC);
}
```

The endDrag method completes the line drawing operation by releasing the display context when the mouse button comes up.

```
Def endDrag(self, wP, point)
{ releaseContext(self, dragDC);
}
```

Finally, a method is also entered for using the right mouse button to clear the screen.

```
Def WM_RBUTTONDOWN(self, wp, lp)
{ repaint(self);
}
```

Although this program does not do very much, it is still a fully functioning program as far as it goes. This is quite attractive given the extremely small amount of code that was written to produce it. And it is not of trivial interest in the sense that all interactive graphics programs can be written in essentially the same way, with the same three mouse control methods: **beginDrag**, **drag**, and **endDrag**. Below is a formal class description of the scribble class.

■ THE SCRIBBLE CLASS DESCRIPTION

Source file:	SCRIBBLE.CLS
Inherits from:	Window

Instance Variables:

dragDC

Object methods:

beginDrag	Initializes mouse dragging by getting a display context for drawing.
drag	Responds to a mouse drag message by drawing a line to the given point from the current position.
endDrag	Concludes mouse dragging by releasing the display context. WM_RBUTTONDOWN Responds to MS-Window's right-button-down message, erasing the window when the right button is pressed.

■ RECTANGLES

Geometrically speaking, a rectangle is just a special type of polygon, so one might expect that the Rectangle class would be a subclass of WinPolygon. However, in Actor, this is not the case. Rect is a peer class with WinPolygon. The reason for this is the special attention given rectangles by the Windows API, since rectangles are used so ubiquitously by it to create windows and controls (Figures 7.1 and 7.2). Rectangle does not need to inherit its capability. It is built upon Windows functions.

Here is an interactive session that creates a rectangle R1 and then asks it for its width and height.

```
R1 := rect(5, 5, 15, 10);
Rect(5 5 15 10 )

width(R1);
10

height(R1);
5
```

The following definition is a method that computes the area of a rectangle:

```
Def area(self)
{ ^abs(right(self) - left(self)) * abs(bottom(self) - top(self));
}
```

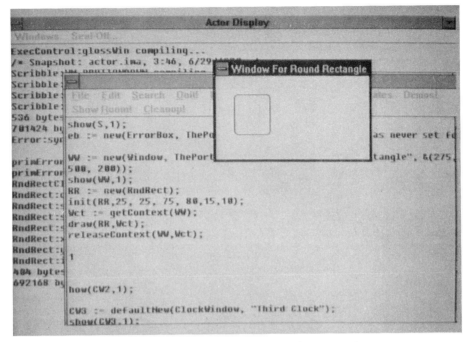

Figure 7.1 Drawing a round rectangle in a window.

Applying it to our previous rectangle simply involves the message:

area(R1);
50

In a similar way, we can also define a perimeter method:

Def perimeter(self)
{ ^(2 * abs(right(self) - left(self)) + (2 * abs(bottom(self) - top(self)))));
}

perimeter(R1);
30

Finally, here is a method that uses the Pythagorean Theorem to compute a rectangle's diagonal:

Def diagonal(self)
{ ^(square(abs(right(self) - left(self))) + square(abs(bottom(self) - top(self)))) **.5;
}

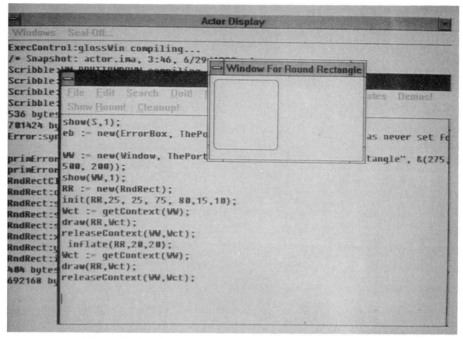

Figure 7.2 The previous round rectangle inflated in size.

diagonal(R1);
11.18033989

■ ROUND RECTANGLES

Round rectangles are implemented in Actor using the RndRect class. Here is an interactive session that first creates a RndRect object and then initializes its size:

RR := new(RndRect);
RndRect(0 0 0 0 0 0)

init(RR,5, 5, 15, 10,10,2);
RndRect(5 5 15 10 10 2)

To draw a RndRect object we must create a window in which it will be drawn.

WW :=
new(Window, ThePort, nil, "Window For Round Rectangle", &(275, 60, 500, 200));
show(WW,1);
RR := new(RndRect);

```
init(RR,25, 25, 75, 80,15,10);
Wct := getContext(WW);
draw(RR,Wct);
releaseContext(WW,Wct);
```

To expand the size of the round rectangle and redraw it, it is simply necessary to send
the messages:

```
inflate(RR,20,20);
Wct := getContext(WW);
draw(RR,Wct);
releaseContext(WW,Wct);
```

■ ELLIPSES

Drawing an ellipse is almost the same idea as drawing a round rectangle (Figure 7.3).
First an appropriate window is created. Then, the ellipse is initialized as an object of
the WinEllipse class, the context is saved, and the graphics is displayed.

```
WW := new(Window, ThePort, nil, "Window For Ellipse", &(275, 60, 500, 200));
show(WW,1);
```

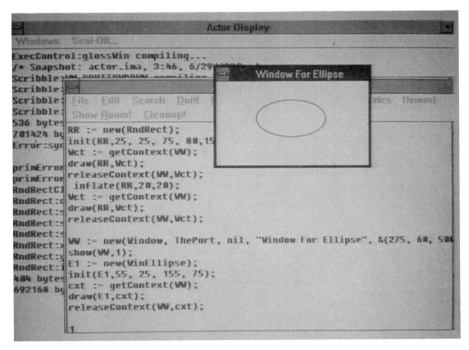

Figure 7.3 Drawing an ellipse in a window.

E1 := new(WinEllipse);
init(E1,55, 25, 155, 75);
cxt := getContext(WW);
draw(E1,cxt);
releaseContext(WW,cxt);

■ POLYGONS

Actor uses the WinPolygon class to implement polygons (Figure 7.4). A WinPolygon object is essentially a collection of Point objects. This is a more complex graphic object than we have dealt with before, but it is really an extension of the same design used for rectangles.

The following messages can be evaluated to utilize the WinPolygon class for drawing a parallelogram:

WW := new(Window, ThePort, nil, "Window For Parallelogram", &(275, 60, 600, 300));
show(WW,1);
P1 := new(WinPolygon, #(100@50 200@50 250@150 150@150 100@50));
cxt := getContext(WW);

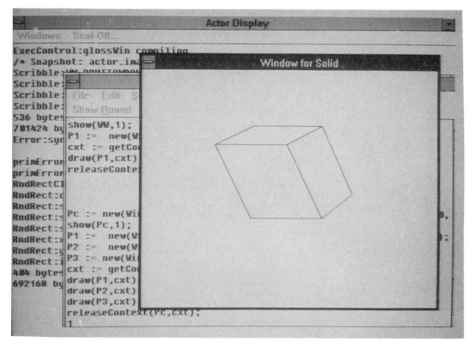

Figure 7.4 A pseudo 3-D polygon.

```
draw(P1,cxt);
releaseContext(WW,cxt);
```

The **draw** method of WinPolygon is written in only a single line of code:

```
Def draw(self, hdc)
{ Call Polygon(hdc, self, size(self)/4);
}
```

As you can see, the **draw** method of the WinPolygon class simply calls the Polygon Windows function, but divides the size of it by four to supply the proper nCount argument. The real key to the Polygon class is its new class method, which is defined:

```
Def new(self, aColl | aPoly)
{ aPoly := variableNew(self:Behavior, size(aColl) * 4);
 do(over(0, size(aColl)),
 { using(idx) putWord(aPoly, x(aColl[idx]), idx * 4);
  putWord(aPoly, y(aColl[idx]), (idx * 4) + 2)
 });
 ^aPoly;
}
```

What is happening here is that this method enumerates over a collection of points and uses the putWord method inherited from the Struct class to allocate memory for each point in the collection to store data for the polygon. The **variableNew** method is provided in the Behavior class for this very usage in defining new methods for Collection classes.

These messages utilize the WinPolygon class to draw a pseudosolid:

```
Pc := new(Window, ThePort, nil, "Window for Solid", &(175, 50, 600, 400));
show(Pc, 1);
P1 := new(WinPolygon, #(100@100 200@100 250@200 150@200 100@100));
P2 := new(WinPolygon, #(100@100 154@75 250@75 200@100 100@100));
P3 := new(WinPolygon, #(250@200 293@167 250@75 200@100 250@200));
cxt := getContext(Pc);
draw(P1,cxt);
draw(P2,cxt);
draw(P3,cxt);
releaseContext(Pc,cxt);
```

When using WinPolygon, it is important to remember that the underlying Polygon function will always close the figure, so the points for the entire quadrilateral have to be specified, otherwise an unwanted diagonal will be automatically inserted to close the figure.

Here is a message sequence that illustrates the use of a call to the Windows PolyPolygon function:

```
PP1 := new(Window,ThePort,nil, "Window For PolyPolygon",&(175,50,600,400));
show(PP1,1);
cxt := getContext(PP1);
Call PolyPolygon(cxt,#(#(20@20 40@20 60@80 40@80 20@20)),#(5),1);
releaseContext(PP1,cxt);
```

An example of an alternative way of drawing and animating a "pseudo cube" is provided by the Actor Hypercube demo. If you want to run the Actor Hypercube animation demo from an interactive session in an Actor workspace, evaluate the messages:

```
CW := defaultNew(CubeWindow, "HyperCube");
show(CW,1);
run(CW);
```

One of the things you may have noticed about all the graphics objects you have drawn so far is that they disappear as soon as input focus is transferred to another window, or the window is moved or resized. What is happening is that the window repaints itself and has no way of knowing that there is an object there to be redrawn too. In order to make sure that the contents of windows are redrawn when **paint** messages are received, a special class with a new version of the **paint** message is needed.

The Actor manual suggests the following **paint** method for a new GraphicsWindow class:

```
Def paint(self, hDC | theRect)
{
theRect := rect(10, 10, width(clientRect(self))/2,
          height(clientRect(self))/2);
draw(theRect, hDC);
}
```

Let's look for a moment at what it does. If you are using Actor, enter the method under the GraphicsWindow class and then evaluate these messages in a workspace:

```
W := defaultNew(GraphicsWindow, "Try Me");
show(W,1);
```

As you can see, the window has a rectangle already drawn in it and redraws it each time the window receives the message to paint from Windows. This is exactly what you see in the code too. So what we have is something very ad hoc, in the sense that the **paint** method as it is written is devoted to always redrawing this particular rectangle.

One way of doing this more generically would be to provide an instance variable that maintained a collection of all graphics objects drawn in the window. Part of the job for the **draw** method would be to append the object drawn to this collection. In this case, the **paint** method would iterate through the collection and redraw each of the objects listed. One important detail here would be finding the appropriate way for passing the name of the particular window to the **draw** method so that it would know which windows object list to update. Ideally, the **draw** methods would be rewritten so that they would still work for windows that did not support this mechanism.

■ COLOR BITMAPS

As we have seen, in Windows 3.0 and later, device-independent color bitmaps are supported. Code can be written that does not, in principle, need to be changed for applications to run on different platforms. As with menus and dialogs, bitmaps can be declared as static resources. The smallest bitmap that can be used in a pattern brush is 8 by 8. Although built-in Actor classes do not include a great deal of explicit handling for color bitmaps, any of the built-in Windows bitmap processing functions can be called from within Actor. Some of the relevant functions are listed in Table 7.1.

In the Actor environment, the overall screen size is stored in the system, and to inspect what it is, you only have to send the **screenSize** system message as follows:

screenSize();

If you have a VGA monitor, the message will return the value:

640@480

This is really the coordinate address of the farthest point in the lower right corner in the screen coordinate system.

Besides the screen coordinate system there is also the one relative to a window, which is called the client coordinate system.

Before drawing something in a window you must first get a display context. After drawing is completed, the display context is then released. These operations are performed with the **getContext** and **releaseContext** messages. Just drawing a graphics object in a simple window is not enough to ensure the survival of that graphics when conditions change. Ordinarily, covering it up with another window, resizing its window, and other modifications will not result in the graphics being redrawn. The best way to ensure that

Table 7.1 Windows Bitmap Functions.

CreateDIBitmap	BitBlt
LoadBitmap	PatBlt
GlobalUnlock	PolyLine

graphics objects are redrawn is to draw them in a type of window that has a **paint** method, which handles redrawing them.

■ POINT3-D

Given what has been covered so far, it is obvious that all the built-in graphics facilities that I have been discussing are valid only for two dimensions (2-D). They not only are used for drawing on a 2-D display—practically all computer graphics have this limitation—the graphics objects that are described are themselves only 2-D. In this section (Listing 1) I will conduct a simple exercise in object-oriented graphics programming, which will consist solely in developing a new point class, one that describes points of three dimensions (3-D).

Listing 1. Point3-D.

```
/***********************/
/*    The Point3-D Class    */
/*                          */
/***********************/

Def z(self)
{
  ^z
}

Def setZ(self, zVal)
{ ^z := zVal;
}

Def set(self, xVal, yVal, zVal)
{ x := xVal;
  y := yVal;
  z := zVal;
}

Def round(self)
{ ^point(asInt(
  if x < 0
  then x - 0.5
  else x + 0.5
  endif), asInt(
  if y < 0
  then y - 0.5
  else y + 0.5
```

```
    endif), asInt(
    if z < 0
    then z - 0.5
    else z + 0.5
    endif));
}

Def asStruct(self | struct)
{ struct := new(Struct, 6);
 putWord(struct, x, 0);
 putWord(struct, y, 2);
 putWord(struct, z, 4);
 ^struct;
}

Def +(self, arg)
{ ^point(x(arg) + x, y(arg) + y, z(arg) + z);
}

Def -(self, arg)
{ ^point(x(arg) - x, y(arg) - y, z(arg) - z);
}

Def =(self, a3DPt)
{ ^class(a3DPt) == class(self) cand x = x(a3DPt) cand y = y(a3DPt) cand z = z(a3DPt);
}

Def printOn(self, aStream)
{
 printOn(x, aStream);
 nextPutAll(aStream, "@");
 printOn(y, aStream);
 nextPutAll(aStream, "@");
 printOn(z, aStream);
}


Def point3D(self, yVal, zVal | a3DPoint)
{ a3DPoint := new(Point3D);
 set(a3DPoint, self, yVal,zVal);
 ^a3DPoint
}

3D1 := point3D(30,40,50);
30@40@50
```

The **moveTo** method of the Point class changes the current window position to the receiver point using the device context handle specified. The **lineTo** method draws a line from the current position up to, but not including, self, using the specified display context handle. Then it resets the current window position to that of the receiver Point. The **draw** method for drawing a point simply calls the Windows Rectangle function with arguments requesting it to draw a dimensionless rectangle:

```
Def draw(self, hdc)
{ Call Rectangle(hdc, x, y, x, y);
}
```

■ CHARTS

Because of the enormous variety of graphics applications that are possible for different purposes, in conventional programming it is very typical that each graphics program has to be written completely from scratch. It is only with the emergence of object-oriented systems that the question really arises of how a wide variety of graphics applications can be developed on a common foundation. In this section I will provide some rather practical examples of building simple bar and pie charts based on a few supplied Actor classes that are simple and easy to extend. From these examples some

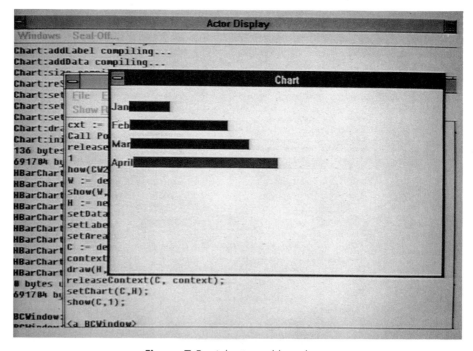

Figure 7.5 A horizontal bar chart.

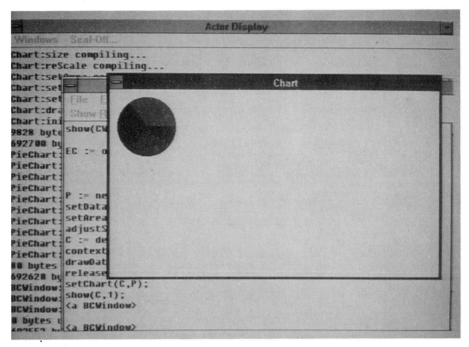

Figure 7.6 A pie chart in a window.

of the relevant issues will emerge of how truly generic graphic systems can be designed. The supplied Actor classes for drawing charts are contained in this branch of the class hierarchy:

Object
  Chart
    HBarChart
    PieChart
    VBarChart
  WindowsObject
    Window
      BCWindow

The BCWindow class is a specialization of Window that has a chart instance variable for storing chart data and a special paint method that utilizes this data for redrawing charts in the window. If the BCWindow and HBarChart classes are loaded into the system, the following messages create the horizontal bar chart shown in Figure 7.5.

```
H := new(HBarChart);
setData(H, #(7, 15, 18, 22));
setLabels(H, #("Jan", "Feb", "Mar", "April"));
setArea(H, 100@100);
```

```
C := defaultNew(BCWindow, "Chart");
context := getContext(C);
draw(H, context);
releaseContext(C, context);
setChart(C,H);
show(C,1);
```

A very similar thing can be done with the PieChart class to create pie chart graphics:

```
Pie := new(PieChart);
setData(Pie, #(7, 15, 18, 22));
setArea(Pie,100@100);
adjustScale(Pie,80);
C := defaultNew(BCWindow, "Chart");
context := getContext(C);
drawData(Pie, context);
releaseContext(C, context);
setChart(C,Pie);
show(C,1);
```

The result is shown in Figure 7.6.

■ ANIMATION

Animation poses special problems in the Windows environment because of the multitasking issue. If Windows is able to interrupt your animation procedure for even the shortest time, you never have control over how the animation sequence will appear. Windows gains control when an application asks for its next message. It is at that point that the multitasking may result in it sending messages to a different application. Typically, it does this when the message queue for the original application is empty. Therefore, one way to keep control during an animation sequence is to guarantee the message queue is never empty. To avoid flicker in an animation sequence, it is necessary to avoid having any time at all when the screen has either no image or an abruptly different one than just before.

One animation technique in Windows is to make a child window the exact size of an image, and then just move the child window across the screen rather than having to repeatedly draw and redraw an image in a larger window. Another animation approach is to make the object to be animated an icon and use the DrawIcon Windows function rather than MoveWindow.

If you know the direction of an animation procedure in advance, then sometimes it is possible to create a bitmap that includes a blank space that is sufficient to automatically erase a previous image when the bitmap is redrawn. This eliminates the need for a special procedure to erase the image.

One way to control the timing of an animation is by use of the WM_TIMER message. The following Actor animation demo routines use the 'alive' message to handle the multitasking issue.

```
Def flipActor(self | idx, array, count)
{ idx := -1;
  array := #(0 1 2 3 2 1);
  count := (size(array) * 4) + 1;
  loop
   alive(self) cand checkMessage();
  while alive(self) cand (count := count - 1) >= 0
  begin
   doDraw(self, bitmaps[array[idx := (idx + 1) mod size(array)]],
   {using(bitmapArray, hDC, hMemDC)
    Call BitBlt(hDC, bitmapArray[1], bitmapArray[2],
    bitmapArray[3], bitmapArray[4],
    hMemDC, 0, 0, bitmapArray[5]
    );
   });
   delay(self, 30);
  endLoop;
}


/* Draw the People strings. */
Def flipPeople(self | hDC, count, idx, rect)
{ rect := rect(150, 85, 400, 112);
  loop
   alive(self) cand checkMessage();
  while alive(self)
   idx := 2000;
   do(findNumbers(self, loadString(idx)),
   {using(number | oc, sz, str, which)
    if alive(self)
    then oc := new(OrderedCollection, number);
     do(number, {using(i) add(oc, loadString(idx := idx + 1));});
    loop
    while alive(self) cand (sz := size(oc)) > 0
    begin
     hDC := getContext(self);
     Call SetTextColor(hDC, 0xFFFFFFL);
     Call SetBkMode(hDC, TRANSPARENT);
     which := random(sz);
     Call DrawText(hDC, asciiz(oc:Object[which]), -1, rect,
      0x25 /*DT_CENTER, DT_VCENTER & DT_SINGLELINE*/);
```

```
    releaseContext(self, hDC);
    remove(oc, which);
    delay(self, 1000);
    scrollRect(self, rect,
     point(#(-1 1)[random(2)], #(-1 1)[random(2)]), height(rect)
     );
    endLoop;
   endif;
  });
  endLoop;
 }
```

▪ OBSERVATIONS

One of the most attractive things about Actor is that it is an interactive environment. This means that, in theory at least, you can try some code and see the results almost immediately, without having to enter the compile-link cycle. Among other things, this frees the programmer from having to take time out and cope with extraneous errors and issues that are unrelated to the problem at hand. One of the things that can disrupt this advantageous situation in Actor is having to deal with compiling resources like menus. For this reason—although it involves a little more work—I recommend that when an application is still under development, that dynamic resources be used. Then, when you have finished your program, the conversion can be made to compiled resources.

▪ GRAPHICS CLASS DESCRIPTIONS

Turtle

Source file: TURTLE.CLS

Inherits from: Object

Instance Variables:

position,

heading,

visibility,

penDown,

stepSize,

kitchenFloor,

kitchenFloorDC,

turConstants

Class methods:

Object methods:

b	Backs the turtle up. If the pen is down, then any tracks will be erased.
backup	" "
down	Lets the "pen" down so that the turtle will leave a trail.
draw	Shell method for drawing the turtle on the screen.
erase	Erases the turtle from the screen by redrawing itself in white.
f	Moves the turtle forward x steps.
face	Faces the turtle at "angle" degrees, where 0 is due North (straight up)
faceRad	Point the turtle in a direction in radians.
form	Draws the shape of the turtle on the screen.
forward	Moves the turtle forward x steps.
getWindowDC	Gets the display context for the kitchen floor window.
goTo	Moves the turtle absolutely to the point specified in nextPosition.
hide	Hides the turtle (makes it invisible).
home	Places the turtle in center of the window.
init	Sets the step size, initializes the turtle's window, creates the turConstants collection, and centers the turtle in the window.
koch	Draws a Koch type fractal curve of order n.
l	Turns the turtle left (counterclockwise) x degrees.
left	Turns the turtle left (counterclockwise) x degrees.
leftRad	Turn turtle to the left in radians.
letGoWindowDC	Releases the display context for the kitchen floor window.
next	Returns the next point the turtle is to travel to.
peano	Draws a peano pattern of this size and order n.
peanoRecurse1	Provides recursion for drawing peano curves.
peanoRecurse2	" "
r	Turns the turtle right (clockwise) x degrees.
recurseKoch	Provides the recursion for the koch method.
recurseSqKoch	Provides the recursion for the sqKoch method.
right	Turns the turtle right (clockwise) x degrees.
rightRad	Turn turtle to the right in radians.
setWindow	Resets the kitchen floor window.

show	Un-hides the turtle (draws it on the screen).
sqKoch	Draws a "square" fractal Koch curve of order n.
star1	Draws a five-pointed star with no intersecting lines.
star2	Draws a star with intersecting lines.
starry	Draws n randomly sized and oriented stars.
up	Lifts the "pen" up so that the turtle will not leave a trail.

ShapesWindow

Source file:	SHAPESWI.CLS
Inherits from:	Window
Inherited by:	TrackWindow
Class Variables:	
$Native Literals	
Instance Variables:	
shapes	An array of shape types.
currentShape	The current drawn shape.
blackBrush	A black brush.
pen	The current pen object.
outline	The set shape outline rect.
Class methods:	
Object methods:	
command	Receive the command message and check the selected menu item after unchecking the old menu item.
init	Set the inital shape and brush color. Also add an "about" choice for this app to the system menu.
paint	Set the pen color and brush color for the shape, then draw it.
setup	Set up the coordinate system that the window will use when drawing. Also, set it so that the shape won't be altered when resizing occurs.

TrackWindow

Source file:	TRACKWIN.CLS
Inherits from:	ShapesWindow
Inherited by:	
Class Variables:	

$Native Literals

Instance Variables:

dragDC	The display context for drag.
pOrigin	The "shape" box origin point.
pOld	The old "shape" box end point.

Class methods:

Object methods:

beginDrag	Direct all mouse messages to this window and set the fill brush to black.
drag	Wipe out the previously drawn "shape" rectangle and draw a new one (this routine is called every time the mouse moves to a new point).
endDrag	Erase the "shape" rectangle, release the display context and send an invalidate message to the window(to cause a repaint).

DemosWindow

Source file:	DEMOSWIN.CLS
Inherits from:	TurtleArea

Instance Variables:

demos

Object methods:

addDemo	Adds a demo with the specified attributes to the demos collection.
command	Responds to command messages.
eol	Transfers eol messages sent to self to the objects in OutPorts.
init	Initializes the DemosWindow.
initDemos	Initializes the Demos list box with the appropriate choices.
recreate	Recreate method for demos window.

Chart

Source file:	CHART.CLS
Inherits from:	Object
Inherited by:	HBarChart, PieChart, VBarChart

Class Variables:

$Native Literals

Instance Variables:

data	A collection of data.
labels	Associated with data.
scale	A point for scale.
area	A point for area size.
prarea	A point for page size.
lead	A point for lead space.
space	The space between items.
brushes	Stores color table.

Class methods:

Object methods:

addData	Adds a data item.
addLabel	Adds a label item.
checkError	Gets the error number returned from a file operation and displays the appropriate error box on the screen.
draw	Draws a chart in the given display context. The area must have been set before drawing.
drawBox	Accepts a rectangle as input and will output a filled box defined by the rectangle.
drawKey	Accepts a rectangle and color index as input and will output a filled box defined by the rectangle. After a brush is created and the box has been filled, the new brush MUST be deleted and the old brush should be made active again.
drawText	Writes text to the screen when given the windows Device Context and a x,y position.
getData	Gets the data from a chart.
getLabels	Gets the labels from a chart.
init	Initializes a new chart object.
load	Reads chart data in from a file and passes it into the Chart's instance variables given the ASCII filename.
prReScale	Rescales the chart based on data and area.
reScale	Rescales the chart based on data and area. Converts the max into a real to force fractional scales to be used.
save	Saves the chart data when given an ASCII file name as the argument.
setArea	Sets the area of a chart. This must be done before drawing.

setData	Sets the data of a chart.
setLabels	Sets the labels of a chart.
size	Returns the size of the data.

HBarChart

Source file:	HBARCHAR.CLS
Inherits from:	Chart
Object methods:	
adjustPrScale	Adjusts the scale based on the data and area.
adjustScale	Adjusts the scale based on the data and area. Only uses fractional scales if < 1.
drawData	Draws the data elements for the chart in a horizontal bar format. The lead instance variable will decide where the chart starts in relation to the bottom and left side of the window. The scale instance variable adjusts the chart for window resizing.
drawLabels	Draws the labels at positions corresponding to the locations of the bars. Converts the label into a string just in case it is not one already.
getClkRgn	Takes an x/y coordinate pair and finds out what bar is being clicked on.
resetLead	Resets the lead to the proper value for this chart.
resetPrLead	Resets the lead to the proper value for this chart.
resetPrSpace	Resets the space between bars to a spacing that's appropriate for this type of chart
resetScale	Resets the scale to the proper scale for this type of chart.
resetSpace	Resets the space between bars to a spacing that's appropriate for this type of chart.

VBarChart

Source file:	VBARCHAR.CLS
Inherits from:	Chart
Inherited by:	
Class Variables:	
$Native Literals	
Instance Variables:	

Class methods:

Object methods:

adjustPrScale	Adjusts the scale based on the data and area.
adjustScale	Adjusts the scale based on the data and area. Only uses fractional scales if < 1.
drawData	Draws the data elements for the chart in a vertical bar format. The lead instance variable decides where the chart starts in relation to the top and left side of the window. The scale instance variable adjusts the chart for window resizing.
drawLabels	Draws the labels at positions corresponding to the locations of the bars. Converts the label into a string just in case it is not one already.
getClkRgn	Takes an x/y coordinate pair and finds out what bar is being clicked on.
resetLead	Resets the lead to the proper value for this chart.
resetPrLead	Resets the lead to the proper value for this chart.
resetPrSpace	Resets the space between bars to a spacing that's appropriate for this type of chart.
resetScale	Resets the scale to the proper scale for this type of chart.
resetSpace	Resets the space between bars to a spacing that's appropriate for this type of chart.

PieChart

Source file:	PIECHART.CLS
Inherits from:	Chart
Inherited by:	
Class Variables:	
$Native Literals	
Instance Variables:	
Class methods:	
Object methods:	
adjustPrScale	Adjusts the scale of the graph. This makes the pie chart 80% of the vertical area of the window.
adjustScale	Adjusts the scale of the graph. This makes the pie chart 80% of the vertical area of the window.

drawData	Draws a pie chart on the screen with it scaled to a size appropriate to the current chart settings and window size. The lead instance variable sets up the distance from the top and left at which the chart is drawn. Scale resizes the chart based on the height of the window.
drawLabels	Draws a key box and a text label for every pie color used in the chart. Converts the label into a string just in case.
getClkRgn	Takes an x/y coordinate pair and finds out what bar is being clicked on.
resetLead	Sets the space from the top and left at which the pie chart starts.
resetPrLead	Sets the space from the top and left at which the pie chart starts.
resetPrSpace	Resets the space between key bars to a spacing that's appropriate for a pie chart.
resetScale	Resets the scale to the proper scale for the type of chart.
resetSpace	Resets the space between keys based on the area. Uses a default if the area hasn't been set.

8

PROGRAMMING WITH OBJECT GRAPHICS

Although Windows 3.0 provides a strong foundation for impressive graphics applications, the construction of the rest of the edifice upon the foundation provided is left completely up to the application programmer. What this really amounts to is a tremendous need for support tools for graphics programming for the Windows environment. With the increased popularity of object-oriented tools, the need for this type of support in Windows graphics programming is at the very top of many developers' wish lists. But up to now, in the graphics area particularly, wishing was about all that serious developers could do. The Whitewater Group's Object Graphics fills both of these two important needs at once. Object-oriented graphics programming for Windows 3.0 is now possible without programmers feeling that they have launched out in virgin territory without a map or a compass.

This object-oriented graphics library demonstrates, as effectively as anything can, what the advantages and potentials are of the Actor programming environment for Windows 3.0 developers. Object Graphics was designed to provide three related types of support: rendering tools, platform filters, and graphics objects. As its accompanying demonstration program ObjectDraw amply proves, the support library is particularly aimed at applications in the object-oriented Draw and CAD (Computer Aided Design) arena. ObjectDraw is a highly usable program as is. Many users will undoubtedly find it of great value in various professional projects. And since all the source code is provided, programmers will also be prompted to use it as a launching pad for even more sophisticated graphics applications. At a later point, I will take a look at how programs like this are built in Object Graphics and discuss some obvious enhancements that can be made to it.

■ AN OVERVIEW OF OBJECT GRAPHICS

Before discussing how Object Graphics is implemented, let's go over some of the things that can be done with an object-oriented graphics library like this. As I mentioned previously, besides the tools for the graphics objects themselves, Object Graphics also provides object-oriented rendering tools and platform filters. The primary applications the library has in view are 2-D drawing, design, and CAD programs. The rendering tools in Object Graphics include things like pens, brushes, text pens, and graph spaces. And, of course, Object Graphics supports the six line styles provided in MS-Windows.

The design approach of Object Graphics uses the idea of a graphic space whose properties can be mapped onto the actual display. One of its key features is the ability to group graphics objects into larger assemblies and later ungroup them, if needed. Object Graphics also provides Picture objects that are collections of graphics objects. By providing Picture objects a protocol is established for broadcasting the rendering messages to unified assortments of graphics and text. Special classes are also supplied for auxiliary tools like horizontal and vertical rulers, polymarks, and palette windows.

The tables in this chapter are supplemental information that you may not find in other Object Graphics Programming manuals.

■ SAMPLEDRAW

One of the quickest ways to grasp the power of Object Graphics is by taking a look at the SampleDraw demo program. The SampleDraw class is a descendant class of Window, which with just three new instance variables and seven new methods implements a simple line drawing program. SampleDraw lets you produce straight lines with the mouse and make selections from the Width! or Color! menus to determine how the lines will actually look. SampleDraw uses the three instance variables: theLine, width, and rgbBox. As you might expect, theLine is used to store new line objects as they are being made by dragging the mouse. The rgbBox variable is used to store an instance of the RGBDialog class that, you may not be surprised to hear, is a dialog used to select colors based on a Red Green Blue scale of primaries (Figure 8.1). The width variable simply stores an integer that is the current value of the width of the line. Trying out SampleDraw involves just evaluating the messages:

```
S1 := defaultNew(SampleDraw, "Window for Drawing Lines");
show(S1,1);
```

SampleDraw's seven methods include: **init**, **command**, **gPaint**, **drag**, **beginDrag**, **endDrag**, and **getWidth**. These methods are of interest because versions of most of them will be necessary for almost any application written with Object Graphics. The **init** method initializes all the instance variables and objects that the SampleDraw program will utilize. This includes the port and the picture variables, as well as the dialogs and menus. The trio of mouse methods mirror the internal Actor messages triggered by mouse input by the user. The **beginDrag** message corresponds to

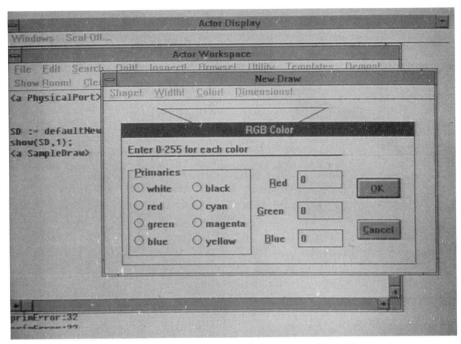

Figure 8.1 The RGB Color dialog shown in SampleDraw.

WM_LBUTTONDOWN. The **drag** message corresponds to WM_MOUSEMOVE, and **endDrag** to WM_LBUTTONUP. The **command** method contains just two case statements, both of which open dialogs that get further input for the color and shape of the line to draw. The **gPaint** method ensures that any lines that are already drawn will be redrawn when the SampleDraw window receives WM_PAINT messages.

As mentioned earlier, there are four main rendering tools in Object Graphics: pens, brushes, text pens, and graph spaces.

■ ADDING A MENU AND MORE SHAPES TO SAMPLEDRAW

What are some simple ways to extend a program like SampleDraw into something that is more useful? To experiment with adding functionality to this program, the first step is really to add a dynamic menu system to it. Once that is done then you are relatively free to experiment with adding various functions and menu options to activate them. To this end, a new **init** method has to be written, which handles the initialization of the dynamic menu system. The best way to proceed, therefore, is to create a subclass of SampleDraw called something like NewDraw.

Here is a sample init method for such a NewDraw class:

```
Def init(self)
{
port    := new(Port);
picture := new(Picture);
RGBox   := new(RGBDialog);
setCursor(self, #graphic);
width   := 0;
createMenu(self);
changeMenu(self, 0, asciiz("&Shape!"), 100, MF_APPEND);
changeMenu(self, 0, asciiz("&Width!"), 101, MF_APPEND);
changeMenu(self, 0, asciiz("&Color!"), 102, MF_APPEND);
changeMenu(self, 0, asciiz("&Dimensions!"), 103, MF_APPEND);
drawMenu(self);
}
```

Besides the original Width! and Color! menus, Shape! and Dimensions! menus have been added. It is up to you what shapes and dimensions options to put as items on this menu and how you will implement them. To see one approach to doing this, you can study how the Track! demo program was written with the Actor built-in graphics functions. With the features of Object Graphics at your disposal, there are some very interesting possibilities to explore.

To make the new menus of the draw program work, a new command method is needed too. This can be written in the following way:

```
Def command(self, wP, lP)
{ select
  case wP == 100
   getShape(self);
  endCase
  case wP == 101
   getWidth(self);
  endCase
  case wP == 102
   runModal(RGBox, RGBBOX, self);
  endCase
  case wP == 103
   runModal(DIMBox, DIMBOX, self);
  endSelect;
}
```

This sketch of the command method assumes that you will want to use the DimensionDlg class of Object Graphics to implement a dialog to use with the new Dimensions! menu. I think you will find this an interesting little laboratory to explore new ideas and see relatively quickly some results of how you have implemented your ideas. This rapid feedback made possible by creating a relatively simple exploratory environment can result in speeding up the learning process in a very noticeable way.

■ OBJECTDRAW

ObjectDraw is a far more sophisticated program than SampleDraw. It demonstrates just about every feature of the Object Graphics library extensions. Although a full understanding of the implementation of the program will require a good grasp of the concepts and issues presented in subsequent sections of the chapter, getting a good feel for some of the more basic things about the program is one of the best ways of grasping what the Object Graphics library is all about.

The main window of ObjectDraw is shown in Figure 8.2. As you can see, like most paint and draw programs, it has both a top menu bar and a palette bar or toolbox strip to the side. The graphics tools provided include: selection, zoom, line, rectangle, round rectangle, ellipse, polygon, poly line, curve, icon, bitmap cropper, and text. The File menu of ObjectDraw supports saving, loading, and printing of graphics. There is also a provision to allow you to open Windows version 2.0 format bitmaps.

Certainly the most unique part of the program is provided by the Arrange Menu. This menu allows the rearranging of the positions of objects according to a particular order.

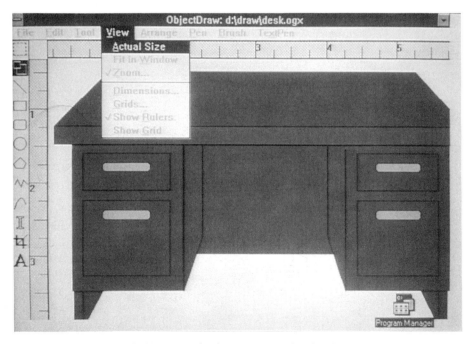

Figure 8.2 A sample drawing created with ObjectDraw.

The Bring to Front and Send to Back commands set the position of the selection in the stacking order of graphics objects. The graphics objects brought to the front will subsequently cover objects behind them, as you would expect. The Group command collects the selected objects into pictures so that they can be manipulated as a single unit. Choosing Ungroup separates all selected pictures back into individual objects once again. Finally, choosing Align to Grid will align the origins of all selected objects with the currently active grid. This should give you some idea of the unique power of the program. Now I'll attempt a quick overview of how ObjectDraw is designed.

The two key classes that are essential for understanding the ObjectDraw program are Draw and ObjectDraw, both of which are peer descendants of Window. ObjectDraw supplies the parent window for the program, and Draw supplies the large child window that displays drawings. An interesting feature of the design is that ObjectDraw is designed in such a way that each of the four child windows respond to paint messages in a different way. The ObjectDraw class handles the initialization of all child windows, including the large Draw object that forms the main graphics drawing area and also governs the control and modifying of all the rendering tools. ObjectDraw provides the basis for creating a composite object composed of the ObjectDraw master object and the various child window objects such as the Draw window, the toolbox, and the vertical and horizontal rulers.

The Draw class implements windows with the interactive drawing and refresh behavior needed for ObjectDraw. It is equipped for allowing zooming, horizontal and vertical scrolling, copy and paste with the clipboard, and interactively aligning any selected graphics objects to the sides, center, horizontal middle, and the grid. The Draw window also allows its graph space to be modified interactively.

Each time it receives a **gPaint** message, a Draw object does five things:

1. Draws a box around the world rectangle of the window's graph space to designate the page.

2. Draws the graph space's grid, if that option has been selected.

3. Draws the complete drawing image present in the window, which is stored as a collection of graphic objects in the picture instance variable.

4. Draws the marking handles of any graphics objects that are currently chosen.

5. Resets the scroll bar markers to reflect whatever the current view of the drawing might be.

The Draw window object is able to create graphic objects of different types by making use of the class name stored in ObjectDraw's tool instance variable, depending on which tool in the tool palette the user has selected. Whenever a graphics object has been selected, it is stored in the instance variable of Draw called theChosen.

The **toolBox** method of the ObjectDraw is simply written:

```
Def toolBox(self)
{
 ^tool;
}
```

It just returns the value of the tool instance variable.

The **toolBox** method is used by Draw's **beginDrag** method. The **beginDrag** method has four case statements. The default case is to execute the code:

```
theGraphic := build(toolBox(parent), aPoint, aPoint);
```

This message supplies the class of the graphics object to be drawn as an argument to the build method.

An excellent example of animation with Object Graphics is provided by the spin-Dividers method of the AboutObjGfx class.

```
Def spinDividers(self | index2)
{
 associate(port, self);
 loop
  alive(self) cand checkMessage();
 while alive(self)
 begin
  fastDraw(centerAt(frames[index], 98@153), port);
  index2 := if (index > 5) index- 6 else index+6 endif;
  fastDraw(centerAt(frames[index2], 190@153), port);
  if (index := index+1) > 11
   index := 0;
  endif;
  delay(self, 5);
 endLoop;
 dissociate(port);
}
```

/* New-style repaint message. Respond by drawing:

1. A box around the world, to look like a page.

2. If appropriate, the Window's GraphSpace's grid.

3. The Window's Picture object.

4. If appropriate, the marking handles.

```
/*
Def gPaint(self, aPort, badRect | page)
```

```
{
page := asRectangle(worldRect(space));
setPattern(brush(page), #invisible);
setPen(page, normal(Pen, primary(Color, #black)));
setCombo(pen(page), #nxor);
draw(page, aPort);
/*
setColor(pen(page), primary(Color, #blue));
setStyle(pen(page), #dot);
inflate(page,
*/
if isMenuChecked(parent, DW_GRID)
 drawGrid(aPort);
endif;
draw(picture, aPort);
draw(theMarks, aPort);

Call SetScrollPos (hWnd, SB_HORZ, left(mappingRect(space)), 1);
Call SetScrollPos (hWnd, SB_VERT,  top(mappingRect(space)), 1);
}
```

If you feel a little fuzzy about some of the things discussed in this chapter that's to be expected. Some of the concepts on which ObjectDraw is based have not yet been explained. You will find them well represented in the sections coming up. A good idea is to return to this section and reread it after you have read the rest of the chapter. At that point some of the things that were unclear to you at first will hopefully make a great deal more sense.

■ EXTENDING ACTOR

Before going any further, I should mention that Object Graphics makes some important changes to the Actor system. When the support classes are loaded, substantial modifications to the Actor Window and Printer classes are made, and it is conceivable that this will interfere with existing code. Four new instance variables are added to Windows: port, space, picture, and cursor. These are the key items involved in creating windows that support the ObjectGraphics protocols. One of the important differences introduced to the Window class is that when a window's port variable has been initialized by being assigned a port, the **gPaint** message automatically becomes operative, instead of paint, for updating the window. The most essential things are enabling the Object Graphics class library by assigning a graphic space and a port to a window. Assigning objects to the picture instance variable of Windows provides them with automatic repaint services, but it is not as essential as assigning a port and graph space to a window.

Object Graphics adds over thirty new object methods to the Window class. This might have been reason enough to create a separate graphic window class, but the intention at the Whitewater Group was clearly to make any and all windows accessible to the Object Graphics facilities. A summary of the new object methods of the Window class are provided in the reference section. As we have just seen, one of the most important of the new methods is **gPaint**, which, for graphics purposes, replaces the old **paint** method of the Window class.

■ PLATFORM FILTERS

Platform filters are intermediate layers of code that allow device-independent graphics to run in specific hardware environments. The main filter classes of Object Graphics are: Port, PhysicalPort, Bitmap, and Color. All graphics output with Object Graphics, whether for the screen or hard copy, is done through the Port and PhysicalPort classes. Any Port object has a graph space associated with it, and all drawing to the Port is done with respect to that graph space. Port is an abstract class, which is device-independent. The real interfacing to display hardware is done by the descendant of Port called PhysicalPort.

These classes are implemented in such a way that the object-oriented approach allows device independence to be taken farther than Windows itself has taken it. Although to

Table 8.1 Instance Variables of the Port Class.

theDisplay	The current association
thePen	The current Pen
theBrush	The current Brush
theTPen	The current Font
theSpace	The current GraphSpace
invRect	The current update Rect
invRegion	The current update Region
palette	The Color palette (OC)

Table 8.2 Instance Variables of the PhysicalPort Class.

hDC	The handle to Window, Printer or Bitmap to which the Port's associated
hBrush	The handle to the current brush
hPalette	The handle to current palette
stockPen	The standard platform pen
stockBrush	The standard platform brush
stockFont	The standard platform font

the programmer the code looks as though it is the Port class that is being initialized, in reality it is always an instance of PhysicalPort that is created instead. In this way, the device-specific aspects of PhysicalPort do not enter into an application's code at all.

■ COLOR

The Color class in Object Graphics is characterized by just four instance variables: red, green, blue, and physical. But it also employs a class variable $Primaries, which is actually a symbolic color dictionary with primary color symbol keys. The Color class also has an interesting set of class methods: **addSymColor**, **primary**, **read**, and **RGB**. The approach to color implemented by Object Graphics combines both the RGB primaries and the CMY (cyan magenta yellow) primaries as well as black and white as do most MS-DOS based systems.

However, the Object Graphics color system is also extensible in the sense that you are free to add new symbols and their primary value components to the color symbol dictionary. You can define a new color symbol with the **RGB** class method and use the addSymColor class method to formally add it to the color dictionary.

■ BITMAPS

Facilities for explicitly handling bitmaps in object-oriented fashion are provided by the LogBitmap, Bitmap, and HugeBitmap classes. A quick overview of some of the things these classes do can be gleaned from examining their instance variables. Naturally the messages provided with these classes are important, but only some brief descriptions will be made here. The **asBitmap** message can convert any graphics object into a corresponding Bitmap object. Objects of the Bitmap and HugeBitmap classes are the only

Table 8.3 RGB Color Component Values.

Symbol	Red	Green	Blue
#black	0	0	0
#white	255	255	255
#red	255	0	0
#green	0	255	0
#blue	0	0	255
#cyan	0	255	255
#magenta	255	0	255
#yellow	255	255	0

Table 8.4 Instance Variables of the LogBitmap Class.

height	# pixels tall
width	# pixels wide
scanBytes	scanline data size
bitsPixel	pixel data size
planes	# of color planes
clipRect	local clipping Rect
bits	image bits
brush	background Brush
color	#mono or #color
theSpace	Bitmap's GraphSpace
pen	foreground Pen

ones in the ObjectGraphics class library that are simultaneously displayable images and output devices, which graphics can be drawn on.

■ RECTANGLES

Given the central importance of rectangles in both the Windows and Object Graphics design schemes, it's not surprising that a couple of new classes are devoted to handling them. The Rectangle class supersedes the Rect class that had previously been used in Actor for graphics. The MathRect class is an idea that is new to the Object Graphics extension, that of using a separate class entirely just to keep track of the mathematical aspects of rectangles. The **asMathRect** method of the Rectangle class is designed to return an equivalent MathRect object for any Rectangle instance. Rectangles are one shape you might think that are self-explanatory. To some degree this is true, but the fact that separate objects are used for the mathematical and displayable aspects, respectively, of rectangles, does add some complications. Generally speaking, though, the handling of rectangle objects is not self-explanatory in Object Graphics simply in the sense that Rectangle and its descendants are descendants of the Shape class and must adhere to the protocol defined there. So before going any further with rectangles, we will first have to learn some things about the way shapes in general are handled.

■ SHAPES

The Shape class provides the basis for all graphic objects that can draw themselves by first outlining a series of points with a Pen object, and then filling the interior space bounded by the shape with a Brush object. Shape objects have the two new instance variables pen and brush, besides origin and corner, which are inherited from the Graphic class. Descendants of the Shape class use a drawMethod message to tell the sender what method of the PhysicalPort class to use to draw them. For example, with its **drawMethod** message, Rectangle returns the method of the PhysicalPort class used to render a rectangle, which is **drawRect**.

■ GRAPH SPACES

Graph spaces govern the following parameters: axis direction, world size, coordinate system, dimensional units, coordinate constraints to grid points, scaling, panning, and gridding. Panning is synonymous with scrolling in a graphics context. In short, graph spaces control the entire scope and degree of detail of an image that will be displayed. GraphSpace objects are composites that contain three different rectangles, all instances of the MathRect class: a world rectangle, a mapping rectangle, and a display rectangle. Unlike Rectangle objects, MathRect objects cannot be drawn to the screen. They are used for representing rectangles in their actual measurements as opposed to the sizes that will be displayed. Although a graph space defines a graphic world, this world does not actually contain graphic objects as it is defined.

A GraphSpace object is created by defining its world rectangle. The origin and corner point coordinates for the world rectangle determine both the allowed ranges and the directionality of coordinates in the space. If minus values are supplied for any of the coordinates to the world rectangle, this establishes a world in which coordinates decrease in the corresponding direction rather than increase.

All graphic objects inherit the two instance variables origin and corner from the Graphic class. These variables are used to hold the coordinates of the two points, which define any graphics object's bounding rectangle. This bounding rectangle is used as a key leveraging area for the most diverse manipulations of graphic objects.

Inspectors are particularly handy for having a look at the contents of different graphics objects. Here are some messages that create and inspect a graphics object:

Table 8.5 Instance Variables of the GraphSpace Class.

worldRect	logical world Rect
mappingRect	logical window Rect
displayRect	physical window Rect
units	unit of measure
granularity	#ticks per unit
aspectLock	true = isotropic map
zoom	Zoom Factor, percent
grid	x@y grains/grid point

```
g1 := build(Graphic, 20@20, 100@75);
Graphic<20@20 20@20>
inspect(g1);
```

In general, a uniform protocol is provided for certain operations that all graphic objects should be able to do. As is customary in true object-oriented systems, the message names are the same even when the implementations differ in various descendant classes. So, for example, any graphics object can be displayed by either the **draw** or **fastDraw** messages. Also, the **invert** message performs a color inversion on graphics objects that flips each of an object's colors into the complementary color.

■ ICONS

As the class hierarchy indicates, Icons are objects that descend from the Graphic class and so inherit all the protocol by which any graphics object can be manipulated. Anything you can do with any other graphics object you can do with an icon. Among other things, this means that, as unlikely as it may sound, even icons can be managed and manipulated by your code in a way that is independent of the hardware and software platform. The Icon class is designed so that even such display-specific things as icons can be handled by a generic coding scheme. So as with other graphic objects you can use the build and inspect messages. As you may have noticed, Icon objects have an additional instance variable called name, which is used to store the icons resource script ID. Of course, it is here that particular care must be taken to provide a scheme that will remain portable over different platforms.

■ POLYSHAPES AND POLYLINES

PolyShape objects determine their visual appearance by manipulating collections of points. PolyShape has two instances variables, vertices, which stores an Ordered-Collection of Point objects, and physical, which stores the data structure. PolyShape is an abstract or formal class used to provide the common basis for its descendants: PolyLine, Curve, and Polygon. PolyShape implements only a single new instance variable: vertices. Apart from this, it manages quite well with those it inherits from the Shape class.

PolyLines are descendants of PolyShapes that can be used to create rather complex and interesting line figures. These two groups of messages record an ongoing session with an evolving PolyLine object. The two **size** messages show the effect of the various additions.

```
PL := new(PolyLine);
setOrigin(PL,20@20);
size(PL);
0
```

```
add(PL,20@20);
add(PL,100@20);
add(PL,20@50);
size(PL);
3
```

■ CURVES

The Curve class and its descendants provide an important extension to the MS-Windows GDI engine, which, in itself, has no specific support for curves. The Curve class implements curves by mapping them onto PolyLine approximations. PolyLines and Curves are both collections of points. With PolyLine and Polygon objects collections of points are used as vertices to which straight lines are drawn. In the Curve class these point collections instead are used as control points. Control points do not necessarily lie on the curve but operate as reference points or pivots for sections of the curve. The approxPoly instance variable contains a Polygon object that forms a straight line approximation of the curve. The step instance variable defines the size of line segments to be used in this approximation. Besides Curve itself, its descendants Bezier and Cubic are also provided. The various subclasses of Curve provide alternative ways that control points affect the shape of the curve.

■ DRAWING TRIANGLES

With a library as rich as Object Graphics, there is almost always more than one way of getting a job done. Typically, there will be some advantages and trade-offs for each method. Let's take the simple example of drawing a triangle in a window (Figure 8.3). As you can probably see from the previous discussion, it should be fairly simple to draw triangles using the PolyLine class. Here are some messages for drawing a right triangle:

```
W1 := defaultNew(Window, "Drawing a Triangle: First Way");
P1 := new(Port);
show(W1,1);
setPort(W1,P1);
PL := new(PolyLine);
```

Table 8.6 Instance Variables of the Curve Class.

step	# of line segments per curve patch.
approxPoly	The Polygon that approximates the curve.
oldVertices	The last known state of the control points.

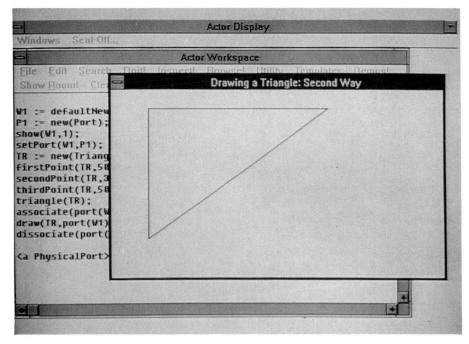

Figure 8.3 Drawing a triangle in a window (second method).

```
setOrigin(PL,50@25);
add(PL,50@25);
add(PL,300@25);
add(PL,50@200);
add(PL,50@25);
associate(port(W1),W1);
draw(PL,port(W1));
dissociate(port(W1));
```

To provide a more routine way of drawing triangles, we might want to create a separate Triangle class as a direct descendant of PolyLine, with instance variables point1, point2, and point3. To make it work, we would then add the five following methods:

```
/* sets the first point */
Def firstPoint(self,aPoint)
{
 point1 := aPoint;
}

/* sets the second point */
Def secondPoint(self,aPoint)
```

```
{
  point2 := aPoint;
}

/* sets the third point */
Def thirdPoint(self,aPoint)
{
  point3 := aPoint;
}

/* adds the 3 points to a Polyline and returns to the origin */
Def triangle(self)
{
  add(self, point1);
  add(self, point2);
  add(self, point3);
  add(self, point1);
}

/* prescribes the drawing method to use */
Def drawMethod(self)
{
  ^#drawPolyLine
}
```

The messages using the Triangle class to draw the same right triangle are then:

```
W1 := defaultNew(Window, "Drawing a Triangle: Second Way");
P1 := new(Port);
show(W1,1);
setPort(W1,P1);
TR := new(Triangle);
firstPoint(TR,50@25);
secondPoint(TR,300@25);
thirdPoint(TR,50@200);
triangle(TR);
associate(port(W1),W1);
draw(TR,port(W1));
dissociate(port(W1));
```

A sixth method for Triangle will gather all the steps into one, so that triangles can be specified in one message.

```
Def createTriangle(self,aPoint1,aPoint2,aPoint3)
{
```

```
point1 := aPoint1;
point2 := aPoint2;
point3 := aPoint3;
triangle(self);
}

W1 := defaultNew(Window, "Drawing a Triangle: Third Way");
P1 := new(Port);
show(W1,1);
setPort(W1,P1);
TR := new(Triangle);
createTriangle(TR,50@25,300@25,50@200);
associate(port(W1),W1);
draw(TR,port(W1));
dissociate(port(W1));
```

If necessary, a special TriangleWindow class could be built with an automatic dialog that asks for the points of a new triangle as soon as the window opens. The code would all be contained in its init method, so that creating it would involve only writing the two messages:

```
TW := defaultNew(TriangleWindow, "Drawing a Triangle");
show(TW,1);
```

The same strategy can be used for drawing parallelograms. Listing . . . provides the sample code for a first attempt at defining a parallelogram class.

```
/***********************/!!
/* The Parallelogram class file */!!
/*          First Version      */!!
/***********************/!!

inherit(PolyLine, #Parallelogram, #(origin corner originAngle secondAngle pen
brush side1 side2), 2, nil)!!

now(class(Parallelogram))!!

now(Parallelogram)!!

/* set the origin point */
Def setOrigin(self,aPoint)
{

    add(self,aPoint);
```

```
}
!!

/* set the rest of the points */
Def setPoints(self)
{
secondPoint(self);
thirdPoint(self);
fourthPoint(self);
endPoint(self)

}!!

/* return the angle at the origin */
Def originAngle(self)
{
 originAngle
}!!

/* return the complementary angle */
Def secondAngle(self)
{
 ^secondAngle
}!!

/* return the first side */
Def side1(self)
{
 ^side1
}!!

/* return the second side */
Def side2(self)
{
 ^side2
}!!

/* set the point to return to */
Def endPoint(self)
{

add(self,at(vertices(self),0));

}!!
```

```
/* set the fourth point */
Def fourthPoint(self)
{

add(self,point(x(at(vertices(self),0))
 - (side2(self) * cos(degToRad(secondAngle))),
  y(at(vertices(self),2))));

}!!

/* set the third point */
Def thirdPoint(self)
{
add(self,point(x(at(vertices(self),1))
  - side2(self) * cos(degToRad(secondAngle)),
  side2(self) * sin(degToRad(secondAngle))
  + y(at(vertices(self),1))));
}!!

/* set the second point */
Def secondPoint(self)
{
add(self,point(side1 + x(at(vertices(self),0)), y(at(vertices(self),0)) ));
}!!

/* set the angles */
Def setAngles(self, a1)
{
originAngle := a1;
secondAngle := 180 - a1;
}!!

/* set the sides */
Def setSides(self,s1,s2)
{
side1 := s1;
side2 := s2;
}!!

/* the draw method of the PhysicalPort class to use */
Def drawMethod(self)
{
 ^#drawPolyLine
}!!
```

As you will see, if you try out this implementation of the Parallelogram class, it is frankly not the most desirable approach to solving this problem. Although conceptually right, the trigonometric routines make the drawings far too sensitive to the initial parameters for this method to be satisfactory. What adds difficulty to the problem is the constraint of being able to define any parallelogram from just the two sides and an angle. To make this program more accurate and efficient various techniques can be applied, such as the use of trig tables. Readers are invited to experiment with methods that can preserve the generic design while providing the needed improvement in accuracy and performance in the trig calculations.

■ PICTURES

The Picture class extends behaviors and protocols for graphic objects to collections of graphic objects. It does this through the elements instance variable, which holds OrderedCollection objects. These graphic collections are nestable, and one of the keys to developing powerful interactive object-oriented graphics applications is learning to manipulate these collections of graphic objects adroitly and efficiently. A version of the asBitmap message can transform entire collections of graphic objects into Bitmap objects.

If a **draw** message is sent to a Picture object, draw messages are then broadcast to each of the graphics objects in its collection.

```
pic1 := new(Picture);
Picture<0@0 0@0>
```

Picture objects follow the standard eleven message protocols for OrderedCollections, which include: **add**, **insert**, **put**, **at**, **find**, **first**, **last**, **remove**, **collect**, **do**, and **extract** messages.

■ REGIONS

Objects of the Region class have a variety of uses, including hit testing, clipping, and motion feedback. The **boundsRegion** method of the Graphic class, which creates and returns a Region object, is defined simply:

```
Def boundsRegion(self | aRgn)
{
  add(aRgn := new(Region), self);
  ^aRgn;
}
```

Unfortunately, WinPolygon objects cannot be collected in Picture objects because they are not descendants of the Graphic class. Only objects that descend from Graphic can be added to a Picture object.

Table 8.7 Instance Variables of the Pen Class.

width	pen width
color	Color object
style	Symbolic line style
combo	Symbolic combine mode
transparent	gap-fill boolean

Table 8.8 Instance Variables of the TextPen Class.

color	text Color
backColor	background Color
style	font facing Symbols
height	in world units
font	font Symbol
combo	combo mode Symbol
transparent	transparency Symbol
dirty	A boolean flag that tells if a size-affecting attribute has changed

RichText objects are specialized descendants of Pictures that restrict the members of their collections to Label objects and other RichText objects.

■ PALETTES

The Palette class is simply a general mechanism for constructing panels of iconic buttons like a toolbox or a color palette. It utilizes two class variables, $Maps, to store the names of the iconic buttons, and $IDs to store their ID numbers.

```
$Maps := #("chooser", "zoomer", "line", "rect", "roundRect",
        "circle", "polygon", "polyline", "curve", "icon",
        "cropper", "text");
```

The beginDrag method of the Palette class illustrates accessing the picture instance variable.

```
Def beginDrag (self, wP, aPoint)
{
if selectTool(self, contains(picture, aPoint))
  command(parent, $IDs[find(picture, selectedTool)], 0L);
```

```
    endif;
}
```

■ GROUPINGS

One of the most useful and powerful things in the Object Graphics library is its support for the interactive grouping and ungrouping of graphics objects. This is handled by the **groupChoice** and **unGroupChoice** methods of Draw. The **groupChoice** method is defined:

```
Def groupChoice(self)
{
 add(picture, theChosen);
 do(theChosen,
  {using(aGraphic)
   remove(picture, aGraphic);
  });
 updateChoice(self);
}
```

On the other hand, the definition of **unGroupChoice** is:

```
Def unGroupChoice(self)
{
 do(theChosen,
  {using(aGraphic)
   if isAncestor(class(aGraphic), Picture)
    remove(picture, aGraphic);
    do(aGraphic,
    {using(element)
     add(picture, element);
    });
   endif;
  });
 updateChoice(self);
}
```

```
    start(new(ObjectDraw));
```

In ObjectDraw, the DimensionDlg object is used to allow the user to set the main parameters of a drawing's graph space. You can choose measurement units, set a parameter for granularity, and specify the width and height of the page size of the graph space. The **sizeKids** method of the ObjectDraw class utilizes the statement:

```
    setCRect(toolBox, rect(0, 0, 25, bottom(cRect)));
```

setCRect is a method inherited from the WindowsObject class that sets a window's sizing rectangle to the specified rectangle size. The cRect argument to the bottom message is an instance variable also inherited from WindowsObject.

Table 8.9 Instance Variables of the Draw Class.

theGraphic	object while dragged
thePoly	PolyShape while dragged
theChosen	selected graphics Pic
theMarks	marker handle PolyMark
startStop	timer state
editor	Text editor for labels
clipRect	Used for Bitmap crop
fName	File name String
startPt	drag chosen from here
marker	Graphic used to mark selections

Table 8.10 Instance Variables of the ObjectDraw Class.

display	Draw object
hRuler	horizontal ruler window
vRuler	vertical ruler window
toolBox	graphical palette
tool	Current Tool
colorDlg	RGB dialog
dimDlg	dimensionDlg
thePen	defaulting Pen
theBrush	defaulting Brush
theTPen	defaulting TextPen
fileDlg	file open dialog

```
$Colors := static(%Dictionary(
        810->#black    811->#white
        812->#red      813->#green
        814->#blue     815->#cyan
        816->#magenta  817->#yellow));



$BrushStyles := static(%Dictionary(
        761->#solid    762->#invisible
        763->#ten      764->#fifteen
```

```
765->#thirty    766->#fifty
767->#seventy   768->#eighty5
769->#vertical  770->#horizontal
771->#diagonal  772->#hatch
773->#pebble    774->#brick));!!


colorBox := newChild(Palette,   1040, self, nil);


cbBrush := new(Brush);
colors := new(Picture);
patterns := new(Picture);
```

■ APPLYING RENDERING TOOLS

Using the rendering tools to draw graphics in a window is relatively straightforward. A port must be initialized as well as pens, and brushes and colors must be selected. A pen must be explicitly set in a port. Once these preparations are made, any supported graphic object can be drawn. Below are two examples of using the Object graphics rendering tools to draw a rectangle in a window. The second example illustrates the use of Brush objects.

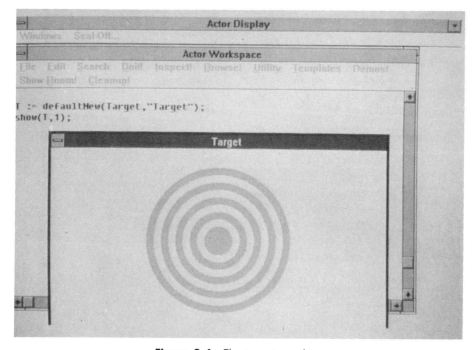

Figure 8.4 The target graphic.

```
W1 := defaultNew(Window, "Graphics Drawing");
P1 := new(Port);
setPort(W1,P1);
p1 := new(Pen);
setColor(p1,primary(Color,#red));
setPen(port(W1),p1);
show(W1,1);
R1 := new(Rectangle);
setOrigin(R1,120@20);
setCorner(R1,200@100);
associate(port(W1),W1);
draw(R1,port(W1));
dissociate(port(W1));
```

```
W1 := defaultNew(Window, "Graphics Drawing");
P1 := new(Port);
setPort(W1,P1);
show(W1,1);
R1 := new(Rectangle);
setOrigin(R1,120@20);
setCorner(R1,200@100);
B1 := new(Brush);
setBrush(R1,B1);
setColor(brush(R1), RGB(Color,255, 0, 0));
associate(port(W1),W1);
draw(R1,port(W1));
dissociate(port(W1));
```

The rest of this section explores various ways of producing the same graphic result with increasingly less code, passing, if you like, from the nearly ridiculous to the nearly sublime. The problem we will be addressing is the apparently simple task of drawing a target from scratch, much in appearance like the sort of target you might see at an archery range. The first version of the Target program will be done by sheer brute force in all its cumbersome, verbose glory (Figure 8.4). All of the action takes place in the init method of the TargetWindow class:

```
/* initialize an instance of the Target class by brute force */

Def init(self)
{
  port := new(Port);
```

```
picture1 := build(Ellipse, 0@0, 200@200);
picture2 := build(Ellipse, 0@0, 180@180);
picture3 := build(Ellipse, 0@0, 160@160);
picture4 := build(Ellipse, 0@0, 140@140);
picture5 := build(Ellipse, 0@0, 120@120);
picture6 := build(Ellipse, 0@0, 100@100);
picture7 := build(Ellipse, 0@0, 80@80);
picture8 := build(Ellipse, 0@0, 60@60);
picture9:= build(Ellipse, 0@0, 40@40);
setColor(brush(picture1),primary(Color, #red));
setStyle(pen(picture1), #invisible);
setColor(brush(picture2),primary(Color, #white));
setStyle(pen(picture2), #invisible);
setColor(brush(picture3),primary(Color, #red));
setStyle(pen(picture3), #invisible);
setColor(brush(picture4),primary(Color, #white));
setStyle(pen(picture4), #invisible);
setColor(brush(picture5),primary(Color, #red));
setStyle(pen(picture5), #invisible);
setColor(brush(picture6),primary(Color, #white));
setStyle(pen(picture6), #invisible);
setColor(brush(picture7),primary(Color, #red));
setStyle(pen(picture7), #invisible);
setColor(brush(picture8),primary(Color, #white));
setStyle(pen(picture8), #invisible);
setColor(brush(picture9),primary(Color, #red));
setStyle(pen(picture9), #invisible);
setCursor(self, #finger);
^self
}
```

To ensure the target is repainted when anything happens to the window, we write the following **gPaint** method:

```
/* repaint the objects in the window */
Def gPaint(self,aPort, invalidRect | bullsEye )
{
bullsEye := point(right(displayRect(self))/2,bottom(displayRect(self))/2);
centerAt(picture, bullsEye);
centerAt(picture2, bullsEye);
centerAt(picture3, bullsEye);
centerAt(picture4, bullsEye);
centerAt(picture5, bullsEye);
centerAt(picture6, bullsEye);
centerAt(picture7, bullsEye);
```

```
    centerAt(picture8, bullsEye);
    centerAt(picture9, bullsEye);
    draw(picture,  aPort);
    draw(picture2, aPort);
    draw(picture3, aPort);
    draw(picture4, aPort);
    draw(picture5, aPort);
    draw(picture6, aPort);
    draw(picture7, aPort);
    draw(picture8, aPort);
    draw(picture9, aPort);
}
```

It can safely be said that, while this program works, it is not at all the best way to do the job. But in the course of improving on the program we will discover some of the powerful capabilities of the Picture class and the most efficient ways of utilizing it.

In the next version, the picture instance variable is initialized, and various images are added to the picture by using **build** messages for ellipses embedded within **add** messages:

```
/* initialize the Target instance */
Def init(self)
{
port := new(Port);
picture :=  build(Picture, 40@40);
add(picture, build(Ellipse, 0@0, 200@200));
add(picture, build(Ellipse, 0@0, 180@180));
add(picture, build(Ellipse, 0@0, 160@160));
add(picture, build(Ellipse, 0@0, 140@140));
add(picture, build(Ellipse, 0@0, 120@120));
add(picture, build(Ellipse, 0@0, 100@100));
add(picture, build(Ellipse, 0@0, 80@80));
add(picture, build(Ellipse, 0@0, 60@60));
add(picture, build(Ellipse, 0@0, 40@40));

setColor(brush(at(picture,0)),primary(Color, #red));
setStyle(pen(at(picture,0)), #invisible);
setColor(brush(at(picture,1)),primary(Color, #white));
setStyle(pen(at(picture,1)), #invisible);
setColor(brush(at(picture,2)),primary(Color, #red));
setStyle(pen(at(picture,2)), #invisible);
setColor(brush(at(picture,3)),primary(Color, #white));
setStyle(pen(at(picture,3)), #invisible);
setColor(brush(at(picture,4)),primary(Color, #red));
setStyle(pen(at(picture,4)), #invisible);
```

```
        setColor(brush(at(picture,5)),primary(Color, #white));
        setStyle(pen(at(picture,5)), #invisible);
        setColor(brush(at(picture,6)),primary(Color, #red));
        setStyle(pen(at(picture,6)), #invisible);
        setColor(brush(at(picture,7)),primary(Color, #white));
        setStyle(pen(at(picture,7)), #invisible);
        setColor(brush(at(picture,8)),primary(Color, #red));
        setStyle(pen(at(picture,8)), #invisible);
        setCursor(self, #finger);
        ^self
    }


    Def gPaint(self,aPort, invalidRect | bullsEye )
    {
      bullsEye := point(right(displayRect(self))/2,bottom(displayRect(self))/2);
      alignCenter(picture, bullsEye);
      draw(picture, aPort);
    }
```

The final version compresses the amount of code still further by using a couple of iteration loops rather than setting up all the rendering tools by brute force.

```
    /*  initialize the Target instance */
    Def init(self | i j)
    {
    port := new(Port);
    picture :=  build(Picture, 40@40);
    add(picture, build(Ellipse, 0@0, 200@200));
    add(picture, build(Ellipse, 0@0, 180@180));
    add(picture, build(Ellipse, 0@0, 160@160));
    add(picture, build(Ellipse, 0@0, 140@140));
    add(picture, build(Ellipse, 0@0, 120@120));
    add(picture, build(Ellipse, 0@0, 100@100));
    add(picture, build(Ellipse, 0@0, 80@80));
    add(picture, build(Ellipse, 0@0, 60@60));
    add(picture, build(Ellipse, 0@0, 40@40));

    { i := 0;
    loop
    while i < 9
     setColor(brush(at(picture,i)),primary(Color, #red));
     i := i + 2;
    endLoop;
    };
```

```
{ j := 1;
loop
while j < 9
 setColor(brush(at(picture,j)),primary(Color, #red));
 j := j + 2;
endLoop;
};

do(picture,
 {using(pic) setStyle(pen(at(picture,pic)), #invisible)});

setCursor(self, #finger);
 ^self
}
```

■ POLYMARKS

Object Graphics provides a class called PolyMark that is used for creating objects that can be seen in a window but will not be part of the final picture (Figure 8.5). PolyMarks are composite objects composed of collections of small marker rectangles, circles, or

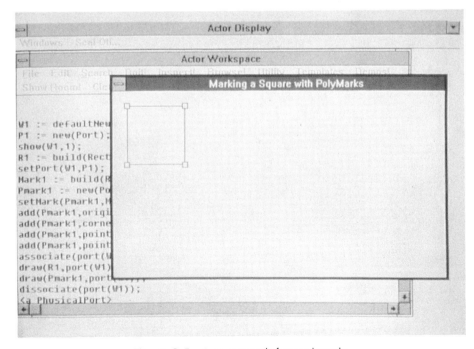

Figure 8.5 A square with four polymarks.

other graphics that are used to mark the boundaries of other graphics objects. PolyMark is designed to make use of other graphics that are created in the standard way and multiply them as needed and depict them at the vertices of graphics objects. Several of the methods of Polymark are class methods. A class variable called $StdSize is also used. This means that at any given time, only one standard size for all PolyMarks is used. The **standardMark** message is used to retrieve the dimensions of the standard marker object, measured in pixels.

The following example demonstrates drawing a square and then marking each of the vertices of the square with a square marker:

```
W1 := defaultNew(Window, "Marking a Square with PolyMarks");
P1 := new(Port);
show(W1,1);
R1 := build(Rectangle, 20@20,100@100);
setPort(W1,P1);
Mark1 := build(Rectangle, 20@20, standardMark(PolyMark));
Pmark1 := new(PolyMark);
setMark(Pmark1,Mark1);
add(Pmark1,origin(R1));
add(Pmark1,corner(R1));
add(Pmark1,point(left(R1),bottom(R1)));
add(Pmark1,point(right(R1),top(R1)));
associate(port(W1),W1);
draw(R1,port(W1));
draw(Pmark1,port(W1));
dissociate(port(W1));
```

■ OBJECT GRAPHICS CLASS HIERARCHY

Object

GraphSpace	Encapsulates axis direction, world size and dimensional units, and coordinate constraint to grid points. GraphSpaces can convert between their own logical, their associated window's offset physical, and true physical coordinates.
Pen	Implements logical pen for drawing both text and graphics.
TextPen	Specializes the Pen Class for the purpose of drawing text.
Brush	Implements logical graphics brushes, used to fill Shape objects. Brushes bundle diverse attributes of lines.

Color	Implements a platform-independent color specification standard, which is a variation of the common RGB color model. Each of the three primaries is represented by an integer in the range of (0–255).
IndexColor	Allows colors to be specified as an index into whatever Color palette is installed in the Port when the color is used.
Graphic	The Formal class that unites all objects capable of drawing themselves, given a Port as an argument.
Icon	Implements drawable Icons.
LogBitmap	Implements the platform-independent portions of bitmap behavior.
Bitmap	Implements the platform-specific portions of ObjectGraphics Bitmap behavior.
HugeBitmap	Supports bitmaps larger than 16K in size.
Shape	Unites all Graphics that draw themselves by outlining (framing) with a Pen object and then filling with a Brush object.
Picture	Contains a collection of depth-ordered Graphics. It fully supports OrderedCollection's protocol, as well as Pen and Brush defaulting.
PolyMark	Devices used for marking the corners or vertices of other graphics.
Region	Implements Regions as a collection of closed graphics.
RichText	Implements collections of attributed text Labels.
Rectangle	Implements objects of the Rectangle Shape.
Chooser	Implements interactive selection behavior.
MathRect	Used for mathematical manipulations rather than drawing. Since these objects don't create or use a Pen or Brush, they fastDraw whether draw or fastDraw messages are sent to them.
RoundRect	Implements round-cornered Rectangles of fixed curvature.
PolyShape	Unites all Shapes, which are defined by a collection of Points.
Curve	Unites all the ObjectGraphics curves.
Bezier	Creates and draws a Bezier Parametric Cubic Curve.
Cubic	Creates and draws a Parametric Cubic Curve.

Picture	Contains a collection of depth-ordered Graphics. It fully supports OrderedCollection's protocol, as well as Pen and Brush defaulting.
Region	Implements Regions as a collection of closed graphics.
RichText	Implements collections of attributed text Labels.
Port	Encapsulates display behavior across windowing environments.
PhysicalPort	Implements the windowing platform-specific portion of the Port-PhysicalPort partnership for MS-Windows.

■ OBJECT GRAPHICS WINDOW CLASS EXTENSIONS

Object methods:

attachPort	Each Output Device implements the attachPort method, which, in cooperation with PhysicalPort:associate, prepares it to be drawn to. (See Bitmap:attachPort and Printer:attachPort.)
setResolution	Sets the GraphSpace environment resolution to reflect the printer represented by the given display context.
newWClass	Creates a new window class Struct. Symbolic cursor switching requires a zero at offset 14, indicating a null cursor.
checkMenuGroup	Clears checkmarks from the portion of the menu defined by the low and high IDs. Then, checks menuID.
create	Creates a window in MS-Windows according to parameters specified in the arguments. The style argument determines new window style.
detachPort	Releases the display context for self when a Port frees the Window from service. This message is part of the common Output Device protocol shared by Window, Bitmap, and Printer.
isMenuChecked	Determines whether the specified menu item is checked.
displayRect	Returns the Window's area Rectangle. This method is part of the common Output Device protocol shared by Windows, Printers, and Bitmaps.
getCursorPos	Gets the cursor's current position, in world coordinates.
hideCursor	Hides the cursor.

setCursorPos	Resets the cursor's position (world coordinates) to the one supplied.
fenceCursor	Constrains cursor movement to the supplied Rectangle (world coordinates).
free	Allows a formerly constrained cursor the freedom of the entire screen.
gPaint	New-style repaint message. aPort is a Port that has been associated with self for painting. badRect defines the currently invalid rectangle that requires update. ObjectGraphics will automatically reject attempts to draw time-critical graphics outside badRect. Use badRect if you wish to limit unnecessary drawing even further.
greyMenuGroup	Greys (and disables) the portion of the menu defined by the low and high IDs.
modMenuGroup	Applies the method, specified in modifier, to the portion of the menu defined by the low and high IDs.
physicalOffset	Returns the coordinates of the upper-left corner where printing or drawing will begin on the page. A Window, unlike a Printer, has no physical offset.
picture	Returns the Window's Picture object.
port	Returns the Window's Port object.
scroll	Calls on the services of the Window's Port to adjust both the Window's and Port's GraphSpaces. This method is part of the common Output Device protocol.
setBackColor	Changes the background color, of all windows of a given MS-Windows class, to the supplied Color. If color is nil, the Windows' backgrounds will not be painted during WM_ERASEBKGND messages. Currently open class members will reflect the change only after invalidation.
setCursor	Resets the Window's cursor to the one supplied.
showCursor	Shows the cursor.
space	Returns the Window's GraphSpace object. Formal behavior gives a fresh Space to the requestor if none was found in IVar space. Descendants may redefine to select from multiple spaces, build custom spaces at run time, etc.
toggleMenuItem	Toggles the checkmark of the menu entry identified by menuID.

unGreyMenuGroup	Un-Greys (and enables) the portion of the menu defined by the low and high IDs.
wait	Initiates a wait for a lengthy operation.
endWait	Ends a wait for a lengthy operation.
setSpace	Sets the Window's GraphSpace.
setPicture	Sets the picture IVar to the supplied Picture.
setPort	Sets the Window's Port object. Initializing a Window's port IVar tells Actor to allow it access to ObjectGraphics facilities.

9

A SAMPLE WINDOWS 3.0 APPLICATION

This chapter describes some very prevalent issues and problems all graphic user interface (GUI) developers must face and shows how object-oriented techniques can be a major help in addressing them. Although the GUI used is Windows 3.0 and the language Actor, many of the techniques described are valid for any object-oriented GUI. I decided to put the object-oriented approach to a test in the Windows 3.0 environment by writing a program that I would find useful myself, which would give me both multidocument editing and "executive control" over all development and user applications—and all in a single main window. The program that resulted is therefore called Executive Control. It is a master controller/editor used specifically in the Windows 3.0 environment. Although this type of application seems reasonable from a user's viewpoint, the convenience derived from packing so much power in one place can be a logistical nightmare for the GUI programmer.

■ EXECUTIVE CONTROL: A BRIEF OVERVIEW

As is sometimes the case with the current generation of GUIs, along with all its advantages, the Windows environment has its cumbersome quirks and inconveniences too. More than likely the average Windows user and programmer ends up feeling that it would be rather nice if somehow you could access most of the things you want to do from a single place. Just how much can be successfully packed into a single command window, without it getting forced and cluttered? That's the question I set out to answer with this program. My discovery was that, using an object-oriented approach, techniques were available to allow a programmer to rather quickly put together a program that has a single main window, which can handle most of the things a user/developer typically does during a Windows session, without the rather huge amount of menus and commands turning into an incomprehensible nightmare of complexities and overhead.

But I should make clear that this is not just a program to answer a question. It is a program that I use myself and that I wrote because I wanted to make life easier. What you have here in the listings is a useful working prototype of a program that will also have a commercial version. As is, it is extremely easy to customize it for your own system and to extend it as you like.

The Executive Control program provided here is especially designed for fulfilling the needs of those who are both users and developers of Windows applications. It utilizes the Windows Multiple Document Interface (MDI) to create a control window that can instantly execute numerous programs in the Windows environment from its menu system as well as provide all the expected facilities for multidocument editing. I found it relatively straightforward to write it using the Actor object-oriented programming environment.

Figure 9.1 shows the main menu bar for the Executive Control program.

In this user interface design I only had to use one hierarchical popup menu assembly. As you can see, there is plenty of room to put more choices here as well as room for additional hierarchical popups too. In spite of all that can be done from this one main

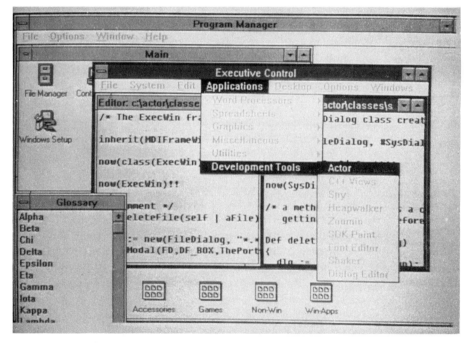

Figure 9.1 The Executive Control Main Window showing two documents in adjacent child windows, the Glossary Window and the Applications/Development Tools submenu.

menu bar, if necessary more could still be added without any real clutter. No attempt was made to enlarge the client area of the main frame window because there has been no need to. It can be increased quite a bit if the need arises.

The Desktop popup menu allows you to execute any Windows desktop accessory just by clicking its name on the menu. The Applications menu is a hierarchical popup menu system that rather easily lets you access applications by category. The Development tools branch, for example, provides instant access to the Windows SDK tool set.

The Executive Control application is built with three surprisingly simple derived classes: ExecApp, a subclass of the Application class; ExecWin, a subclass of the MDIFrameWindow class; and SysDialog, a specialization of the FileDialog class. In an object-oriented GUI, much of the battle is won by finding the right classes to use or create. In this case, it turned out that the most efficient approach was to create a few new subclasses where some key methods could be overridden by supplying alternative ways of doing things. Although at first it might seem like looking for a needle in a haystack, when the right solution is found it is usually quite clear why it is the best or at least a very good answer to the design problem.

The tool used was Actor 3.0, an interactive object-oriented programming (OOP) system that behaves like Smalltalk while using a syntax like C. Since Actor 3.0 allows you to call any Windows function interactively, it's a superb laboratory for exploring all Windows 3.0 features.

The only thing previously holding Actor back was memory capacity. Now that you can use multiple megabytes under the 386 Enhanced Mode of Windows this is no longer a problem. The main advantages of Actor as I see it are four: 1) the syntax is similar to C, 2) it is object-oriented, 3) it is interactive, and 4) it has a large class library for Windows all ready to use.

▪ MULTIPLE-DOCUMENT INTERFACE (MDI)

The MDI is one of the most attractive new aspects of Windows 3.0. However, taming some of the complex interactions between the controls of the frame window and the optional number of child windows that a user can open can be a real bear both at the design and the debugging stages. But, as it turns out, this is just the sort of problem that object-oriented systems excel at solving.

▪ ACTOR MDI SUPPORT

Actor is shipped with a set of classes that provide full support for the Windows 3.0 MDI standard. As its name indicates, the MDIFrameWindow class is used for creating MDI Frame Windows. It redirects the appropriate Windows messages to its own procedures and keeps track of the child windows that it contains. In order to create an application specific MDI Frame window you usually only need to create a descendant of this class that contains an appropriate command method. Whenever processing a message that creates a new MDI Child window the processMenu method is called with the desired caption so that the "Windows" menu in your frame window will have a correct list of its children.

The MDIFileWindow class is a descendant of MDIFrameWindow that is designed to handle command message processing, which supports the use of MDI with FileWindow objects. The MDIChild class contains the modifcations needed to allow a window to function as an MDI Child window. Those parts of MDI applications intended for use as child windows should be descendants of it. To use MDIChild with existing code you either make a copy of it and make it descend from your child window class, or make your class descend from MDIChild.

The FileChildMDI class is a descendant of the FileWindow class that has the necessary facilities enabling it to be used in an MDI application. The MDIClient class handles the creation and maintenance of an MDI Client window. An MDI Client must be created with an MDIFrameWindow as its parent and is automatically destroyed by the MDIFrameWindow's default window procedure on closing. Finally, there is FileApp. This is a simple class that contains all the necessary methods for initializing a finished MDI File Window program. It is used to seal off the MDIFileWindow classes and create a stand-alone application. It defines the main window that initializes all the others. These, then, are the basic classes that define Actor's MDI support. Let's look at some of the relevant details of their implementation.

■ MDIFRAMEWINDOW

As is quite common, the instance variables of MDIFrameWindow provide the key to understanding how this subclass of Window does its work. They are listed for your convenience in Table 9.1.

The clientWindow variable stores the instance of the MDIClient class associated with the main frame window. An instance of the Dictionary class is stored in the childList variable to keep tally of the currently open child windows. Another instance variable stores the handle of the currently active child so that the focus of control is unambiguous. The windowMenu instance variable is used to store the dynamic menu item "Window," which provides various options for rearranging child windows.

Table 9.1 Instance Variables of MDIFrameWindow.

clientWindow	points to client window space
childList	dictionary of children
activeHWnd	keep track of active child
childClass	keep track of child class type
windowMenu	keep "Window" menu

▪ MDIFILEWINDOW

An application specific command method must be created for each MDI application so that it knows how to handle creation of a new MDI child. Once the MDI child is created there should be no problems in passing command statements on to the child windows command method.

The portion of the command processing concerned with child windows in the Executive Control program is localized in the childCommand method, which is defined as follows:

```
Def childCommand(self,wP,lP)
{
 if (wP == FILE_OPEN) or (wP == FILE_NEW)
 then createMDIChild(self, childClass, "(Untitled)", nil);
 command(childList[activeHWnd], wP, lP);
 processMenu(self, getText(childList[activeHWnd]));
 else if childList[activeHWnd]
 command(childList[activeHWnd], wP, lP);
 endif;
 endif;
 execWindowProc(self:ancestor, #WM_COMMAND, wP, lP);

}


Def init(self, cmdLine | dlg fName)
{ init(self:ancestor, cmdLine);
 mainWindow := newMain(MDIFileWindow, "FileEditMenu", "File Editor", nil);
 setClassType(mainWindow, #FileChildMDI);
 show(mainWindow, CmdShow);
}
```

The FileApp class provides a way that an MDI editor can be created and used, either in the Actor environment or as a stand-alone application. The messages for creating it are just:

```
F := new(FileApp);
init(F, nil);
```

There is a problem, though, if the goal is to create a stand-alone application, or even one that can operate in the Actor environment whose window can stay open when the main Actor Display window closes. The window created by FileApp is not a main window such as the type created with the newMain message in Actor. Sending the message:

```
F := newMain(FileApp);
```

produces an error because of the way this class's initialization is designed.

An alternative might be to initialize the MDIFrameWindow object directly. The following works:

```
W1 := newMain(MDIFrameWindow,"editmenu","K",nil);
show(W1,1);
```

That is, it succeeds in creating an MDI main window. However, the edit menu is the standard one and has no provision for file operations. And, of course, without that there is no real MDI. Even after the appropriate menu system has been defined, it will not work until the right command method is written to handle the menu commands, rather than modifying the command method. The Executive Control program was designed to solve these and other problems in providing a stand-alone MDI application with a truly massive assembly of menus.

■ MDI CLASS HIERARCHY

As mentioned, the Executive Control (Figure 9.1) application is built with three rather simple derived classes: ExecApp, a subclass of the Application class; ExecWin, a subclass of the MDIFrameWindow class; and SysDialog, a descendant of the FileDialog class. The relevant branch of the Actor class hierarchy with the new classes in place looks like this:

Object
  Application
    ExecApp
  WindowsObject
    Control
    MDIClient
    Dialog
      FileDialog
        SysDialog
    Window
    MDIChild
    MDIFrameWindow
      ExecWin
    TextWindow
      EditWindow
        WorkEdit
          FileWindow
        FileChildMDI

Evaluating these messages opens an Exec Control main window:

```
EW := new(ExecApp);
init(EW, nil);
```

The important new application specific methods are the init method of the ExecApp class and the command method of the ExecWin class. The main window utilizes the "ExecMenu" compiled menu resource, which is defined in Listing 1.

Hierarchical menus are created simply by nesting POPUP statements. The main routine of the ExecWin's command method reads:

```
if (wP == FILE_OPEN) or (wP == FILE_NEW)
then createMDIChild(self, childClass, "(Untitled)", nil);
  command(childList[activeHWnd], wP, lP);
  processMenu(self, getText(childList[activeHWnd]));
else
    if childList[activeHWnd]
    command(childList[activeHWnd], wP, lP);
    endif;
endif;
execWindowProc(self:ancestor, WM_COMMAND, wP, lP);
```

What is happening is that the wP parameter of the WM_COMMAND message is being tested so that clicking on a File Open menu item sends the createMDIChild message that creates a new open file as a child window, which is an instance of the MDIChild class (Figure 9.2). The imbedded childList message is used to broadcast menu commands to any open child windows.

The nested conditional:

```
else
    if childList[activeHWnd]
    command(childList[activeHWnd], wP, lP);
    endif;
```

is to test if any children exist before sending any command messages to them. The rest of the command method is the proverbial case statement litany that is common in Windows programs. With Executive Control, there are so many menu commands that it was physically necessary to partition the command method into different command modules. It was the only way they could be compiled. But it turns out that there are good reasons for partitioning the command method in any cases, as we'll see.

■ HANDLING LARGE COMPLEX MENU SYSTEMS

There are important things to consider at two different design levels for getting the most for the least in a user interface design. First of all there is the layout of the menu bar. Given the familiar layout, it is still possible to create user interfaces that range from excellent to nearly unusable. At this point, most good ideas will expand upon and improve the most common designs rather than result from trying utterly new ap-

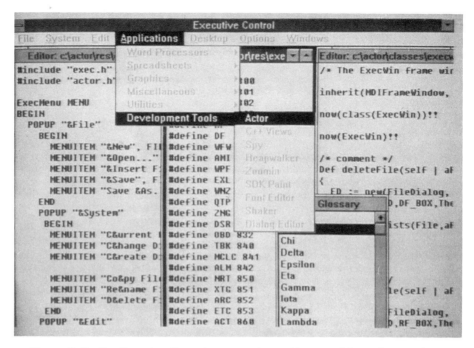

Figure 9.2 The Executive Control main window in Maximized form showing three documents open in adjacent child windows.

proaches. But there are still plenty of important refinements to make from within the familiar framework.

Example: Important irreversible action items on a popup menu should be situated where the likelihood of an accidental click is minimized and confirm dialogs used to give the user a chance to back up.

■ HIERARCHICAL MENUS

Hierarchical or cascading menus provide a very important means for packing a lot of functionality into a single menu bar while avoiding clutter. However, as with any good thing, it's important to know when you're overdoing it. A hierarchical menu is really like adding the equivalent of another whole menu bar of options. But it requires screen space for those options to pop out to the side. For my taste, two hierarchical menus are the most that should be attempted in a single window. In my program I decided to put plenty of options on just one. Although hierarchical menus can be created either dynamically or statically, it turns out that the static resource script approach to creating them is so simple, that this is very often going to be the way to go right from the outset.

Like any other menu, a hierarchical menu can be either created from a compiled static resource, or created on the spot dynamically using the Windows interface. In Actor, there are various different ways of creating menus dynamically. An example of a dynamic hierarchical menu using the MenuItem class is provided by:

```
Def appsPopup(self | popup)
{ popup := newPopup(MenuItem, "A&pplications");
addItem(popup, wpPopup(self));
addItem(popup, ssPopup(self));
addItem(popup, graphPopup(self));
addItem(popup, miscPopup(self));
addItem(popup, utilityPopup(self));
addItem(popup, develPopup(self));
^popup
}


Def wpPopup(self | popup)
{ popup := newPopup(MenuItem, "&Word Processors");
addItem(popup, new(MenuItem, "Word for Windows", 228, #word));
addItem(popup, new(MenuItem, "Ami", 229, #ami));
addItem(popup, new(MenuItem, "Word Perfect", 230, #ami));


^popup
}
```

Dynamic popups are useful when you're still uncertain what the final form of the menu system will be. The disadvantage in the case of hierarchical popups is that it takes a special procedure to create them. In the case of static hierarchical menus, the procedure is quite a bit simpler as far as the coding is concerned. Writing the resource script for them is simply a matter of nesting POPUP statements in defining a menu resource. For example, the same hierarchical menu defined dynamically above would be defined statically as follows:

```
POPUP "&Applications"
BEGIN
 POPUP "&Word Processors"
 BEGIN
  MENUITEM Word for Windows", WFW
  MENUITEM "Ami", AMI
  MENUITEM "Word Perfect", WPF
 END
```

■ COMBINING STATIC AND DYNAMIC MENUS

The user interface to the Executive Control program also demonstrates the use of both static and dynamic menus on the same menu bar. My first attempt at doing it was not as successful. The dynamic menus just took over the whole menu bar, so the attempt succeeded in providing a working program, but with dynamic menus only. The first attempt used the Menu and MenuItem classes. This one utilizes the features of the MDIFrameWindow class to create the Windows menu, which is the only menu system on the menu bar that is a dynamic menu. The rest are defined in the resource script in the listing. Much of the action is in the init method of MDIFrameWindow:

```
windowMenu := Call CreatePopupMenu();
Call AppendMenu(windowMenu, MF_STRING, 9997, asciiz "&Cascade"));
Call AppendMenu(windowMenu, MF_STRING, 9998, asciiz("&Tile"));
Call AppendMenu(windowMenu, MF_STRING, 9999, asciiz("&Arrange Icons"));
Call AppendMenu(hMenu, MF_POPUP, windowMenu, asciiz("&Windows"));
```

■ DYNAMIC FILE DIALOGS

One of the drawbacks of static resources is that every single aspect is predefined. If you have a need for a large number of controls that differ from one another only in minute details, rather than defining a separate resource item for each, it might be preferable to use dynamic resources. A case in point is the use of various different types of file dialog. Often, identical file dialogs can be used for many of the different operations you want to do on files. To solve this, the SysDialog class was created as a direct subclass of FileDialog; methods were defined in it that created dialogs dynamically. For example, the copyDlg method was defined:

```
Def copyDlg(self | dlg)
{
  dlg := new(DialogDesign);
  setText(dlg,"Copy File");
  setSize(dlg,0@0,200@70);
  addItem(dlg,newStatic(DlgItem, "From:",925,10@10,60@16,0));
  addItem(dlg,newStatic(DlgItem,"To:",925,15@40,60@16,0));
  addItem(dlg,newEdit(DlgItem,"",101,40@10,150@10,0));
  addItem(dlg,newEdit(DlgItem,"",101,40@40,150@10,0));
  runModal(dlg,nil,ThePort);

}
```

■ FACTORING COMMAND METHODS

One of the main enemies of complex menu systems in GUIs is the prospect of a seemingly endless succession of case statements that becomes increasingly difficult to debug. The whole spirit of OOP is oriented toward building functioning packages that will always work, even though any number of new packages are designed and added to the system. For this reason good object-oriented design requires that a single huge command method for processing all menus be avoided. By factoring the processing of

Windows command messages into a number of separate command methods each of which can work autonomously as well as in mutual cooperation, programs compile faster, are far easier to debug, require less memory resources, and are much easier to update (see Listings 1–3).

The basic concept is fairly simple. When a command method is defined for an Actor class, it enables that class to receive Windows WM_COMMAND messages and interpret them. The coding of the command method ordinarily takes the form of a series of case statements that test for the control IDs of various menu items and then send the appropriate messages. The command method either must be in the class defining window on which the menu bar is located, or the notification messages must be transmitted to other objects. However, in cases where there are a truly huge number of menu items, this approach cannot be used. Instead, the main command method can be written to call subcommand methods that are designed to operate with the various separate functional packages. This way, subcommand methods can be written that will always work with each menu or other control, regardless of the context in which they are used. The master command method is responsible for calling upon the subordinate command methods that it requires.

Listing 1. ExecWin Class Listing.

```
/* The ExecWin frame window class for the Executive
Control program, a Windows 3.0 combined master control window and multidocument
editor combined. */ !!

inherit(MDIFrameWindow, #ExecWin, nil, 2, nil)!!

now(class(ExecWin))!!

now(ExecWin)!!

/* runs file dialog for deleting files */
Def deleteFile(self | aFile)
{
FD := new(FileDialog, "*.*");
runModal(FD,DF_BOX,ThePort);

copyAll(exists(File,aFile,0));

}
!!

/* runs file dialog for renaming files */
Def renameFile(self | aFile)
{
```

```
    FD := new(FileDialog, "*.*");
    runModal(FD,RF_BOX,ThePort);

    copyAll(exists(File,aFile,0));

    }
    !!

    /* creates a dynamic file dialog */
    Def fileDlg(self | fDlg cBox lBox)
    {
     fDlg := new(DialogDesign);

    }
    !!

    /* runs a file dialog for copying files */
    Def copyFile(self | aFile)
    {
     FD := new(FileDialog, "*.*");
     runModal(FD,CF_BOX,ThePort);

     copyAll(exists(File,aFile,0));

    }
    !!

    /* subcommand  method for handling system commands */
    Def systemCommand(self,wP)
    {
    select
     case wP == CUD
     is currentDir(self);
     endCase
     case wP == CHD
     is changeDir(self);
     endCase
     case wP == CRD
     is createDir(self);
     endCase
     case wP == CF
     is copyFile(self);
     endCase
     case wP == RF
     is renameFile(self);
```

```
            endCase
            case wP == DF
            is deleteFile(self);
            endCase
          endSelect;

}
!!


/* create a Directory */
Def createDir(self | path dlg)
{
  dlg := new(InputDialog, "Create Directory", "Enter path to create.", "");
  runModal(dlg,INPUT_BOX,ThePort);
  path := getText(dlg);
  create(Directory,path);
}!!


/* remove a Directory */
Def removeDir(self | path dlg)
{
  dlg := new(InputDialog, "Remove Directory", "Enter path to remove.", "");
  runModal(dlg,INPUT_BOX,ThePort);
  path := getText(dlg);
  remove(Directory,path);
}!!


/* change a Directory */
Def changeDir(self | newPath dlg)
{
  dlg := new(InputDialog, "Change Directory", "Enter new path.", "");
  runModal(dlg,INPUT_BOX,ThePort);
  newPath := getText(dlg);
  makeCurrent(Directory,newPath);
}!!


/* returns the current Directory */
Def currentDir(self | aString)
{
  aString :=  fullName(current(Directory));
  new(ErrorBox,ThePort, "The current directory is"
  + aString, "Current Directory", 0);
}!!


/* subcommand method for handling application options  */
```

```
Def optionCommand(self,wP)
{
sdkCommand(self,wP);
if wP == GLS
glossWin(self,wP);
endif;
}
!!

/* subcommand method for executing applications */
Def appCommand(self,wP)
{
  select
  case wP == WFW
  is word(self,wP);
  endCase;
  case wP == AMI
  is ami(self,wP);
  endCase;
  case wP == EXL
  is excel(self,wP);
  endCase;
  case wP == ZNG
  is zing(self,wP);
  endCase;
  case wP == OBD
  is obdraw(self,wP);
  endCase;
  case wP == TBK
  is tbook(self,wP);
  endCase;
  case wP == NRT
  is norton(self,wP);
  endCase;
  case wP == XTG
  is xtree(self,wP);
  endCase;
  case wP == CPV
  is cppv(self,wP);
  endCase;
  endSelect;
}
!!


/*************************************************
```

*The command module that handles the creation and
control of child windows for holding documents*

```
**************************************************/
Def childCommand(self,wP,lP)
{
 if (wP == FILE_OPEN) or (wP == FILE_NEW)
  then createMDIChild(self, childClass, "(Untitled)", nil);
  command(childList[activeHWnd], wP, lP);
  processMenu(self, getText(childList[activeHWnd]));
  else if childList[activeHWnd]
  command(childList[activeHWnd], wP, lP);
  endif;
  endif;
  execWindowProc(self:ancestor, #WM_COMMAND, wP, lP);


}
!!


/*****************************************

The SDK Tool Menu command method module

**********************************************/

Def sdkCommand(self,wP)
{
 select
 case wP == SPY
 is spy(self,wP);
 endCase;
 case wP == HPW
 is heapwalk(self,wP);
 endCase;
 case wP == ZMN
 is zoomin(self,wP);
 endCase;
 case wP == SDP
 is sdkpaint(self,wP);
 endCase;
 case wP == FED
 is fontedit(self,wP);
 endCase;
 case wP == SHK
```

```
  is shaker(self,wP);
  endCase;
  case wP == DED
  is dlgedit(self,wP);
  endCase;
 endSelect;
 }
 !!


/***********************************************

The Windows Menu command method module that
creates the Windows dynamic menu system

***********************************************/

Def windowsCommand(self,wP)
{
 select
  case wP == IDM_CASCADE
  is Call SendMessage(getHWnd(clientWindow),
   messageID(#WM_MDICASCADE), 0, 0L);
  endCase
  case wP == IDM_TILE
  is Call SendMessage(getHWnd(clientWindow),
   messageID(#WM_MDITILE), 0, 0L);
  endCase
  case wP == IDM_ARRANGEICONS
  is Call SendMessage(getHWnd(clientWindow),
   messageID(#WM_MDIICONARRANGE), 0, 0L);
  endCase
 endSelect;
 }
 !!

/* opens the sample glossary window */
Def glossWin(self, wp | WW)
{
WW := new(Window, ThePort, nil, "Glossary", &(375, 63, 535, 300));
show(WW,1);
L := new(ListBox, 375, WW);
setCRect(L, &(0,0,153,223));
moveWindow(L);
addString(L, "Alpha");
show(L,1);
```

```
addString(L, "Beta");
addString(L, "Gamma");
addString(L, "Delta");
addString(L, "Epsilon");
addString(L, "Zeta");
addString(L, "Eta");
addString(L, "Theta");
addString(L, "Iota");
addString(L, "Kappa");
addString(L, "Lambda");
addString(L, "Mu");
addString(L, "Nu");
addString(L, "Xi");
addString(L, "Omicron");
addString(L, "Pi");
addString(L, "Rho");
addString(L, "Sigma");
addString(L, "Tau");
addString(L, "Upsilon");
addString(L, "Phi");
addString(L, "Chi");
addString(L, "Psi");
addString(L, "Omega");
}
!!


/*****************************************

The Desk Accessory Menu command method module

*****************************************/
Def deskCommand(self,wP)
{
  select
  case wP == CLC
  is calc(self,wP);
  endCase;
  case wP == CLK
  is clock(self,wP);
  endCase;
  case wP == NPD
  is note(self,wP);
  endCase;
  case wP == CNP
  is cpanel(self,wP);
```

```
    endCase;
    case wP == CDF
    is card(self,wP);
    endCase;
    case wP == CLD
    is cal(self,wP);
    endCase;
    case wP == WRT
    is writer(self,wP);
    endCase;
    case wP == PTB
    is pbrush(self,wP);
    endCase;
    case wP == PRM
    is printman(self,wP);
    endCase;
    case wP == RCR
    is record(self,wP);
    endCase;
    case wP == STP
    is setup(self,wP);
    endCase;
    case wP == CLB
    is clipbrd(self,wP);
    endCase;
    case wP == TRM
    is terminal(self,wP);
    endCase;
   endSelect;
   }
   !!
   /* executes the Zoomin SDK utility */
   Def zoomin(self,wp)
   {
    exec("D:\WINDEV\ZOOMIN.EXE");
   }
   !!
   /* executes Zing */
   Def zing(self,wp)
   {
    exec("E:\ZING\ZING.EXE");
   }
   !!
   /* executes Xtree */
   Def xtree(self,wp)
```

```
{
 exec("C:\XTREE\XTG.EXE");
}
!!
/* executes MS write */
Def writer(self,wp)
{
 exec("E:\WINDOWS\WRITE.EXE");
}
!!
/* executes MS Word */
Def word(self,wp)
{
 exec("C:\WINWORD\WINWORD.EXE");
}
!!
/* launches terminal program */
Def terminal(self,wp)
{
 exec("E:\WINDOWS\TERMINAL.EXE");
}
!!
/* executes SDK spy utility */
Def spy(self,wp)
{
 exec("D:\WINDEV\SPY.EXE");
}
!!
/* launches the Shaker utility */
Def shaker(self,wp)
{
 exec("D:\WINDEV\SHAKER.EXE");
}
!!
/* runs Windows setup */
Def setup(self,wp)
{
 exec("E:\WINDOWS\SETUP.EXE");
}
!!
/* executes SDK sdkpaint utility */
Def sdkpaint(self,wp)
{
 exec("D:\WINDEV\SDKPAINT.EXE");
}
```

```
!!
/* executes recorder */
Def record(self,wp)
{
 exec("E:\WINDOWS\RECORDER.EXE");
}
!!
/* executes print manager */
Def printman(self,wp)
{
 exec("E:\WINDOWS\PRINTMAN.EXE");
}
!!
/* executes Windows paintbrush accessory */
Def pbrush(self,wp)
{
 exec("E:\WINDOWS\PBRUSH.EXE");
}
!!
/* executes object draw */
Def objdraw(self,wp)
{
 exec("D:\DRAW\OBJDRAW.EXE");
}
!!
/* executes Windows notepad accessory */
Def note(self,wp)
{
 exec("E:\WINDOWS\NOTEPAD.EXE");
}
!!
/* executes Norton Integrator */
Def norton(self,wp)
{
 exec("E:\NORTON\NI.EXE");
}
!!
/* method that executes the MS Windows SDK Heapwalker program */
Def heapwalk(self,wp)
{
 exec("D:\WINDEV\HEAPWALK.EXE");
}
!!
/* executes SDK font editor */
Def fontedit(self,wp)
```

```
{
  exec("D:\WINDEV\FONTEDIT.EXE");
}
!!
/* executes excel spreadsheet */
Def excel(self,wp)
{
  exec("D:\EXCEL\EXCEL.EXE");
}
!!
/* executes SDK dialog editor */
Def dlgedit(self,wp)
{
  exec("D:\WINDEV\DIALOG.EXE");
}
!!
/* launches C++ Views browser */
Def cppv(self,wp)
{
  exec("D:\CTV\CB.EXE");
}
!!
/* executes Windows control panel accessory */
Def cpanel(self,wp)
{
  exec("E:\WINDOWS\CONTROL.EXE");
}
!!
/* comment */
Def clock(self,wp)
{
  exec("E:\WINDOWS\CLOCK.EXE");
}
!!
/* opens clipboard */
Def clipbrd(self,wp)
{
  exec("E:\WINDOWS\CLIPBRD.EXE");
}
!!
/* executes Windows cardfile accessory */
Def card(self,wp)
{
  exec("E:\WINDOWS\CARDFILE.EXE");
}
```

```
!!
/* executes Windows calculator accessory */
Def calc(self,wp)
{
 exec("E:\WINDOWS\CALC.EXE");
}
!!
/* executes Windows calendar accessory */
Def cal(self,wp)
{
 exec("E:\WINDOWS\CALENDAR.EXE");
}
!!
/* executes ami word processor */
Def ami(self,wp)
{
 exec("D:\AMI\AMI.EXE");
}
!!
/******************************************************

The main command method module that calls all the
other command methods such as the childCommand method,
which knows how to handle creation of new MDI children.

******************************************************/

Def command(self, wP, lP)
{
childCommand(self,wP,lP);
windowsCommand(self,wP);
systemCommand(self,wP);
deskCommand(self,wP);
appCommand(self,wP);
optionCommand(self,wP);
}!!

/* The ExecApp class */!!

inherit(Application, #ExecApp, nil, 2, nil)!!

now(class(ExecApp))!!

now(ExecApp)!!
```

```
/* Create and show the application mainWindow
   Load a data file, if necessary. */
Def init(self, cmdLine | dlg fName)
{
 init(self:ancestor, cmdLine);
 mainWindow := newMain(ExecWin, "ExecMenu", "Executive Control", nil);
 setClassType(mainWindow, #FileChildMDI);
 show(mainWindow, CmdShow);
}!!



/* The SysDialog class creates various types of file dialogs */!!

inherit(FileDialog, #SysDialog, nil, 2, nil)!!

now(class(SysDialog))!!

now(SysDialog)!!

/* a method that creates a custom dialog for
   getting file names before deleting */

Def deleteDlg(self | dlg)
{
 dlg := new(DialogDesign);
 setText(dlg, "Delete File");
 addItem(dlg,newEdit(DlgItem,"",101,30@20,60@15,0));
 runModal(dlg,nil,ThePort);
}!!

/* a method that creates a custom dialog for
   getting file names before renaming */

Def renameDlg(self | dlg)
{
 dlg := new(DialogDesign);
 setText(dlg, "Rename File");
 setSize(dlg,0@0,200@70);
 addItem(dlg,newStatic(DlgItem,"From:",925,10@10,60@16,0));
 addItem(dlg,newStatic(DlgItem,"To:",925,15@40,60@16,0));
 addItem(dlg,newEdit(DlgItem,"",101,40@10,150@10,0));
 addItem(dlg,newEdit(DlgItem,"",101,40@40,150@10,0));
 runModal(dlg,nil,ThePort);
```

```
} !!

/* a method that creates a custom dialog for
   getting file names before copying */

Def copyDlg(self | dlg)
{
  dlg := new(DialogDesign);
  setText(dlg,"Copy File");
  setSize(dlg,0@0,200@70);
  addItem(dlg,newStatic(DlgItem,"From:",925,10@10,60@16,0));
  addItem(dlg,newStatic(DlgItem,"To:",925,15@40,60@16,0));
  addItem(dlg,newEdit(DlgItem,"",101,40@10,150@10,0));
  addItem(dlg,newEdit(DlgItem,"",101,40@40,150@10,0));
  runModal(dlg,nil,ThePort);

} !!

/* Handle file dialog events (OK, Cancel, etc.). Selecting Open
   will always do something, if only to reload the lists according
   to the current filter. */
Def command(self, wP, lP | action)
{ action := high(lP);
  select
  case wP == IDCOPY
  is end(self);
  copyDlg(self);
  endCase
  case wP == IDRN
  is renameDlg(self);
  endCase
  case wP == IDDL
  is deleteDlg(self);
  endCase
  case wP == IDCANCEL
  is resetDir(self);
  end(self, 0);
  endCase
  case wP == FILE_LB and action = LBN_SELCHANGE
  is sendDlgItemMessage(self, FILE_DIRLB, LB_SETCURSEL, -1, 0);
  endCase
  case wP == FILE_DIRLB and action = LBN_SELCHANGE
  is sendDlgItemMessage(self, FILE_LB, CB_SETCURSEL, -1, 0);
  setItemText(self, FILE_LB, getLoadDir(self) + fileSpec);
  endCase
```

```
case (wP == FILE_DIRLB and action = LBN_DBLCLK)
cor (wP == IDOK and getLBSel(self, FILE_DIRLB))
is newDir(self);
endCase
case wP == FILE_LB and action = LBN_DBLCLK
is
 if getLoadFile(self)
 then resetDir(self);
  end(self, IDOK);
 endif;
endCase
case wP == IDOK
is open(self)
endCase
endSelect;
 ^1;
}!!
```

Listing 2. The Executive Control Resource Script File.

```
#include "exec.h"
#include "actor.h"

ExecMenu MENU
BEGIN
 POPUP "&File"
  BEGIN
   MENUITEM "&New", FILE_NEW
   MENUITEM "&Open...", FILE_OPEN
   MENUITEM "&Insert File...", FILE_READ
   MENUITEM "&Save", FILE_SAVE
   MENUITEM "Save &As...", FILE_SAVEAS
  END
 POPUP "&System"
  BEGIN
   MENUITEM "C&urrent Directory", CUD
   MENUITEM "C&hange Directory", CHD
   MENUITEM "C&reate Directory", CRD

   MENUITEM "Co&py File", CF
   MENUITEM "Re&name File", RF
   MENUITEM "D&elete File", DF
  END
 POPUP "&Edit"
```

```
    BEGIN
     MENUITEM "Cu&t\tShift+Del", EDIT_CUT
     MENUITEM "&Copy\tCtrl+Ins", EDIT_COPY
     MENUITEM "&Paste\tShift+Ins", EDIT_PASTE
     MENUITEM "C&lear", EDIT_CLEAR
     MENUITEM SEPARATOR
     MENUITEM "Select &All\tCtrl+A", EDIT_SELALL
    END
   POPUP "&Applications"
   BEGIN
    POPUP "&Word Processors"
     BEGIN
      MENUITEM "Word for Windows", WFW
      MENUITEM "Ami", AMI
      MENUITEM "Word Perfect", WPF
     END
    POPUP "&Spreadsheets"
     BEGIN
      MENUITEM "Excel", EXL
      MENUITEM "WingZ", WNZ
      MENUITEM "Quattro Pro", QTP
     END
    POPUP "&Graphics"
     BEGIN
      MENUITEM "Zing", ZNG
      MENUITEM "Designer", DSR
      MENUITEM "Object Draw", OBD
     END
    POPUP "Miscellaneous"
     BEGIN
      MENUITEM "Toolbook", TBK
      MENUITEM "Macrocalc", MCLC
      MENUITEM "Almanac", ALM
     END
    POPUP "Utilities"
     BEGIN
      MENUITEM "Norton", NRT
      MENUITEM "Xtree Gold", XTG
      MENUITEM "Archive", ARC
      MENUITEM "Other", ETC
     END
    POPUP "Development Tools"
     BEGIN
      MENUITEM "Actor", ACT
      MENUITEM "C++ Views", CPV
```

```
                    MENUITEM "Spy", SPY
                    MENUITEM "Heapwalker", HPW
                    MENUITEM "Zoomin", ZMN
                    MENUITEM "SDK Paint", SDP
                    MENUITEM "Font Editor", FED
                    MENUITEM "Shaker", SHK
                    MENUITEM "Dialog Editor", DED
                  END
                END
                POPUP "&Desktop"
                  BEGIN
                    MENUITEM "&Calculator", CLC
                    MENUITEM "Cloc&k", CLK
                    MENUITEM "&Notepad", NPD
                    MENUITEM "C&ontrol Panel", CNP
                    MENUITEM "C&ardfile", CF
                    MENUITEM "Ca&lendar", CLD
                    MENUITEM "&Write", WRT
                    MENUITEM "Paint&brush", PTB
                    MENUITEM "&Print Manager", PRM
                    MENUITEM "&Recorder", RCR
                    MENUITEM "&Setup", STP
                    MENUITEM "Cl&ipboard", CLB
                    MENUITEM "&Terminal", TRM
                  END
                POPUP "&Options"
                  BEGIN
                    MENUITEM "&Glossary...", GLS
                    MENUITEM "&Menus", MNS
                    MENUITEM "&Child Windows", CWS
                    MENUITEM "&Buttons", BTS
                    MENUITEM "Me&ssages", MSS
                  END
              END
              CF_BOX DIALOG DISCARDABLE 27, 23, 170, 116
              STYLE WS_DLGFRAME | WS_POPUP | DS_ABSALIGN
              BEGIN
                CONTROL "" FILE_LB, "ComboBox", CBS_SIMPLE | CBS_SORT |
                  WS_VSCROLL | WS_TABSTOP | WS_CHILD, 4, 30, 55, 80
                CONTROL "Files:" 3, "static", SS_LEFT | WS_CHILD, 4, 19, 31, 10
                CONTROL "" FILE_DIRLB, "ListBox", LBS_STANDARD | WS_TABSTOP
                  | WS_CHILD, 65, 42, 55, 68
                CONTROL "Directories:" 3, "static", SS_LEFT | WS_CHILD, 65, 31, 38, 10
                DEFPUSHBUTTON "&Copy", IDCOPY, 130, 37, 30, 15, WS_CHILD
                PUSHBUTTON "&Cancel", IDCANCEL, 130, 63, 30, 15, WS_CHILD
```

```
    CONTROL "Directory:" 3, "static", SS_LEFT| WS_CHILD, 4, 7, 32, 11
    CONTROL "" FILE_DIR, "static", SS_LEFT| WS_CHILD, 39, 7, 146, 11
END
RF_BOX DIALOG DISCARDABLE 27, 23, 170, 116
STYLE WS_DLGFRAME| WS_POPUP| DS_ABSALIGN
BEGIN
    CONTROL "" FILE_LB, "ComboBox", CBS_SIMPLE| CBS_SORT|
WS_VSCROLL| WS_TABSTOP| WS_CHILD, 4, 30, 55, 80
    CONTROL "Files:" 3, "static", SS_LEFT| WS_CHILD, 4, 19, 31, 10
    CONTROL "" FILE_DIRLB, "ListBox", LBS_STANDARD| WS_TABSTOP
| WS_CHILD, 65, 42, 55, 68
    CONTROL "Directories:" 3, "static", SS_LEFT| WS_CHILD, 65, 31, 38, 10
    DEFPUSHBUTTON "&Rename", IDRN, 130, 37, 34, 15, WS_CHILD
    PUSHBUTTON "&Cancel", IDCANCEL, 130, 63, 30, 15, WS_CHILD
    CONTROL "Directory:" 3, "static", SS_LEFT| WS_CHILD, 4, 7, 32, 11
    CONTROL "" FILE_DIR, "static", SS_LEFT| WS_CHILD, 39, 7, 146, 11
END
DF_BOX DIALOG DISCARDABLE 27, 23, 170, 116
STYLE WS_DLGFRAME| WS_POPUP| DS_ABSALIGN
BEGIN
    CONTROL "" FILE_LB, "ComboBox", CBS_SIMPLE| CBS_SORT|
WS_VSCROLL| WS_TABSTOP| WS_CHILD, 4, 30, 55, 80
    CONTROL "Files:" 3, "static", SS_LEFT| WS_CHILD, 4, 19, 31, 10
    CONTROL "" FILE_DIRLB, "ListBox", LBS_STANDARD| WS_TABSTOP
| WS_CHILD, 65, 42, 55, 68
    CONTROL "Directories:" 3, "static", SS_LEFT| WS_CHILD, 65, 31, 38, 10
    DEFPUSHBUTTON "&Delete", IDDL, 130, 37, 34, 15, WS_CHILD
    PUSHBUTTON "&Cancel", IDCANCEL, 130, 63, 30, 15, WS_CHILD
    CONTROL "Directory:" 3, "static", SS_LEFT| WS_CHILD, 4, 7, 32, 11
    CONTROL "" FILE_DIR, "static", SS_LEFT| WS_CHILD, 39, 7, 146, 11
END
```

Listing 3. The Executive Control Header File.

```
#define CHD 800
#define CRD 801
#define CUD 802
#define CF  803
#define RF  804
#define DF  805
#define WFW 810
#define AMI 811
#define WPF 812
#define EXL 820
```

```
#define WNZ 821
#define QTP 822
#define ZNG 830
#define DSR 831
#define OBD 832
#define TBK 840
#define MCLC 841
#define ALM 842
#define NRT 850
#define XTG 851
#define ARC 852
#define ETC 853
#define ACT 860
#define CPV 861
#define SPY 862
#define HPW 863
#define ZMN 864
#define SDP 865
#define FED 866
#define SHK 867
#define DED 868
#define CLC 870
#define CLK 871
#define NPD 872
#define CNP 873
#define CDF 874
#define CLD 875
#define WRT 876
#define PTB 877
#define PRM 878
#define RCR 879
#define STP 880
#define CLB 881
#define TRM 882
#define GLS 890
#define MNS 891
#define CWS 892
#define BTS 893
#define MSS 894
#define HLP 895
#define CF_BOX 896
#define RF_BOX 897
#define DF_BOX 898
#define IDCOPY 899
```

#define IDRN 900
#define IDDL 901

MDIFrameWindow

Source file:	MDIFRAME.CLS
Inherits from:	Window

Instance Variables:

clientWindow	point to client window space
childList	dictionary of children
activeHWnd	keep track of active child
childClass	keep track of child class type
windowMenu	keep "Window" menu

Object methods:

add	Adds a new child window to the childList ivar.
close	Steps through all of the applications child windows and makes sure that they are ready to be closed, before closing the MDI Frame Window.
command	Processes all MDI Frame Window specific command messages.
createMDIChild	Calling this method with a class name, caption text, and a rectangle in which to display the window will create a new MDI child. It will then add that child windows pointer to the childList dictionary, keying it on the hWnd of that child.
defWndProc	Default for dialogs is to do nothing. Return 0 to let Windows do normal processing. WARNING: Do not remove this method! May be redefined in descendants if they register a private window class with Windows for their dialogs.
execWindowProc	Makes sure that any messages not processed by an Actor method are passed on to the DefFrameProc in Windows, so that the frame window is managed properly.
getActiveHWnd	Returns the windows handle to the active MDI Child.
getClient	Gets a pointer to the Frame windows client space.
init	Sets up the Frame Window so that it creates an MDIClient to go with it. Also, dynamically creates a "Windows" menu that is initialized with the "Cascade," "Tile," and "Arrange Icons" menu choices, for MDI Child management.

processMenu	Since, many times, the caption text of a window will change after it has been created, this method will take care of modifying that MDI child entry in the "Windows" menu.
remove	Removes an MDI child from the childList dictionary.
setActiveHWnd	Sets the handle to the active child window of the MDI application.
setClassType	Sets the class type that the MDI application will use when creating a new child in its client space.

FileChildMDI

Source file:	FILECHIL.CLS
Inherits from:	FileWindow
Object methods:	
close	Makes sure that the window is ready to be closed.
command	Handles menu events. It has been changed from the one present in the FileWindow class. Instead of using the command method of its ancestor (WorkEdit) it will use the command method of EditWindow. This essentially removes the ability to execute a line of Actor code or inspect the environment (neither of which is possible in a sealed off application). These menu choices could be removed from the FileEditMenu in the resource file if one wants to use FileChildMDI in a stand-alone application. This command method could also be removed if the FileChildMDI object is only to be used in the Actor environment.
create	Creates an MDI child window according to certain specifications. Par is the parent of this child. It should be set to the Frame window that controls the MDI application. The wName is the text that will appear in the caption bar. Rect is a rectangle representing the area in which the window should be displayed. Style defines what attributes the window should have. It should be noted that, once the WM_MDICREATE message is sent to the MDIClient, a window will be created and shown.
defWndProc	Default for dialogs is to do nothing. Returns 0 to let Windows do normal processing. WARNING: Do not remove this method! May be redefined in descendants if they register a private window class with Windows for their dialogs.

destroy	Destroys the MDI Child window by passing the WM_MDIDESTROY message to the MDI Client window.
execWindowProc	Sets up this window's default procedure so that it will execute the DefMDIChildProc function if the message is not handled by the Actor system.
setText	Sets the window text (the window caption) to the given string.
WM_MOVE	Handles the movement of a child window within the frame window. NOTE: This message must be passed on to the default child procedure
WM_SETFOCUS	Received whenever the focus has been set to this instance of the child window. This takes care of notifying the MDI frame window that it is the currently active MDI child. NOTE: This message must be passed on to the default child procedure.
WM_SIZE	Received whenever the window has been resized. NOTE: This message must be passed on to the default child procedure.

MDIChild

Source file:	MDICHILD.CLS
Inherits from:	Window
Class methods:	
new	Creates and returns a new Window object. In the case of an MDI child window the window will be automatically displayed when it is created. This call accepts a parent for the child (this should be an MDI Frame window), a name for the caption bar, and a rectangle in which the window should be displayed.
newStyle	Creates and returns a new Window. Par is the parent window. The wName is a string containing the caption for the Window. Rect determines where and how big the Window will be. If rect is nil, the default is used. Style is a numeric value that is a combination of Windows style values. If style is nil, the default style is used.
Object methods:	
close	Ensures that window is ready to be closed. MDIClient

create	Creates an MDI child window according to certain specifications. Par is the parent of this child. It should be set to the Frame window that controls the MDI application. The wName is the text that will appear in the caption bar. Rect is a rectangle representing the area in which the window should be displayed. Style defines what attributes the window should have. It should be noted that, once the WM_MDICREATE message is sent to the MDIClient, a window will be created and shown.
defWndProc	Default for dialogs is to do nothing. Return 0 to let Windows do normal processing. May be redefined in descendants if they register a private window class with Windows for their dialogs.
destroy	Destroys the MDI Child window by passing the WM_MDIDESTROY message to the MDI Client window.
execWindowProc	Sets up this windows default procedure so that it will execute the DefMDIChildProc if the message is not handled by the Actor system.
setText	Sets the window text (the window caption) to the given string.
WM_MOVE	Handles the movement of a child window within the frame window. NOTE: This message must be passed on to the default child procedure.
WM_SETFOCUS	Received whenever the focus has been set to this instance of the child window. This will take care of notifying the MDI frame window that it is the currently active MDI child. NOTE: This message must be passed on to the default child procedure.
WM_SIZE	This message will be received whenever the window has been resized. NOTE: This message must be passed on to the default child procedure.
Source file:	MDICLIEN.CLS
Inherits from:	Control
Inherited by:	
Class Variables:	
$Native Literals	
Instance Variables:	
Class methods:	

new	Creates a new instance of the MDIClient class. As arguments it accepts a pointer to the parent window (this should be an MDIFrame window) and client structure. This client structure should be a four byte struct containing a popup menu handle in the first word and an ID for the first MDI child window in the second word. Make sure the ID for the MDI child is high enough so that it will not conflict with any numbers passed into the MDIFrame windows command method.
newStyle	Takes care of the actual creation of an MDIClient. The parameters passed can be seen in the "new" method, with the exception of style. If no style is defined in the newStyle statement a style will be obtained from the "style" class method of MDIClient. This style should be appropriate for most MDI applications.
style	Returns the default window style.

Object methods:

create	Creates a new MDI client window. Certain parameters should be the same no matter the client window that is being created, thus, these values have been hardcoded. For example, MDIClient should not have a menu, will always be registered with the "mdiclient" class, and has its position and size determined by the MDIFrame window.
defWndProc	Default for dialogs is to do nothing. Return 0 to let Windows do normal processing. May be redefined in descendants if they register a private window class with Windows for their dialogs.
destroy	An MDI Client Window should be destroyed via its Frame Window so this disables the normal destroy method.
WM_DESTROY	An MDI Client window will be destroyed via its Frame Windows default Frame procedure.
WM_MDIDESTROY	The message that is called every time an MDI Child makes a request to be destroyed. The default procedure for the MDI Client will handle the destruction of the child window. That child's pointer will then be removed from the child window dictionary of the frame window.
WM_NCDESTROY	Removes the property created for the Client Window when it has been destroyed.

10

TOPICS IN OBJECT-ORIENTED WINDOWS DESIGN

This chapter concerns several different issues in object-oriented design for the Windows environment. There are two basically different viewpoints represented here: design with respect to the user, and design with respect to the resources of the computer. As a reflection of this, the chapter is divided into roughly two different parts. The first part deals with object-oriented design, both generally and in the Windows environment. It does this from the point of view of the application, without reference to the issues of memory management on the computer. The second part takes up the latter issue, and, in particular, covers the topics of: 1) memory management in Windows 3.0, 2) object-oriented memory management, and 3) memory management in Windows using Actor.

■ DESIGNING FOR USERS

The first principle of software design is that software must be designed to be used by someone, and therefore, its design must be conducted from the point of view of the people who will be the intended users. Although everyone will agree with this principle, it continues to be violated far more frequently than it is followed. It cannot be true that the principle is so seldom adhered to because of the sheer incompetence of software designers. The fact of the matter is that there is still very much to learn, and a surprising amount to take into consideration when designing for users. It would naturally take at least a book to expound on this topic in adequate detail, so the intention here is to introduce some insights that can guide readers to further study and exploration.

As all programmers know, a computer must be first loaded with data before its instructions are executed. A human being can begin to engage in an activity and then go out in search of the data that will be needed to carry out or complete the activity. Obviously, it is sometimes very important to a particular type of human work that it be able to proceed in precisely this way. Software applications have to be designed with this sort of thing in view. Although these are very sweeping generalities, I have in mind some very specific examples.

Most readers will be familiar with popular paint programs, like the Paintbrush application that comes as an accessory with Windows 3.0 and later. In these programs there will typically be a toolbox composed of icons that stand for different kinds of operation that a user might want to perform. The aspiring electronic artist feels at home with this to a certain degree. Just as a traditional painter often uses a paintbox with different colors that can be dipped into with a brush, the electronic artist can use the mouse to dip into different drawing tools. The graphics tools are verbs, if you like, and the graphics lines and shapes are the nouns of a sentence that this kind of program speaks. Sometimes you must first select the noun before selecting the verb, but with the paintbox style, the typical case is the reverse: you first choose the verb and then create or add to the noun. On the whole, this can work well for creating things like drawings, because there is no set place where you have to work next. You can stay with one tool for a while, going from one area of a drawing to another and using it where it seems needed. As long as the final result is what you want, the order in which you do things doesn't really matter.

It is interesting to compare this with applications that involve sequential rather than spatial compositions, such as music compositions, animations, and computer programs. Here you are by no means as free to browse about at will within the work that's being created. It has to unfold as a continuous sequence, so there usually is a next place where you have to work. This next frame, next measure, or next line is the natural, built-in focal point. It is the noun that is primary over any verb. What's important is how the next noun behaves, not what tool you happen to be using. As a matter of fact, if elaborate tools are attempted in this type of application, they can end up getting in the way to the extent that the result is unusable for many people. The reason is that you end up imposing a style of working on the user that is rather foreign to the type of work being done, and many people will refuse to accept that.

■ WHAT'S THE COMPUTER REALLY DOING?

The second principle of software design is that programs must, to the greatest degree possible, reflect the primary function for which the hardware is being used. In designing any artifact that is to be used repeatedly—so in designing computer programs—you always need to ask what primary function the machine is really performing for the user. As obvious as this sounds, it is overlooked surprisingly often. What is the main function that personal computers generally perform today? I suggest that it is this:

One of the most important roles of desktop computers is that of allowing a very large amount of information to be made visible rapidly at one time, in a way that can be easily modified as desired.

A key word here is 'visible'. Computers excel at making graphic, textual, and numeric information visible. If this is true, then it follows that the best designed software applications are those that allow this function to be performed the best. Of course, I'm using a trick word here, for who's to say what is 'best'?

Well, of course, it's the users who ultimately decide, but it's the designer's job to anticipate them as much as possible. If you design an application so that you allow the users to see as much or as little information at one time on the screen as they wish, and provide a wide variety of options for how that information is displayed, it's hard to see how you will be going wrong. As basic a principle as this is, it is surprising how many commercially available programs violate it.

▪ PARTITIONING PROCEDURES AND PROTOCOLS

The first step in designing an object-oriented system is making lists of the important data items and procedures that the application will require. This is probably not something that's going to remain fixed throughout the course of the program's life, but the important thing is to get off to good start by developing a reasonable partitioning of some of the essential things the program will be dealing with. If the essentials are clarified and understood, the details can be added to this. Then the initial skeleton will have muscle connected to it. Once you have an idea of what the main classes will be for your application, then you will need to design a message protocol for it. A message protocol includes a plan of which messages will be understood by which objects, and how these messages will circulate through the program, and how descendant classes will utilize them.

The use of formal classes has an important role in the design of object-oriented systems. One of their most important features is providing functionality that is of the greatest generality without specifics that are useless for many applications. When an ancestor class has features that are undesirable, they have to be overridden by descendant classes, which means redefining them. This means additional labor and potential problems. Ideally, a set of formal classes should be designed so that nothing ever has to be overridden. Though it's impossible to completely achieve this, it should be one of the goals of object-oriented design.

In an object-oriented system the typical situation is that there is more than one possible design solution to creating a system of objects to fulfill a given program requirement. Quite often there are actually several solutions. Which one is selected depends on the main goals and criteria that have to be solved. There are consequently at least two levels to object-oriented design: the strategic level and the tactical. At the tactical level, design does not occur apart from coding. It is primarily the result of trying out the coding of an initial design that results in redesign and recording, and ultimately proves which design option works best. At the strategic level, the view is toward the perfect generic design where no line of code is wasted or redundant. Wherever code can be reused it is inherited rather than rewritten, both within an application, and across many similar programs.

■ DESIGNING CLASSES

There are really several different viewpoints from which considerations can be made for designing classes. From a strictly formal viewpoint, you can consider all the variables that are nearly always used together with the same procedures and package them together into a class. Or you can look at the full scope of not just a single application, but all similar ones, and design a class that will play a desired role within a functional hierarchy. This latter approach is particularly clear, for example, when designing a formal or abstract class. It's often advantageous to create a new specialized subclass object for a special job, so that because of the design of the new object, the coding becomes tremendously simplified.

For the advanced designer of object-oriented systems, it is not only the current application that is kept in view when a system of classes are being designed, but many other applications that can or may be written as well. The very nature of object-oriented systems is that a host of different application programs can be assembled from a growing set of autonomously functioning classes. To make good on this inherent quality of the technology the designer has to look to the desirable applications that can be built while designing the current application that will be built. Ideally, there will be a kernel of classes from the application that will form the basis for many applications in the future as well as for the current one.

■ MULTIPLE APPLICATION INSTANCES

It is often desirable to design applications in such a way that there can be multiple instances present at the same time. It is when an application consists of a number of cooperating objects that send messages to one another that special design considerations are needed. The reason is that to send messages, each object has to know the name of the instance of the object in its particular copy of the application. For multiple instances of the whole multiobject application to work properly, the names of corresponding objects have to be different, and each object within an application must know the name of those objects in the same copy of the application as itself. From this, it's clear that the instance names cannot appear in the code directly. The solution is simple and elegant. First, some mechanism must be adopted for generating unique names for the instances. Second, each object has instance variables that hold the names of the objects to which it must send messages. Messages access these instance variables to determine the object to which they will be sent. Here we see yet another important technique in which instance variables play the key role.

■ OBJECT-ORIENTED DESIGN FOR GUIS

The following sections describe some very prevalent issues and problems all graphic user interface (GUI) developers must face and attempt to show how object-oriented techniques can be a major help in addressing them. An important question to ask before getting absorbed in various details is whether object-oriented design makes any difference to end users or whether it is a refinement that only affects developers. Initially, it may seem that the benefits of object-oriented systems are only for the programmers who do the development work on applications. However, it is becoming clear that if the object-oriented methodology is carried to its consistent logical conclusion, then it is also quite relevant to what the end user will be seeing in the way of applications. In the future, there will be a different type of application program emerging from which users will also derive great benefit. To illustrate this point, let's look at a familiar enough type of computer software: spreadsheets. Would an object-oriented spreadsheet work any differently than one built using conventional design? In the next section we will attempt to answer this.

In commercial programming, another important issue to consider in designing programs and user interfaces is portability to different computer platforms. For example, if a programmer wants to port a program being written under Windows to the Macintosh or X Windows, then there are some general things to consider to make this easier. For example, there is mouse control. The Macintosh has only a one button mouse. Therefore in developing a class for mouse control it is important to remember that it must be possible to produce a version of one's program that can work with only a single mouse button.

▪ EXAMPLE: DESIGNING AN OBJECT-ORIENTED SPREADSHEET

If spreadsheets were constructed entirely by the principles of object-oriented design, then they would be built quite differently in certain respects than they currently are. Existing spreadsheets are cell-oriented systems for the editing, storage, and recalculation of arrays of dependent numbers. They are cell-oriented because all the important formulas and operations are defined in terms of cells. But what is a cell? It is a rather ambiguous thing, when you get right down to it. It is partly a data structure and partly a display structure. You store data in cells, and yet a cell is something that you define visually by coordinates that tell you where to look for the cell on the screen. The advantages of this scheme have proven themselves in practice over the years, but the object-oriented approach utilizes some concepts that could revolutionize the way spreadsheets are designed.

If spreadsheets were designed exclusively by object-oriented principles, then they would no longer be so uncompromisingly cell-oriented. This would be required by the modular concept of developing models and views independently as consistent modular components. In an object-oriented spreadsheet, the number models would be built out of formulas that applied to the number objects regardless of where they would be displayed on an array of cells. Ideally, you could assign them to cells and be able to edit them much as you do now. But the result would allow you to detach the number models from the display cells and all the formulas would survive intact and be ready for display in any number of different ways, including any possible spreadsheet cells arrangement.

Another important consequence of the modularity of object-oriented design is that any type of object can be assigned to cells for display by them, and more than one object may be assigned to a cell. Although the benefit of this may not be immediately apparent, there is considerable advantage to being able to access the value of a cell as pure data and turn its formula on or off as the need arises. This allows models to be created in which any cell can be either a dependent or independent quantity. Models of this kind are far more versatile than today's spreadsheet models because they are multipurpose. From this discussion it should be apparent that while the most immediate advantages of object-oriented GUIs are for programmers, there will be a new generation of application programs that transmit these benefits to the user, once object-oriented principles of design are both clearly understood and put into effective practice.

■ OPEN ACTIVITY CHAINS

One thing that will help in designing object-oriented software is to have something to fasten onto that can allow the designer to realistically anticipate what users will expect out of a program. This is always going to be a very large challenge, but I would like to suggest some concepts that may often be of help. A useful concept is that of *open activity chains*. The best way to explain what these are is by giving some examples.

In an earlier chapter the HP New Wave architecture was described. If you recall, the design of this system is based on the idea of application objects that can consist of several different files specific to different application programs that are integrated into one final master document by the user environment so that the user does not have to be concerned with the messy details of how this is achieved. There are some clear advantages of this approach, but there are also some potential disadvantages. The most important danger or drawback is that if the user's work is assembled from many files by the higher level software in a way that the user doesn't have to worry about, then the situation might arise that the application becomes too dependent on a black box, which is out of the user's control. If the key of the application is the way numerous files are integrated together, and this linking process is of an unknown nature to the user, then various difficulties can arise. First among them is the likelihood that the application is not portable elsewhere. If the user feels there are advantages to porting the applications to a different environment or platform, that is probably going to be quite difficult unless provision has been made for it. Second, if something goes wrong, and the application becomes unusable for any reason, the user will have all the files, but probably no idea of how to fix the problem that stops them from integrating properly.

In addition to these general kinds of danger or drawback there are some more specific ones that can apply to a certain number of users. This arises from the fact that there are often different application programs that use the same file format, which can make different unique contributions to the same evolving file. For example, a user may use more than one text editor, spreadsheet, or graphics drawing program to create a final result because each has a feature that the others lack. In this way, a work process resembling an assembly line might result. The same file might pass through a series of similar programs before reaching its final form. The file format might even change during this process. Then, there could be a need for several of these resulting files to be integrated into an object such as those in the HP New Wave system.

The difficulties that have been enumerated are not necessarily fatal to an architecture like the New Wave system. However, these issues have to be taken into account when the overall environment is designed. Possibly the most challenging problem in designing software for today's GUI environments is in making the software easy to use for novices without turning the system into a complete black box that cannot be fixed when things go wrong, or reassembled elsewhere. One feature of its solution probably involves the notion of multiple levels of integration and access. This shouldn't be confused with the different levels of object-oriented design itself. What is being referred to here amounts to getting rid of the black box, or keeping it open for those who want to access it. Ideally, a user should be able to ignore what's going on under the hood as long as there's no reason to do otherwise. However, if there's a reason there should be a way to access the lower level of the interface that allows problems to be fixed and applications to be transported in a reasonably straightforward manner.

■ FACTORING COMMAND METHODS

As discussed in the previous chapter, one of the enemies of complex menu systems in GUIs is the proliferation of very long sequences of case statements that can be very difficult to debug. The strategy of object-oriented programming (OOP) is based on building functioning packages that will always work, even though any number of new ones are added to the system. This implies that good object-oriented design requires avoiding a single large command method for processing all menus whenever possible. As was seen earlier, by using the technique of factoring the processing of Windows command messages into a number of separate command methods each of which can work independently, and also in cooperation with other menus, programs compile faster, are simpler to debug, use up less memory resources, and are considerably easier to update.

■ OBJECT-ORIENTED DESIGN FOR MS-WINDOWS

One of the original object-oriented design models is the Model-View-Controller architecture, or M-V-C for short. A key aspect of this architecture is the idea that modularity should prevail between the way information is organized and stored and the way it is accessed and displayed. In other words, the data for an application is stored in an appropriate set of objects, and this data model is independent of the way the information will be ultimately displayed to the user. A number of different objects can be designed for viewing the same data in alternate ways. A standard protocol is usually devised for showing a given set of data in these alternate viewing models. Although this idea may seem obvious or rudimentary, it is by no means the case that mainstream programming has operated in this way. In fact, the contrary has been the rule rather than the exception.

It will be useful to consider a concrete example. In the fields of document processing and desktop publishing, it has become popular to utilize special files known as style sheets. Although the applications that utilize them were not necessarily developed using object-oriented programming, there is a similarity between the use of style sheets and the M-V-C model we are discussing. The similarity lies in the idea of storing the text data in one file, and the style format by which it will be viewed and printed in another. In this way, alternate viewing styles can be quickly and easily assigned to the same text data. The advantages of doing things in this way have been clearly recognized in the industry, and there are many document processing applications that currently use this approach.

The modularity of the M-V-C architecture is, of course, far more fundamental and far-reaching than that of style sheets. The design embraces not just disk files, but application memory as well. And it invites levels of modularity that can have a very noticeable effect on how applications are used.

At this point, there have been three main object-oriented Windows programming systems: Actor, Views, and CommonView. There are striking differences in the approaches taken by all three as is clearly evident in their respective class hierarchies. The C++ Views approach is an explicit implementation of the M-V-C architecture. Views uses the Notifier class, a direct descendant of the root class Object, as the key to its control layer mechanism. In any given application there is always one and only one instance of the Notifier class, which is always globally assigned the name **notifier**. The main event loop of applications is incorporated in the notifier object. All applications also have a top view object that is an instance of a subclass of AppView. All messages between the Views object system and Windows are conducted through the notifier, which waits for the start message before it begins processing events. The formal Window class provides methods to respond to messages of every event type.

The Views Window and View classes are similar to the Actor WindowsObject and Window classes, respectively. View has an instance variable called **model** that is used to store the ID of objects that provide the data model for an application. Views uses three classes to implement menu systems: Menu, PopupMenu, and MenuItem.

Views differs from Actor in forming separate classes for different types of button, such as: PushButton, CheckBox, RadioButton, and TriState. Another major difference is that the TextEditor class is a descendant of Control rather than View, as it would be if a design like that used in Actor were followed. Another major design difference is that the Views Dialog class is a descendant of View. If a design like Actor were followed, Dialog would have instead been a direct descendant of Window and a peer of View. Menu bars in Views are created by making an instance of the Menu class and attaching instances of the PopupMenu class to it.

The difference in the design approaches used by Actor and Views can be quite readily seen in the way these two object-oriented Windows systems implement text editing. Views provides a class called TextEditor, which is a descendant of Control and a direct subclass of EditBox. A TextEditor object is itself actually a window that can hold text and be aligned and justified. TextEditor objects are designed to work as part of a composite of objects also from the String, Stream, and FileStream classes. This composite still has to be integrated into a larger composite that constitutes the main window, particularly if file operations are to be added. The ControlView class is designed to allow instances of the ControlWindow classes to be integrated as child views of a complete application. This handles list box controls, among other things.

■ HIERARCHICAL MENUS

As the example in the previous chapter demonstrated, hierarchical or cascading menus offer a ready means of packing a lot of functionality into a single menu bar while at the same time avoiding a cluttered screen. Yet their use can certainly be overdone. Using a hierarchical menu resembles introducing the equivalent of an additional menu bar of options. Screen space is needed for those options that pop out to the side of the main menu rectangle. For my taste, two hierarchical menus is the most that should be attempted in a single window. In my program I decided to put plenty of options on just one. Although hierarchical menus can be created either dynamically or statically, it turns out that the static resource script approach to creating them is so simple, that this very often is going to be the way to go right from the outset.

■ HANDLING LARGE COMPLEX MENU SYSTEMS

As was mentioned in passing in the previous chapter, there are important considerations with at least two different design levels for arriving at the optimal user interface design. First, there is the layout of the menu bar. As mentioned earlier, given the familiar layout, it is still quite possible to create user interfaces that can range from excellent to almost unusable. There is as yet no instant method for producing the optimal designs in user interfaces or any other area of OOP.

■ COMMONVIEW

Actor and Views are far more similar to one another than either of them is to CommonView. Unlike Actor and Views, CommonView does not have a single common root class like Object. In creating an interface to the Windows environment, it provides a set of independent foundation classes: Control, Event, Menu, Window, and so on. CommonView resembles Views in that DialogWindow is a subclass of Window and Edit is a descendant of Control. The basis for main Windows is provided by App-Window and its two immediate descendants TopAppWindow and ChildAppWindow. Generally speaking, CommonView translates Windows messages into its own internal event handlers and Event objects.

One of the most unique aspects of the CommonView design is typified by the Event class and its descendants. CommonView utilizes a dispatcher that dispatches Event objects to the event handlers of Window objects. Event objects are transient and serve only to convey to Windows that certain events have occurred. The various descendants of Event correspond to the types of events involved. Although interesting because of its substantial differences from Actor and Views, the CommonView architecture cannot be regarded as successful, and a major redesign may be forthcoming in subsequent releases.

■ C++ VIEWS CLASSES

Class
Object
 Assoc
 Clipboard
 Container
  Collection
   OrdCollect
   Stack
  Set
   Dictionary
    Tokens
 Display
  BitMap
  Window
   Control
   Button
    PushButton
    CheckBox
     RadioButton
     TriState
    Group
     InclusiveGroup
     ExclusiveGroup
   ListBox
   ScrollBar
   TextBox
    EditBox
     EditLine
     TextEditor
  View
   AppView
   PopupWindow
    Dialog
     ListSelect
     FileSelect
     Input
     Report
     YesNo
 String

Stream
  File
    Archiver
   ToFMStream
   TagStrm
   TokenStrm
Menu
  PopupMenu
MenuItem
Serial
Timer
Notifier
Port
Printer
Region
  Polygon
  Rectangle
   RoundRect
   Ellipse

■ COMMONVIEW CLASSES

Accel
App
Bitmap
Brush
Color
Control
  FixedIcon
  TextControl
    Button
      CheckBox
      PushButton
      RadioButton
       Edit
        MultiLineEdit
        SingleLineEdit
    FixedText
    ListBox
      FileListBox
  Scrollbar
    HorizScrollbar
      WndHorzScrollbar
    VertScrollbar

WndVertScrollbar

• •

Cursor
DrawObject
  LineObject
  ShapeObject
    EllipseObject
    RectangleObject
  TextObject
Event
  ControlEvt
  ExposeEvt
  FocusChangeEvt
  KeyEvt
  MenuCommandEvt
  MenuInitEvt
  MenuSelectEvt
  MouseEvt
  MoveEvt
  ReSizeEvt
  ScrollEvt
EventContext
Font
Icon
Menu
 SysMenu
MessBox
  ErrorBox
Pair
 Point
 Dimension
 Range
 Selection
Pen
Pointer
Rectangle
ResID
ResString
Window
 AppWindow
  ChildAppWindow
   TopAppWindow
 ControlWindow
  EditWindow

DialogWindow
  ModeLessDialog

• •

FreeStore
  GobalAllocator
  LocalAllocator
Container
Lock
Stack
  Ring

■ WINDOWS MEMORY MANAGEMENT DESIGN

In a multitasking system like Windows, there are often several different applications that will be requesting memory during the same Windows session. Memory management facilities are available to make sure that all applications retain access to the memory needed in as efficient manner as possible. Developers of Windows applications must make use of these facilities to ensure that their application is using the least amount of memory necessary at any given time. Windows has a total of forty different memory management functions to allow the application developer to address both the issues and the memory. In the following paragraphs, I will present a concise overview of the way memory management is handled under MS-Windows.

In Windows, memory can be allocated in two ways: from the global heap and from the local heap. The global heap comprises memory that is available to all applications. A local heap provides memory for just a single application. In Windows, memory is allocated in blocks and is relocatable. It can be moved around and even discarded. Movable memory blocks do not have fixed addresses. At any time, Windows can move them to a different location. Movable memory blocks allow free memory to be consolidated into the largest possible blocks. If an allocated block of memory lies between two free areas, the allocated block can be moved so that the two free areas are combined into one block of consecutive addresses. Discardable memory is memory that can be freed and reallocated. Naturally, this involves destroying any data that may have been contained in it. When a block of memory is allocated in Windows, a handle to it is returned to the application requesting it. This handle is not an address but rather a means of retrieving whatever the memory block's current address may be.

Accessing memory blocks involves locking the memory handle. While the handle is locked Windows cannot move or discard it. An address pointer for the beginning of the block is returned, and the application is given reliable access to the memory. Unlocking the memory handle is up to the application. This means that to provide for the most efficient memory management, developers should adopt the rule that when an application is finished using a block of memory, its handle should be unlocked as soon as possible.

Most Windows applications use mixed memory models. The recommended method is with small code segments of about 4K each so that Windows can easily move these segments about in memory. Applications can allocate memory from either the global heap or from local heaps. The main consideration as to which heap will be used is usually the amount of memory needed. Larger memory blocks are usually allocated from the global heap where it is possible to allocate single blocks larger than 64K. The main Windows functions for managing the global heap are Global Alloc, GlobalLock, GlobalUnlock, GlobalCompact, and GlobalFree. An application's local heap is the free memory in its data segment that can be allocated for various purposes. The local heap is not automatically assigned by Windows but must be requested with the HEAPSIZE statement. Normally, the local heap cannot be larger than 64K, which is the size of an application's data segment.

■ TYPES OF DATA STORAGE

In Windows, seven different types of data storage may be used:

Static data	Used for static variables such as those defined by the static and extern keywords in C.
Automatic data	Used for variables already on the stack when functions are called.
Local dynamic data	Any data in memory areas allocated using LocalAlloc.
Global dynamic data	Any data in memory areas allocated using GlobalAlloc.
Window extra bytes	Used for additional storage that may be requested for a window class.
Class extra bytes	Used for additional storage that may be allocated after the WNDCLASS structure.
Resources	Memory used for resources in an application's .EXE file that have been loaded into memory.

Windows applications that are conversant with advanced memory management issues have to be able to respond to the WM_COMPACTING message.

■ DISCARDABLE MEMORY

In Windows, creating applications with discardable memory must be done explicitly. To create a discardable memory block, both the GMEM_MOVEABLE and the GMEM_DISCARDABLE options to the Global Alloc function must be used. For example, in C the declaration would be:

```
hMem = GlobalAlloc(GMEM_MOVEABLE | GMEM_DISCARDABLE, 4096L);
```

Windows will discard discardable memory when it gets allocation requests that need to be met. Windows determines which discardable blocks to actually discard based on a least recently used algorithm. Using the GlobalDiscard Windows function discards the data stored in the block but retains its handle. The GlobalReAlloc function makes nondiscardable memory blocks discardable and vice versa.

■ ADVANCED MEMORY MANAGEMENT

In the following two paragraphs two advanced Windows memory configurations will be described, the standard and 386 Enhanced Mode configurations.

■ STANDARD MODE

The standard mode Windows memory configuration is the default on 286 computers with at least one megabyte (1M) of memory and 386 with more than one but less than 2 megabytes (2M). Windows uses the protected mode of the 80286 and 80386 processors in the standard memory mode. When Windows runs in this mode, the global heap is usually made up of three distinct blocks of memory. The first block is usually the 640K DOS segment. The second block is in extended memory, which is allocated using the extended memory device driver, but then is accessed directly. Finally, the third block in standard mode is the high memory area (HMA), which is only available if no other software has been loaded into high memory before launching Windows. The Windows global heap is formed by linking these three blocks of memory together. Discardable memory segments are allocated from the top of the heap, fixed segments from the bottom, and movable code and data from just above the fixed segments.

■ 386 ENHANCED MODE

With 368 computers with 2M or more of extended memory, Windows can be run in the 386 Enhanced Mode. In this mode Windows provides a virtual memory scheme that utilizes both extended memory and hard disk space to allow memory spaces as large as 64M. In the enhanced mode, the Windows global heap is composed of a large single virtual address space. The size of this space is based on both the amount of extended memory and the amount of disk space available. Because the structure of this virtual memory space is composed of a single large block, it resembles that of basic memory configuration, and its layout is actually strongly analogous to it, though of course it includes a far larger address space.

■ SOME RULES OF THUMB

1. Avoid far pointers to static data in small and medium models.

2. Do not pass data to other applications by a global handle.

3. Do not assume any relationship between a handle and a far pointer in any mode.

4. Do not perform segment arithmetic.

5. Do not compare segment addresses.

6. Do not read or write past the ends of memory objects.

■ THE WINMEM32.DLL LIBRARY

As part of the Windows 3.0 SDK package Microsoft supplies a dynamic Link library called WINMEM32.DLL that provides functions, which can be used by applications that permit use of the 32-bit addressing capabilities of the 80386 and 80486 processors. The attraction of this DLL is that it can potentially provide the long-hoped-for way beyond the segmented memory addressing in the MS-DOS world. The answer to the question of whether this DLL can allow developers to use a flat memory model at long last is unfortunately an equivocal yes and no. It is true that functions are provided here that utilize the 32-bit registers of the 80386 and 80486 chips. And it is also true that this addressing scheme can be used to define single memory segments larger than anyone is likely to ever need. However, Windows itself is a program that is written in the segmented memory model as is MS-DOS. Because of this, every Windows application must have at least one 16-bit segment in the old 16-bit segmented model. However, despite this limitation, the lion's share of a Windows application's code and data can be put in memory segments that use the new 32-bit addressing.

The important thing about this DLL is that it implements a standard for a flat memory model under Windows that Microsoft says will be adhered to in all future versions of Windows. However, there is a downside to the assurances that code written with the WINMEM32.DLL library will always be supported in future Windows releases. There are problems in using a hybrid memory model that is composed partly of 16-bit and partly of 32-bit addressing, as one might expect. And as is not surprising the trouble becomes particularly acute when interrupts are called. All code written in the 32-bit model has to live with the important limitation that it cannot contain code or data that is accessed at interrupt time. The main consequence for developers is that it is virtually impossible to use a high-level language to write code using WINMEM.DLL. Only assembly language programmers ought to attempt it. What this means is that there will probably be third-party packages appearing that provide the assembly code that can be linked with programs written in C or other languages to provide access to 32-bit memory for developers not initiated in the meticulous art of assembly language programming.

■ MEMORY MANAGEMENT WITH ACTOR

One of the main differences between Actor and a language like C is that Actor provides an automatic memory management system whereas in C memory has to be allocated and deallocated as needed. Actor performs incremental garbage collection in the background, which is a unique and important capability in the Windows environment. Windows itself, you might often think, needs a good garbage collector.

Actor divides memory resources into static and dynamic memory. Static memory is where permanent objects are stored, meaning things like classes and methods. Dynamic memory is used for more volatile constructs like strings and long integers. The purpose of having two different types of memory is so that the garbage collector has less to be concerned with. The garbage collector leaves static memory alone and only looks for garbage in dynamic memory. Actually, though, the garbage collector doesn't really look for garbage. It works by copying the live objects into a new memory area and leaving the rest behind.

The ShowRoom! function on the Workspace menu shows three things: Actor static memory, Actor dynamic memory, and Windows memory free. After you have launched Actor, look at the value of Windows memory. Then evaluate this message:

> *Call GlobalCompact(-1);*

Then compare the new value of free Windows memory. The same thing can be done for local memory using the message:

> *Call LocalCompact(-1);*

If you have a fair amount of memory in your computer and own the MS-Windows 3.0 SDK, you can try this experiment. Load the HeapWalker program. Go to the Alloc menu and select Allocate All of Memory. Now, all of Windows memory is allocated. Go back to the Alloc menu and select the option Free 50K. Without exiting HeapWalker switch to Actor and look at ShowRoom! If you like, evaluate

> *Call GlobalCompact(-1);*

and compare. Now go back to HeapWalker and select Free All from the Alloc menu. Then you can go back and compare the ShowRoom! facility in Actor.

Another informative way of using the HeapWalker program is to start it right at the beginning of a Windows session and take a good look at how the memory is allocated for the different Windows facilities. You might even want to save a snapshot file of the memory map with HeapWalker at this point. Then load several different programs into Windows and compare the difference. If necessary, save one or more snapshots of the state of Windows memory at different points during a session. In this way, with a little practice, you'll begin to get familiar with the way Windows manages memory in situations with several tasks competing for resources.

Practical memory management issues in Actor are of two kinds, those involved with managing memory in the development environment and those involved with memory management in the final user application you are writing. The two are very closely related, however. Generally, what saves memory in the programs you write saves memory in the development environment too. One thing good to know is that since the garbage collector copies objects back and forth between two dynamic memory areas, you need twice as much as you really use. For this reason, any time you can put something in static memory that would ordinarily be dynamic you are saving space.

You might think that even static memory can accumulate garbage over time. This is true, and for this reason a static garbage collector is also included with Actor. This is the Cleanup! function that can be selected from the Workspace window. In real mode the dynamic memory settings for Actor are between 25 and 30K. For the 386 Extended Mode, the setting can be as high as one megabyte and is determined by your development and application requirements. Although applications written with Actor cannot profit from static garbage collection unless that feature is specifically built into them, dynamic garbage collection is built-in and automatic and offers one of the most attractive features of applications built with Actor.

■ SWAPPING STATIC MEMORY

One way of decreasing the amount of memory an Actor program uses under Windows is to utilize the technique of static memory swapping. Static memory swapping works by paging the least recently used memory objects out to disk, and reading them back in when their use is requested.

The practical memory management methods provided in the System class include: checkDynamic, cleanup, dynamicGC, initMemory, staticRoom, staticSwapOff, and staticSwapOn. The latter two provide just what their name indicates, a way of toggling static memory on or off. An additional means exists for controlling the use of static memory swapping by using the SwapFlags and SwapFile keywords in the WIN.INI Windows initialization file. Table 10.1 shows a list of the SwapFlag values in hexadecimal and what they are used for.

■ ACTOR MEMORY CLASSES

The two main supplied classes for memory management in Actor are MemoryObject, and its subclass Handle. The MemoryObject and Handle classes allow memory from the Windows global heap to be allocated as Actor Struct objects. The Struct class has several methods used for the conversion back and forth between object and binary formats. This allows Actor to treat blocks of memory as objects if desired. Methods are provided in the Handle class to allocate memory as either fixed, movable, or shared.

Also included is the Class Description of the MemoryBlock class, which incorporates some interesting features to its design. MemoryBlock provides access to blocks of Windows memory greater than 64K. First of all, interest in its implementation is its $LiveBlocks class variable, which stores the handles of all of its instantiated memory blocks. MemoryBlock's design is something like the MemoryObject and Handle classes combined into one. MemoryBlock uses the same three instance variable as Handle: handle, address, and length.

■ MEMORY CLASS DESCRIPTIONS

The MemoryObject Class

Source file:	MEMORYOB.CLS
Inherits from:	Struct
Inherited by:	Handle
Class methods:	
new	Returns a new MemoryObject instance.
Object methods:	
copyFrom	General copyFrom method.
copyFromLong	Copies the data at the given Long into self. Useful for getting data back from MS-Windows after it has copied it into the area starting at the Long.
fill	Fills receiver Struct with the specified word value.
freeHandle	Frees the block. Assumes a corresponding lock was done.
getData	Returns data at self as a struct.
getText	Returns a string from self with nulls removed.
intCall	Calls an interrupt routine with the parameters in self.
isIdx	Returns true to inspector's indexed query.
keysDo	Evaluates a one-argument block over the keys of the receiver. An IndexedCollection, the keys are the integer indices of the collection, and thus are probably of little interest. However, Do is provided so that any collection can respond to keysDo.
longAt	Returns a Long at the given offset.
lP	Derives a long pointer by locking the block.
putLong	Stores a Long at the given offset.
species	Returns the species type.

The Handle Class

Source file:	HANDLE.CLS
Inherits from:	MemoryObject
Instance Variables:	
handle	global heap memory handle
address	non-nil if locked

length	actual length of allocated memory

Class methods:

set	Creates a new Handle with the given handle value.

Object methods:

addr	Returns the address of the block. Locks it if it is not already locked.
alloc	Allocates a global memory block of the given type and length and stores its information.
asHandle	Returns a global heap handle but returns nil if memory is not allocated.
asString	Returns an Actor object representing the contents of this memory block as a string.
asStruct	Returns an Actor object representing the contents of this memory block as a struct.
byteAt	Returns the byte value at the specified byte offset. Locks the handle temporarily if not already locked.
checkHandle	Checks that memory has been allocated. If not, then issues an error message.
copyInto	Copies a ByteCollection into receiver, adjusts length of receiver if required.
fastPutWord	Stores a word value at the specified byte offset. This method assumes that the receiver's memory had been previously locked in the global heap. Not doing so will produce unknown results, possibly catastrophic in nature.
fastWordAt	Returns the word value at the specified index. This method makes the same assumptions that the previous method makes.
fixed	Returns a new fixed handle.
free	Frees the handle, returning true if freed.
handle	Returns the global heap handle.
length	Returns the actual length of allocated memory. If memory not allocated returns nil. Note that the actual length returned may be different from that requested (never less than) when the memory was allocated. This is a function of how Windows allocates memory in the global heap.
lock	Locks the handle, returning the long address.

lower	Allocates movable memory from nonbanked portion of Windows global heap.
movable	Returns a new movable handle.
putByte	Stores a byte value at the indicated byte offset.
putWord	Stores a word value at the indicated byte offset.
reAlloc	Reallocates a global memory block of the given type and length and stores its information.
setHandle	Sets the memory block's handle.
shared	Returns a new shared-memory handle.
size	Returns the actual length of allocated memory. Same as sending length message.
sysPrintOn	Prints Handle object to a specified stream.
unlock	Unlocks the handle, returning true if ref count goes to 0.

MemoryBlock

Source file:	MEMORYBL.CLS
Inherits from:	Object
Inherited by:	
Class Variables:	
$LiveBlocks	Handles of all blocks currently allocated.
Instance Variables:	
handle	
address	
length	
Class methods:	
destroyAll	Destroys all living MemoryBlocks.
fixed	Returns a new fixed handle.
init	Initialize method.
liveBlocks	Returns the set of live MemoryBlocks.
lower	Allocates movable memory from nonbanked portion of Windows global heap.
movable	Returns a new movable handle.
shared	Returns a new shared-memory handle.

Object methods:

alloc	Allocates a global memory block of the given type and length and stores its information.
asStructAt	Returns a Struct of size sz containing the data starting at offs.
byteAt	Returns the byte value at the specified byte offset. Locks the handle temporarily if not already locked.
checkHandle	Checks that memory has been allocated. If not then reports an error.
copy	Copies the Block with segment wrapping.
destroy	Unlocks and frees self and removes the handle from $LiveBlocks.
fastPutWord	Stores a word value at the specified byte offset. This method assumes that the receiver's memory had been previously locked in the global heap. Not doing so will produce unknown results, possibly catastrophic in nature.
fastWordAt	Returns the word value at the specified index. This method makes the same assumption as the previous one.
free	Frees the handle, returning true if freed.
handle	Returns the handle ivar.
length	Returns the length of the block.
lockLock	Locks the handle, returning the long address.
longAt	Returns a Long at the given offset.
lP	Returns the long address of the MemoryBlock.
putByte	Stores a byte value at the indicated byte offset.
putLong	Stores a Long at the given offset.
putStructAt	Copies nBytes of ByteCollection struct at offs.
putWord	Stores a word value at the indicated byte offset.
removeRef	Removes the MemoryBlock from the LiveBlocks set without freeing it. This is used for MemoryBlocks that will be given to/read from the clipboard.
setHandle	Sets the handle of self. System use only.
setLength	Sets the length of self. System use only.
sysPrintOn	Prints Handle object to specified stream.

| unlock | Unlocks the handle, returning true if ref count goes to 0. |
| wordAt | Returns the word value at the specified index. Note that the index is a byte offset, that is, at (handle, 2) returns the word located at byte offset 2. Locks the handle temporarily if not already locked. |

■ DESIGNING INDEXED SEQUENTIAL FILE DATABASES 1947

In this section, I will address another important area of a computer's resources: massive storage of data. What advantages does the object-oriented approach provide in making efficient use of today's external disk storage media? There are actually several advantages to using the object-oriented approach to implementing traditional random access file type databases, such as those of the familiar indexed sequential type. To illustrate what these advantages are, and how advanced data storage systems may be designed using them, I will first introduce an Actor extension product for object-oriented database construction called Wintrieve.

Wintrieve is a support package for database programming under MS-Windows that supports the X/Open standard of ISAM (Indexed Sequential Access Method) of databases. One of the particular advantages of Wintrieve that many programmers will immediately appreciate is that there is no upper limit to the number of indexes permitted. Two other attractive features of the Wintrieve package are its support for transactions and journaling. Combined together, these facilities help protect the integrity of large, complex database systems. The Wintrieve package includes support for both the Actor and C languages. It is advantageous to have access to an ISAM file system from an OOP language like Actor under Windows, because data in ISAM disk files can be read into predefined objects and from that point, most of the advantages of a full-fledged object-oriented system can be provided for the database. In this way, in an important sense, you are getting the best of two worlds. Before illustrating how such systems are designed, it will be useful first to gain an overview of the Wintrieve architecture.

■ WINTRIEVE: AN OVERVIEW

The most important classes in Wintrieve to first know about are: IsamFile and IsamManager. IsamFile is designed for creating objects that can handle a single data file. It has six instance variables, which are listed in Table 10.1. An ISAM file can be built with the **create** method of the IsamFile class, and when this is done, a record descriptor is stored as a string in the file information section of the file.

The RelFile class provides facilities for linking multiple data files into a relational database. The scheme utilized requires one RelFile object to act as the master for other IsamFile and RelFile objects that comprise the relational database. The **relate** method of the RelFile class can be used to build associations between fields of the master RelFile

Table 10.1 IsamFile Instance Variables.

filename	The name of a file
record	An IsamRecord instance
keys	Dictionary of keyName/key pairs
manager	An IsamManager object
currentIndex	KeyName of currently selected index
block	Global Heap block, used in com with ISAM Server

object and the fields of other files. These relations are only meaningful for read operations.

```
BF := new(BookFile); setFilename(BF, "c:\cbook\book.dat");
MasterFile := initFile(new(RelFile), BF, "book", #book);
RelFile("book")

DependentFile1 := initFile(new(IsamFile), DB, "aut", #author);
IsamFile("author")

DependentFile2 := initFile(new(IsamFile), DB, "pubt", #publisher);
IsamFile("author")

relate(MasterFile, #pubID, DependentFile2, #primary);
```

The dependent file of a RelFile master object can itself be a RelFile object that is master of its own dependents, and so on. In this way, a nested hierarchy of dependent files can be built.

Not all the results of reading ISAM data into objects is necessarily advantageous. There are some circumstances in which some disadvantages might appear. In a relational database, for example, if you had a separate class for each database file, then there are some designs to avoid in which encapsulation might work against you, since the objects of one class might not have immediate access to the data of those of another class. There are, of course, a number of ways around such potential difficulties. By using a C++ interface to Wintrieve, the classes could be defined as friends. In Actor, the data file classes could be descendants of a common superclass that gave a full description of the data of all the data fields of the different files. As common descendants of this single class, the data file classes would have access to each other's data. Still another option would be to collect the different data file objects into a single Collection object.

■ OBJECT-ORIENTED RELATIONAL DATABASE SYSTEMS

An object-oriented relational database system is a specially designed application that provides all the advantages of traditional relational databases while at the same time offering the attractive features that the greatest modularity of design can provide, both in the areas of data access and data presentation.

One of the most attractive features of a system of this kind is that an object-oriented system can be fed by a relational database, as it were, without this being obvious to the end user. It would appear that the object-oriented approach is extremely well suited to providing a front end to a relational database that hides the inner workings of the file access system while allowing the utmost flexibility in presenting the data to users. In the next few sections I will describe the architecture of Wintrieve, the object-oriented relational database system provided as an extension to the Actor language.

■ DESIGNING RELATIONAL DATABASES WITH WINTRIEVE

As you have just seen, fully relational databases can be created with Wintrieve by using the RelFile class and the relate method for actually creating the links. In a traditional relational database, a series of data files are used to represent a large connected information context such as various activities of a business. There is always a data field in common between at least two of the files. Ideally, any file would have at least one other file with a field in common.

Although the Wintrieve data file system is not in itself a hierarchical database system the way a true object-oriented database system can be, it is possible to use Wintrieve to build such a database. A hierarchical database is one that allows a conceptual relationship between data files as well as a field overlap that provides for relational links. For example, in a hierarchical database, all the data files, say, that pertain to vehicles of any kind would have a conceptual relationship, whether or not they had relational links. The instance variables of object classes are similar to the fields in a hierarchical database. However, there is no random access file system usually provided for objects the way there is for a system like Wintrieve.

Despite the fact that relational databases and hierarchical databases are two quite different things, it is possible to simulate a hierarchical database using a relational one. An obvious method of doing this is to include additional fields in each data file such as InheritsFrom, InheritedBy, and InstanceOf. These would be "meta-fields" of the data files, in that they would provide information about the conceptual structure of the file system itself, rather than the real world information it contains.

Corresponding to the simulated hierarchical database, an actual object hierarchy would also be constructed from classes of the object system. Ultimately an object would be created for each database record, but for most applications it would seem wasteful of resources to create the objects until they are needed. Once an object is created, it would handle reading the corresponding record to set the values of it variables on its own. Ideally, such a system would function as though there were really a random access file system for a hierarchical database. In practice, there would be various compromises based on a trade-off between essential requirements of an application and what it is most feasible to implement.

■ WINTRIEVE CLASSES

```
Object
        Collection
                IndexedCollection
                        ByteCollection
                                Struct
                                        MemoryObject
                                                Handle
                        KeyedCollection
                        Dictionary
                                OrderedDictionary
        CStruct
                IsamCStruct
                SubStruct
        CType
                        IsamRecord
                UserType
        FieldInfo
        IsamDesc
        IsamDict
        IsamKey
        IsamKeyParser
        IsamFile
                RelFile
        IsamManager
        WindowsObject
                Window
                        IsamLink
```

IsamCStruct

IsamCStruct is like a CStruct object, but where its data is a Handle object. The Handle's memory is allocated from nonbanked portion (lower) of the global heap.

IsamRecord

An IsamRecord object is also a special kind of CStruct that defines record layouts for Actor ISAM file access.

IsamDict

The IsamDict class provides a protocol for accessing and manipulating ISAM dictionary structures.

IsamKey

IsamKey class provides protocol for instantiating and defining ISAM index keys.

IsamLink

The IsamLink class provides the protocol for managing a connection with an ISAM Server. Usage of an IsamLink object typically involves initiating a session, sending requests, and terminating a session with the ISAM Server. IsamLink inherits from Window because communications between applications in MS-Windows is actually accomplished through windows. A windows handle is used to uniquely identify the communicating agents. When making requests to the ISAM Server the appropriate fields of queryBlock must be filled in, please refer to "ISAM Server Protocol Specification" to for more information.

IsamFile

The IsamFile class provides protocol for managing single ISAM files.

RelFile

The RelFile class provides a protocol for linking record field(s) of a parent RelFile object to key fields of the dependent IsamFile class or its descendant objects.

IsamManager

The IsamManager class provides the basic interface to the ISAM Server. All access to the ISAM Server is made through an IsamManager object. IsamManager provides protocol for managing a session, transactions, journaling, and file access.

IsamDesc

The IsamDesc class is a support class that provides a protocol for managing ISAM record descriptors.

IsamKeyParser

IsamKeyParser is a support class for the IsamKey class. It provides protocol for parsing key attribute and key part descriptors.

▪ UNDERLYING CLASSES USED BY WINTRIEVE

The CStruct class is a C structure support class. A CStruct contains two instance variables, a dictionary of field characteristics and binary data. The CStructs are useful whenever you need to convert between Actor objects and binary data, such as in communication with an operating system, disk files or a window manager. The CStruct makes use of four other classes to implement its objects: FieldInfo, CType, UserType, and SubStruct.

The FieldInfo class holds the information about a field in C structure objects. CType objects describe C language types for C structures and handle the translation from Actor format to the binary Struct format. An instance of CType is needed for every C datatype that will be used as fields in CStruct objects. The CTYPES.ACT file contains some sample C Type definitions. The UserType class provides user extensible types for Actor CStructs. The Substruct class provides CStruct objects that are actually nested fields within other structs.

Structs are fixed-size, indexed collections of word (two bytes) or long (four bytes) data, useful to communicate with MS-Windows and other programming languages. All the Actor geometric object classes, with the exception of Point, are descendants of Struct. The data inside Struct objects is accessed by means of byte offsets, as in, for example, "the word located at byte offset 3." The MemoryObject class is an Abstract parent class for describing blocks of non-Actor memory. The Handle class describes memory objects allocated by the system global memory manager.

■ WINTRIEVE CLASS DESCRIPTIONS

OrderedDictionary

Source file:	ORDEREDD.CLS
Inherits from:	Dictionary
Instance Variables:	
orderKeys	A collection to maintain the keys in order.
Object methods:	
addAssoc	Adds an Association to the Dictionary.
assocsDo	Evaluates the block over each of the receiver's Associations.
do	Enumerates over the elements in the OrderedDictionary.
grow	Copies elements into larger collection and swaps with the old collection.
init	Initializes the KeyedCollection by setting the tally instance variable to 0.
keys	Return the keys in proper order.
keysDo	Evaluates the one argument block over the keys of the Dictionary.
put	Replaces a current element or creates a new one. The put method for this class is identical to the add method except for the order of its arguments.

removeUsing	Removes the element with the specified key from the Dictionary. If there is no element corresponding to aKey, then the 0-argument block is executed. The removeUsing method returns the removed key or the value of the block.
setCompareBlock	Re-sorts itself according to newCompareBlock and returns self.
setOrderClass	Sets the class of the order for the keys

■ SAMPLE CLASS DESCRIPTIONS

BookWindow

Source file:	BOOKWIND.CLS
Inherits from:	TextWindow
Instance Variables:	
keysDict	Dictionary of keys
bookDB	ISAM manager
bookTable	ISAM book file
Object methods:	
changeIndex	Changes to selected index and displays first record in new index ordering.
closeDB	Closes the database.
command	Responds to the menu events. The wp argument gives the selected menu ID. Gets a message symbol from the menu object.
createMenu	Sets up the menu bar.
deleteRec	Deletes the current record.
getISBN	Handles input dialog processing for obtaining ISBN number. Returns ISBN number or nil if user cancels.
getTitle	Handles input dialog processing for obtaining search title. Returns title or nil if user cancels.
init	Initializes the Book Window. Creates the menu and About to control menu.
insertRec	Inserts a record.
nextRec	Reads the next record and displays it.
openDB	Initiates a session with the ISAM manager.

prevRec	Reads the previous record and displays it.
printRecord	Displays the current record in the window.
recDlg	Builds a record dialog.
searchRec	Searches for a record based on current index order.
shouldClose	Closing the window so close the database.
updateRec	Updates a record.
validateInput	Validates record dialog input. If ok, returns dictionary of input field values. If there is an error in one of the input fields, displays error box and then returns nil.

BookDlg

Source file:	BOOKDLG.CLS
Inherits from:	Window
Instance Variables:	
isbn	field edit control
title	field edit control
pubID	field edit control
quantity	field edit control
price	field edit control
isbnVal	field input value
titleVal	field input value
pubIDVal	field input value
quantityVal	field input value
priceVal	field input value
ok	user acceptance flag
bOK	OK button control
bCancel	Cancel button control
bookFile	
op	
Object methods:	
command	Handles command events. Just checks for theOK or CANCEL button being pressed and takes appropriate action. If it's the OK, reads the values of the input fields.
initButtons	Creates the OK and CANCEL buttons.

initEdits	Creates the input fields.
isbn	Returns the isbn input field value.
price	Returns the price input field value.
pubID	Returns the pubID input field value.
quantity	Returns the quantity input field value.
setIsbn	Sets the display value of the ISBN field.
setPrice	Sets the display value of the price field.
setPubID	Sets the display value of the pubID field.
setQuantity	Sets the display value of the quantity input field.
setTitle	Sets the display value of the title input field.
shouldClose	Sends the message back to parent that the reciever is about to close.
title	Returns the title input field value.

INDEX

123/G, 27
386 Enhanced Mode, xi, 2, 6, 325
  application shortcut keys, 14
  Control Panel in, 11–12

Accessories Group, 3
Active Data, 32–33
Actor, xii, 61, 64, 117–60
  3.0, 117
  adding Primitives to, 143–44
  Browser, 118–20, 127–28
  buttons, 170–75
  Callback, 124–25
  class variables, 128
  classes, 120–23
  code blocks, 128
  compared to Smalltalk, 143–44
  controls, 123
  critique of, 143–44, 234
  data storage in, 333–41
  Dating class, 149–52
  dialogs, 124, 170, 175–76
  differs from Views, 318–19
  file formats, 128–29
  graphics programming for Windows, 217–43
  Inspector, 120
  list structures, 125
  managing time in, 144–45
  MDI support, 279–80
  memory classes, 328
  memory management, 326–28

  menus, 124
  Object Graphics in, 243–76, 250–51
  programming environment, 117–18, 125–28
  sample application, 277–79
  sample workouts for, 129–60
  static memory, 328
  Support Packages for, 143
  syntax, 126–28
  Temporal object class, 147
  TextFile class, 176–77
  Timer class, 148–49
  Wintrieve, 333–41
  WorkSpaces, 176
Actor, sample workouts for
  application class, 141–43
  arrays, 133–34
  calling Dynamic Link Libraries (DLL), 138–39
  class variables, 138
  collections, 133, 134–37
  control structures, 131
  debugging, 140
  dictionaries, 136
  Eratosthenes' sieve benchmark, 157
  external programs, 140
  Fibonacci program, 157–58
  Frame Representation Language (FRL), 139–40
  List handling support, 159–60
  loops, 131–32
  number class session, 129–30
  ordered collections, 135–36
  Profiler, 140
  queues, 137–38

sealing-off process, 141
strings, 130–31
text collections, 136–37
Tower of Hanoi, 158–59
ActorApp class, 170, 190
Agent, 16
Algol, 29
Always Warn option, 11
Ami, xi, 8, 17
Ami Professional, 17
Animation, 19
  in Windows, 232–34
Apple, xi, 16
Application shortcut keys, 14
Applications
  launching, 3–4
AppView class, 74–75, 77
Arrange All, 16
AT&T, xi, 43
Autodesk, 28
Autosketch, 28

Borland, xi
Browser, 37, 41–42
Browser, Actor's, 118–20
  Global References, 119
  Implementors, 119
  References, 119
  Senders, 119
  Window Routine Senders, 119
Buttons, 2, 170, 318
  creating, 172–75
  in Windows 3.0, 88
Byte, 6

C Language, xii, 35, 45, 50, 65, 71, 104, 126,
    143–44, 279, 326, 333
C++ Language 2.0, xii, 318, 334
  class specifiers, 43–44
  classes, 44
  constructors, 48–50
  critique of, 54–55
  Debugger, 52–53
  destructors, 48–50
  difference with C Language, 45
  friends, 45–46
  member functions, 45
  Memory model, 52
  methods, 45
  multiple inheritance, 44–45
  overloading, 45–48
  overview of, 43

privacy in, 45
protection of data, 45
prototyping, 47
reserved words, 44
scope in, 49
structs, 44
Views Browser, 72–74
Views classes, 320–21
virtual classes, 47–48
virtual functions, 47–48
Zortech compiler, 50–52
C Languages, 43–80
Calculator, 6–7, 8
Calendar, 5, 7
Cardfile, 7
Channel Computing, 17
Charts, 230–32
CL.EXE, 55
Class hierarcy
  Objective-C Language, 57–59
Classes, 34–39, 43–44
  Actor, 120–23
  designing, 314
  finding correct one, 279
  MS-Windows, 83–85, 121–23
Clipboard, 3, 5–6, 9, 28
  coping from Calculator, 7
  coping from non-Windows applications, 6
  saving as a disk file, 6
  transfering images from Cardfile, 7
Clock, 5
Clocks, digital, 152–54
Codes, reusability of, 39–40
Codeview, 101–02, 104
Collapse Branch, 5
Collapsing windows, 1
Collection structures
  Assoc, 60
  Dictionary, 60
  of Objective-C Language, 59–61
  Sets, 60
Color graphics, 93, 227–28, 252–53, 263–64
  CMY primaries, 252
  LogBitmaps, 253
  RGB color component values, 252
Color Palette, 27–28
Colors, 11
Combo boxes, 90
  creating, 181–83
Command methods
  ExecWin class listing, 287–301
  factoring in GUI, 317
  factoring in MDI, 286–306
  header file, 304–06

resource script file, 301–04
CommonView, 318–20
  classes, 321–23
Communications class, 79
Compound object, 16
Computer Aided Design (CAD), 243–44
Computer Aided Display (CAD), xii
Constructors, 48–50
Container object, 16
Control Panel, 3, 5, 11
  adding special fonts, 5
  configuring printer, 5
  creating custom backgrounds, 5
  setting time and date, 5
Controls
  Actor, 123
  in Windows 3.0, 88
  owner-drawn, 87
Corel Draw, xi, 8
Cox, Brad
  Object-Oriented Programming, 32
Crayon Colors, 27
Crosstalk, 9
Ctalk, xii, 65–71, 78, 80
  Buffer class, 69
  Collection class, 69
  Container class, 69
  critique of, 71
  foundation classes of, 68–69
  Run-time applications, 70
  Stream class, 69
  syntax of, 67–68
  Text Window classes, 69–70
  VIEWS, 28, 65–66, 71–80
Customizing Windows, 5, 13

Data storage, 324, 333–41
Dates
  managing in Windows, 144–56
Debugger, 52–53
  windows of, 53
Debugging
  in Windows, 94, 95
  Spy, 98–99
Debugging, symbolic, 63, 101–02
Design, object-oriented, 311–41
  classes, 314
  command methods, 317
  CommonView, 318–23
  computer oriented, 311–13
  for Windows, 317–33
  GUI, 314–17
  menus, 319

multiple applications instances, 314
open activity chains, 316–17
partitioning procedures for, 313
spreadsheets, 315–16
user oriented, 311–12
Views classes, 320–21
Designer, xi, 8
Desk accessory programs, 5
Desk space, free, 5
Desktop publishing, 8, 9
Desktop, 11
Destructors, 48–50
Detect Idle Time, 14
Device context, 91
Dialog Editor, 95–96
Dialogs, 89–90, 170
  Actor, 124
  creating dynamic, 178–79
  creating file, 175–76
  creating VIEWS, 77
  custom, 180
  modeless, 179–80
Dictionaries, 17
Directory tree display, 4
Display context system, 86
DOS Directories
  DIRECT.RC, 213–15
  DIRECTOR.CLS, 200–213
  FILESTRI.CLS, 197–200
  manipulating, 194–215
  SYSCHNG.ACT, 195–97
DOS Prompt, 3
Drafix CAD, 8
Dword, 6
Dynamic Data Exchange (DDE), 8, 19–20, 93
Dynamic dialogs
  creating, 178–79
  custom, 180
Dynamic Link Libraries (DLL), 19–20, 26–27, 92–93, 326
  initialization of, 93
  termination of, 93
Dynamic menus
  creating, 177–78

EditWindow, 166–68
Electronic libraries, 21
EMM386.SYS, 7
Enumeration functions, 124–25
Eratosthenes' sieve benchmark, 49–50, 157
Excel, xi, 1, 7, 9, 17, 20, 27
Exclusive in Foreground, 12

Executive control, 277–79
  ExecWin class listing, 287–301
  header file, 304–06
  resource script file, 301–04
Executive Controller, 186–90
Executive program, 2
ExecWindow, 186–90
Expand All, 5
Expand Branch, 5
Expand One Level, 5
Expanding windows, 1

Fibonacci program, 157–58
File, 5
File Drawer, 17
File Manager, 2, 3, 4–5
FileChildMDI, 307–08
FileEditor, 168
  class descriptions, 168–69
FileWindow, 168
Font Editor, 11, 96–97
Fonts, 2, 5
  Printer, 11
  Screen, 11
Forest & Trees, 17
FORTRAN, 29
Functions of Windows, 83–86

Games Group, 3
GDI, 90–92
Generic Printer, 5
Glossary, 8
Graph Plus, 17
Graphic design, 9
Graphic Display Interface (GDI), 164
Graphics, xii, 7–8, 19, 28, 312
  animation, 232–34
  charts, 230–32
  color bitmaps, 227–28
  color, 93
  ellipses, 223–24
  polygons, 224–27
  programming for Windows, 217–43
  Rect, 220–22
  rectangles, 220–22
  rendering tools, 266–71
  RndRect, 222–23
  round rectangles, 222–23
  SDKPaint, 96
  three-dimensional points, 228–30
  VIEWS, 79
  WinEllipse, 223–24

  WinPolygon, 220–22
  WinPolygon, 224–27
Graphics class descriptions, 234–36
  Chart, 237–39
  DemosWindow, 237
  HBarChart, 239
  PieChart, 240–41
  ShapesWindow, 236
  TrackWindow, 236–37
  VBarChart, 239–40
Graphics classes, 217–30
  GraphicsObject, 217–18
  Point, 61, 217–18
  Rect, 217–18
  Rectangle, 61
  RndRect, 217–18
  Struct, 217–18
  WinEllipse, 217–18
  WinPolygon, 217–18
Graphics, Object
  See Object Graphics
Graphics User Interface (GUI), 1, 277
  Object-oriented design for, 314–17
Groups
  adding programs to, 3
  creating new, 3–4

Heapwalker, 99–100, 104, 326
Help, 1, 2
Help-building system, 94
Hewlet-Packard, 16
Hierarchy, 34
HIMEM.SYS
Hybrid system, 35–36
Hyperscript, 21–23
  ADD POPUP MENU, 26
  creating applications in, 26
  Dynamic Link Libraries (DLL), 26–27
  executing commands from, 25
  limitations of, 27
  scripts, 25
  user interface, 26

I/O ports, 11
Icon Editor, 8
Icons, 2
  in Windows 3.0, 87
ICs, 32
Idle option, 11
Indexed Sequential Access Method (ISAM), 333–34
Information context, 91
Informix, 21

Inheritance, 34, 36
Initialization files, 5, 12–13
Inspector, Actor's, 120
Instantiation, 34
Integrated circuits, 64–65
Interface programming, xii

Keyboard, 1
Keyname=value statement, 13

Legend, 8
LISP, 35, 46–47, 57
List boxes, 89–90
    creating, 181
List handling support in Actor, 159–60
LOOPS, 57
Lotus, xi
Lotus-Intel-Microsoft (LMI), 15

Macintosh, 21
Macintosh GUI, 1
Macro Recorder, 5, 9–10
    ending, 9
    recording key strokes, 9
    recording mouse movements, 9
Macrocalc, 8
Main Group, 3
Main Window Menu Bars
    creating, 183–86
MDIFileWindow, 279–82
MDIFrameWindow, 280, 286, 306–07
Memory classes, 328–33
    Handle, 329–31
    MemoryBlock, 331–33
    MemoryObject, 329
Memory management, xii–xiii, 5, 7, 15, 311, 323–35
    386 Enhanced Mode, 235
    Actor, 326–28
    advanced mode, 235
    rules of thumb, 235–36
    standard mode, 235
    WINMEM32.DLL, 326
Memory, discardable, 324–35
Memory, partitioning of, 32
Menus
    Actor, 124
    combining static and dynamic, 285–86
    creating dynamic, 177–78
    handling complex ones, 283–84, 319
    hierarchical, 284–85, 319
    in Windows 3.0, 87–88

setting up, 77
Message-passing model, 33–34
Messages in Windows, 83–84
Metaclass, 35
Metafiles, 91–92
Micrografix, 17
Microsoft, xi
Microsoft Codeview, 52, 63
Microsoft Paint, 8
Microsoft Software Development Kit (SDK), 81–82
Microsoft Windows
    See Windows
Microsoft Windows Executive, 17
Minimum Time-Slice, 11–12
Model-View-Control (MVC) interface model, 74–76, 317–18
Modeless dialogs, 179–80
Mouse, 1
Move, 5
MS-DOS, 21
Multi-Document Interface, 91–92
Multidocument editing, 277–78
Multiple applications instances, 314
Multiple Document Interface (MDI), 278–84
    class hierarchy, 282–83
    command methods, 286–306
    dynamic file dialogs, 286
    FileChildMDI, 307–08
    handling complex menus, 283–84
    hierarchical menus, 284–85
    MDIChild, 280–81
    MDIChild, 308–10
    MDIFileWindow, 281–82
    MDIFrameWindow, 279–80
    MDIFrameWindow, 306–07
    static and dynamic menus, 285–86
Multitasking, 2
Multitasking Controls, 11–12
Music, 128
Music Instrument Digital Interface (MIDI), 28
Music Printer Plus, 28

Never Warn option, 11
New Media Graphics, 17
NewWave, 16–17, 316–17
    Compound object, 16
    Container object, 16
    Dictionaries, 17
    encapsulation, 17
    File Drawer, 17
    Office, 17
    Office Tool, 17
    Printers, 17

WasteBasket, 17
Next, xi
Non-Windows Applications Group, 3, 6
    coping to Clipboard, 6
Notepad, 5
Notifier class, 74–75
Numbers, 8

OBJC.EXE, 55
OBJCC.EXE, 55
Object Graphics
    and Actor, 243–76
    Bitmaps, 252–53
    class hierarchy, 272–74
    Color, 252
    Curves, 256
    Draw, 264–65
    Graph spaces, 254–55
    grouping, 264–66
    Icons, 255
    MathRect, 253
    overview of, 244
    Palettes, 263–64
    PhysicalPort filters, 251–52
    Picture, 262
    Platform filters, 251–52
    Polygons, 256
    Polylines, 255–56
    PolyMark, 271–72
    PolyShape, 255–56
    Port filter, 251–52
    programming, 243–76
    Rect, 253
    rectangles, 253
    Region, 262–63
    rendering tools, 266–71
    SampleDraw, 244–47
    Shapes, 253
    Triangles, 256–62
    window class extensions, 274–76
Object Management Facility, 16
Object-Oriented C Language, xii, 43–80
Object-Oriented Programming (OOP)
    classes within, 34–35
    definition of, 32
    importance of, 37–38
    importance of, for Windows, xi-xiii
    introduction to, 29–42
    message passing in, 33–34
    metaphors of, 32–33
    paradigm of, 30–31
    responsibilities, 40–42
    tools, 43–80

Object-Oriented Systems
    advantages of, 39–40
    classes, 38
    degrees of, 36
    how they work, 36–37
    instances, 28
    types of, 35–36
    using, 37
Object-Oriented Tools, 43–80
ObjectDraw, 243, 247–50, 265
    toolBox, 248–50
Objective-C Language, xii, 55–65
    Array class, 58
    AsciiFiler class, 58
    AVL classes, 57, 60
    BalNode class, 57
    class hierarcy of, 57–59
    Collection, 59–61
    critique of, 64–65
    demonstration of, 61–63
    graphics classes, 61
    IdArray, 58
    IPSequence class, 57
    MS-DOS version, 63–64
    ObjGraph class, 58
    Sequence class, 57
    SortCltn class, 57, 60–61
OEM Text, 6
Office Tools, 17
Open a document
    when launching an application, 3
OpenScript, accessing other applications
    by Dynamic Data Exchange, 19–20
    by Dynamic Link Libraries, 19–20
    by external executions, 19–20
Options, 5
Outline processor, 15–16
Overloading, 35
    function, 46–48
    operator, 46–47
Owner Display, 6

Pagemaker, xi, 1, 8, 9
Paintbrush, 5, 7–8, 9
Paradigms, Programming, 29–32
Pascal, 29, 126, 144
PBRUSH.DLL, 20, 27
Pen, 61
Picture Publisher, 8
PIF Editor, 5, 14
    multitasking in, 14
    use with DOS batch files, 14

Popup menus, 278–79
  floating, 90
Presentation Manager for OS/2, 1
Print Manager, 3, 8, 10–11
Printers, 5, 17
  adjusting for reset time, 11
PrintScreen hotkey, 27
Processing time, 14
Profiler, 97–98
Program Manager, 2–3, 4, 27–28
Programming Paradigms, 29–32
PROLOG, 46
Proportional fonts, 2
Prototyping a function, 47

Quattro Pro, 27

Real Mode, 2
Relational database systems, 335–36
Resource Compiler, 94
Resource Editors, 95
Resource File selections, 190–94
Resource Scripts, 103
  syntax, 190–94
Run command, 3

Samna, 17
SampleDraw, 244–47
  adding menus to, 245–47
Scientific mode, 6–7
Screen capture, 6, 9
Screen clutter
  minimizing, 4
Scribble
  class description, 220
  sample demonstration, 218–19
Scroll bars, 1
SDK package, 326
SDK Paint, 96
SDK Tools, 93–105
  critique of, 103–05
Sealing applications, xiii
Setup program, 8
Shaker, 100–101
Smalltalk, 35, 37, 41, 46, 55, 56, 57, 58, 59, 61, 63,
  65–66, 71, 125–26, 128, 279
SMARTDRV.SYS, 7
Spreadsheets
  designing, 315–16
Spy, 98–99, 104
Sta key, 7

Standard Mode, 2
Statistics Box, 7
Streamliner, 79–80
Stroustrup, Bjarne, 43, 48
Style Keywords, 85–86
Subclass, 34, 38–39
Subdirectories (+)
  expanding, 4–5
Sun workstation platform, 21
Superclass, 34, 38–39
Swap, 100
Switch to, 2
Symbolic Debug Utility (Symdeb), 102

Task List, 2, 13
Task Switch, 27
Template
  See Classes
Terminal, 5, 8
Text, 6
Text editing classes, 78
TextFile class, 176–77
TextWindow, 164–66
Three-dimensional points, 228–30
Time
  management class descriptions, 154–56
  managing in Windows, 144–56
Timer class, 78–79
Toolbook, 17–21
  and Windows 3.0, 18
  animation and, 19
  clip art and, 19
  creating hotwords, 21
  electronic libraries, 21
  graphics and, 19
  hypertext capabilities, 17–18
  messages in, 18–19
  objects in, 18–19
  OpenScript and, 19–20
Toolbox, 28
Tools
  graphic rendering, 266–71
Tower of Hanoi, 158–59
Triangles
  methods of drawing, 256–62

Unlisted Printer, 5
User interfaces, 86
  for Windows, 161–215
User interface style, 103

VGA modes, 6

Video Graphics Array modes
See VGA modes
Video New Wave, 17
VIEWS, xii, 318
    AppView class, 74–75, 77
    Browser, 72–74
    C++ Language 2.0, 71
    classes, 76–77, 320–21
    Communications class, 79
    ControlView, 77
    creating dialogs in, 77
    critique of, 80
    Ctalk, 71
    Development tool for Windows, 71–72
    DIALOG.EXE, 77
    graphics, 79
    menus in, 77–78
    Model-View-Control (MVC) interface model,
        74–76
    Notifier class, 74–75
    Objective-C Language, 71
    PopupWindow, 77
    Port class, 79
    PushButton, 76
    RadioButton, 76
    Streamliner, 79–80
    TextEditor, 78
    Timer class, 78–79
    Windows, 76
Virtual classes, 47–48
Virtual functions, 47–48

WasteBasket, 17
WIN.INI file, xii, 5
Window
    ActorApp, 170
    creating, 161–63
    EditWindow, 166–68
    FileEditor, 168
    FileWindow, 168
    management functions, 86
    Text, 164–66
Windows, xi-xiii
    3.0 new functions, 105–11
    3.0 new messages, 111–14
    3.0 new structures, 114–15
    buttons, 88
    class structure of, 85
    Codeview, 101–02
    Color graphics, 93
    Combo box notification messages, 112
    combo boxes, 90
    compatability of 2.0 and 3.0, 102

    controls, 88
    controls, owner-drawn, 87
    customizing, 5
    debugging, 94–95
    design, 311–41
    Device context, 91
    Dialog Editor, 95
    Dialogs, 89–90
    display context, 86
    Dynamic Data Exchange (DDE), 93
    Dynamic Link Libraries, 92–93
    Editing control messages, 105, 112
    enumeration functions, 124–25
    Font Editor, 96–97
    functions, 83–86
    GDI, 90–92
    graphics, color, 93
    graphics, programming for, 217–43
    Heapwalker, 99–100
    Help-building system, 94
    How system works, 82–83
    icons, 87
    Information context, 91
    List box messages, 112–14
    list boxes, 89–90
    managing time in, 144–45
    memory management, 311, 323–35
    menus, 87–88
    messages, 83–84
    Multi-Document Interface, 91–92
    Object-oriented design for, 317–33
    popup menus, floating, 90
    Profiler, 97–98
    program structure, 102–03
    Resource Compiler, 94
    resource editors, 95
    scroll bar, 88
    SDKPaint, 96
    Shaker, 100–101
    software developments of 3.0, 81–115
    Spy, 98–99
    style keywords, 85–86
    Swap, 100
    user interface style, 103
    user interfaces, 86, 161–215
    window classes, 83–85
    writing resource scripts for, 103
    Zoomin, 97, 98
Windows 3.0
    a session with, 27–28
    changing desktop color, 27
    introduction to, 1–28
    new functions, 105–11
    new messages, 111

new structures, 114–15
sample application, 277–310
Toolbook, 18
Windows applications
    types of, 13–14
Windows Applications Group, 3
Windows Help
    See Help
Windows in Background, 12
Windows in Foreground, 12
Windows Setup, 3
Wingz, 21–27
    3-D graphics capabilities, 23
    applications built in DLL, 26–27
    Box-Jenkins in, 25
    Census X-11 Method in, 25
    clip art and, 23
    creating controls for, 23
    database building in, 24
    editing in, 23
    Foran system in, 25
    GOAL, 27
    graphics in, 22
    Hyperscript language, 21–23
    Hyperscript, 25–26
    limitations of, 27
    matrices size possibilities, 24
    Multiple Regression in, 25
    Objects, 24
    Operating Icons, 23
    Operator Icons, 21
    pasting in, 23
    resizing rows and columns in, 23
    Spreadsheets, 21–27
    Time-Series in, 25

Tool Box Icons, 21
Tool Box, 24
WINMEM32.DLL, 326
Wintrieve, 333–41
    BookDlg, 340–41
    BookWindow, 339–40
    class descriptions, 338–41
    classes, 336–41
    classes, underlying, 337–38
    interface with C++ language, 334
    IsamCStruct, 336
    IsamDesc, 337
    IsamDict, 336
    IsamFile, 333, 333–34, 337
    IsamKey, 337
    IsamKeyParser, 337
    IsamLink, 337
    IsamManager, 333, 337
    IsamRecord, 336
    OrderedDictionary, 338–39
    relational database systems, 335–36
    RelFile, 333–34, 337
Word, 6
Word for Windows, 1, 9, 15
    outlining in, 15
Workbench, 28
WorkSpaces, 176

Zing, 8
Zoomin, 97, 98
Zortech C++ Language, xii
Zortech compiler, 50–52
    memory map in, 51–52
Zortech Tools, 53–54